NEW ACCENTS

General Editor: TERENCE HAWKES

Popular Fictions: Essays in Literature and History

IN THE SAME SERIES

Popular Fictions

Essays in Literature and History

Edited by
PETER HUMM,
PAUL STIGANT
and **PETER WIDDOWSON**

METHUEN
London and New York

First published in 1986 by
Methuen & Co. Ltd
11 New Fetter Lane, London EC4P 4EE
Published in the USA by
Methuen & Co.
in association with Methuen, Inc.
29 West 35th Street, New York, NY 10001

Photoset by Rowland Phototypesetting Ltd
Bury St Edmunds, Suffolk
Printed in Great Britain by
Richard Clay Ltd, Bungay, Suffolk

British Library Cataloguing in
Publication Data

Popular fictions: essays in literature
and history. – (New accents)
1. English literature – History and
criticism
I. Humm, Peter   II. Stigant, Paul
III. Widdowson, Peter   IV. Series
820.9   PR83

ISBN 0 416 90040 2
    0 416 90050 X Pbk

Library of Congress Cataloging in
Publication Data

Popular fictions
(New accents)
1. English literature – History and
criticism.
2. Popular literature – Great Britain –
History and criticism
3. Literature and history.
4. Politics and literature.
5. Popular culture.
I. Humm, Peter.
II. Stigant, Paul. III. Widdowson,
Peter. IV. Literature & history.
V. Series: New accents (Methuen & Co.)
PR408.P67P6   1986   820'.9
86-21860

ISBN 0 416 90040 2
    0 416 90050 X (pbk.)

Contents

General editor's preface

It is easy to see that we are living in a time of rapid and radical social change. It is much less easy to grasp the fact that such change will inevitably affect the nature of those academic disciplines that both reflect our society and help to shape it.

Yet this is nowhere more apparent than in the central field of what may, in general terms, be called literary studies. Here, among large numbers of students at all levels of education, the erosion of the assumptions and presuppositions that support the literary disciplines in their conventional form has proved fundamental. Modes and categories inherited from the past no longer seem to fit the reality experienced by a new generation.

New Accents is intended as a positive response to the initiative offered by such a situation. Each volume in the series will seek to encourage rather than resist the process of change, to stretch rather than reinforce the boundaries that currently define literature and its academic study.

Some important areas of interest immediately present themselves. In various parts of the world, new methods of analysis have been developed whose conclusions reveal the limitations of the Anglo-American outlook we inherit. New concepts of literary forms and modes have been proposed; new notions of the nature of literature itself, and of how it communicates, are current; new views of literature's role in relation to society flourish. *New Accents* will aim to expound and comment upon the most notable of these.

In the broad field of the study of human communication, more and more emphasis has been placed upon the nature and function of the new electronic media. *New Accents* will try to identify and discuss the challenge these offer to our traditional modes of critical response.

The same interest in communication suggests that the series should also concern itself with those wider anthropological and sociological areas of investigation which have begun to involve scrutiny of the nature of art itself and of its relation to our whole way of life. And this will ultimately require attention to be focused on some of those activities which in our society have hitherto been excluded from the prestigious realms of Culture. The disturbing realignment of values involved and the disconcerting nature of the pressures that work to bring it about both constitute areas that *New Accents* will seek to explore.

Finally, as its title suggests, one aspect of *New Accents* will be firmly located in contemporary approaches to language, and a continuing concern of the series will be to examine the extent to which relevant branches of linguistic studies can illuminate specific literary areas. The volumes with this particular interest will nevertheless presume no prior technical knowledge on the part of their readers, and will aim to rehearse the linguistics appropriate to the matter in hand, rather than to embark on general theoretical matters.

Each volume in the series will attempt an objective exposition of significant developments in its field up to the present as well as an account of its author's own views of the matter. Each will culminate in an informative bibliography as a guide to further study. And while each will be primarily concerned with matters relevant to its own specific interests, we can hope that a kind of conversation will be heard to develop between them: one whose accents may perhaps suggest the distinctive discourse of the future.

TERENCE HAWKES

List of contributors

Tony Bennett is Associate Professor in the School of Humanities at Griffith University, Australia. He taught previously at the Open University where he chaired a course on popular culture. His publications include *Formalism and Marxism* (1979) and, with Janet Woollacott, *Bond and Beyond: The Political Career of a Popular Hero* (forthcoming).

Roger Bromley teaches literary and cultural studies in the School of Social and Historical Studies at Portsmouth Polytechnic. He has written on popular fiction, on Hardy and Malcolm Lowry, and on Caribbean writing. He is a corresponding editor of the *European Journal of Communication*. Current work includes articles on cultural studies in Britain today, a chapter on forms of Liberalism and recent spy fictions for a forthcoming book on popular fiction, and a book on popular cultural forms and political ideology.

Peter Brooker teaches in the School of Humanities at Thames Polytechnic, London, and is an editor of *Literature and History*. He has published a book on Ezra Pound (1979) and is currently working on a study of Bertolt Brecht.

Michael Denning is Assistant Professor of English and Comparative Literature at Columbia University, New York, and the author of *Cover Stories: Narrative and Ideology in the British Spy*

Thriller (1986) and *Mechanic Accents: Dime Novels and Working Class Culture in Nineteenth-Century America* (forthcoming).

Patricia Duncker is a freelance writer and lecturer. She is working on a novel about the Great War and a study of contemporary feminist fiction.

Norman Feltes teaches in the Departments of English and Social and Political Thought, York University, Toronto, Canada. A slightly revised version of his present essay appears in *Modes of Production of Victorian Novels* (1986).

Kate Flint (Fellow and Tutor in English, Mansfield College, Oxford) is author of *Dickens* (1986) and editor of *Impressionism in England* (1984). She has books forthcoming on *The Woman Reader, 1830–1920* and on late nineteenth-century art criticism.

Graham Holderness has held appointments in the Open University's Arts Faculty and in the English Department of the University College of Swansea. He is currently Staff Tutor in Literature and Drama in Swansea's Department of Adult and Continuing Education. He is author of *D.H. Lawrence: History, Ideology and Fiction* (1982); *Shakespeare's History* (1985); and of the Open University Press publications *Wuthering Heights* (1985) and *Women in Love* (1986). Forthcoming titles include (with John Turner and Nicholas Potter) *The Play of History: Studies in Shakespeare's Historical Imagination*; and (with Christopher McCullough) *The Shakespeare Myth: Further Essays in Cultural Materialism*.

Peter Humm teaches British and American writing and culture in the School of Humanities at Thames Polytechnic, London.

Stuart Laing is a lecturer in the School of Cultural and Community Studies at the University of Sussex. His recent publications include two essays in *Society and Literature 1945–70*, edited by Alan Sinfield (1983), and *Representations of Working-Class Life 1957–64* (1986).

Kathy MacDermott is currently Senior Researcher at the Australian Human Rights Commission. She holds a D.Phil. in literature (University of York), has taught popular culture in the US, and has published on science fiction and detective fiction as well as, more recently, on ideology and discrimination.

Brian Maidment teaches English at Manchester Polytechnic. He has particular research interests in Victorian popular literature and is currently completing two books on early Victorian artisan literary culture: a critical study, and an anthology of writing by and about self-taught writers.

Paul O'Flinn has taught English at Ibibio State College, East Nigeria, and at Trent University, Ontario, and has taught sociology at the University of Reading. He is currently Principal Lecturer in English in the Department of Humanities at Oxford Polytechnic. Previous publications include *Them and Us in Literature* (1975).

Paul Stigant teaches history in the School of Humanities at Thames Polytechnic, London.

Peter Widdowson, Professor of English at Middlesex Polytechnic, was previously a member of the School of Humanities, Thames Polytechnic, London. He has published a book on E.M. Forster's *Howards End* (1976), edited *Re-Reading English* (1982) and is currently writing a book on *Hardy in History: A Case-Study in the Sociology of Literature*.

Editors' note

Nine people are closely involved in editing the journal *Literature and History*: Peter Brooker, Helen Carr, Francis Duke, Peter Humm, Lucy Jeffreys, Jane Maxwell Smith, Roger Richardson, Paul Stigant and Peter Widdowson. Although only three of them have edited this book, the articles it contains have all been read and appraised by the editorial group. Similarly the introduction, written jointly by Paul Stigant, Peter Humm and Peter Widdowson, draws on ideas, arguments and collaborations which continue between the editors and between them and their colleagues at Thames Polytechnic and elsewhere. An introduction containing so many sentences beginning with 'But' reveals the creative tensions of that collective process, and also underlines the gains to be derived from a dialogue between 'Literature' and 'History'.

Literature and History itself has appeared twice a year since 1975. Its continuing success has depended not only on its contributors and subscribers, but also on the considerable support it has received from the School of Humanities at Thames Polytechnic and on the hard work and goodwill of the staff of the Print Room there: from the start the journal has been composed and printed entirely within the Polytechnic. *Literature and History*, and therefore this book, is a truly collaborative enterprise.

The present book contains twelve essays selected not only from the 120 or more articles the journal has published over the last eleven years, but from a sizeable sub-group within that number on 'popular fictions'. In order to accommodate even these twelve contributions, it has been necessary for the editors to cut and slightly amend the essays. Otherwise they stand as they were first published in *Literature and History*. Cuts are indicated by [. . .] in the text, and dates of original publication are given on the Contents page.

Introduction

PETER HUMM,
PAUL STIGANT
and PETER WIDDOWSON

The double-barrelled aspect of this book's title is quite deliberate. All the essays collected here deal in their different ways with
'popular fictions', but they were all, also, first published in the
journal *Literature and History*. In that sense, then, they are quite
literally 'essays in literature and history'. More important,
however, than the literal sense is their relationship to the
academic disciplines of 'Literature' and 'History'. For they are
presented here not simply as interesting pieces in their own
right, but also as significant contributions to an area of knowledge that can legitimately be called Literature-and-History.
Moreover, they bear on this concept in another way: they are
also part of the history of the journal itself, and we would like to
suggest that this is also how they should be read. The appearance of these essays was not fortuitous: the editorial group of
Literature and History was eager to publish them because they
helped the journal explore the concept of 'popular fictions', and
also indicated ways in which the disciplines of Literature and
History could come together to break down the methodologies,
epistemologies and pedagogies that keep them apart.*

  * If a similar project seems to have informed the inception of the Essex Conferences, that
also was not fortuitous. While *Literature and History* did play some direct part in the founding
of the Conference, both developments in fact emerge from the same cultural moment in the
mid-1970s. The closeness of their concerns manifests itself in the papers taken from the
Essex Conferences which are published, in tandem with the present volume, as *Literature,
Politics and Theory*.

The concept of 'popular fictions', however, should not be seen as some kind of marriage broker, disappearing tactfully once Literature and History have met. Reading the essays in this book requires, as writing them must have done, a juggler's skill in keeping all three notions in play. Of the three, however, 'Literature' causes the most anxiety: squeezing it between 'popular fictions' and History calls into proper question the stability of that central and too-long dominant term. Just as deciding to call some fictions 'popular' raises the question of how and why other literature is more valued, so putting History last reinforces that evaluative process. But a recognition that the canon of Literature is a historical construct should not simply lead to a partisan regrouping of past champions and new contenders; rather it should produce a sceptical analysis of what is invested in such hierarchies. The history of literature discernible in this book is, in fact, part of a continuous rewriting of the relations between the artificial categories of Genre, Canon and Tradition. These categories are, however, still held within what the authors of one recent *New Accents* book, *Rewriting English*, call the 'strong magnetic field' of literature.[1] And it is worth staying within that field a little longer if only to resist that traditional treatment of 'popular fictions' which values them solely for their social content. Just as canonic texts receive intensive formalistic reading, so popular fictions should be treated in a way which does not merely allow 'non-canonised texts [to be] collapsed back into the conditions of production from which they derive'.[2] Popular fictions, then, need to be read and analysed not as some kind of sugar-coated sociology, but as narratives which negotiate, *no less than* the classic texts, the connection between 'writing, history and ideology'.

That last phrase can be found printed on the inside cover of more recent issues of *Literature and History*, and it represents a definite shift in the concerns of the journal since its inception. But equally, retaining *Literature* as part of our title also has a strategic importance, both for the journal and for this book. *Literature* is not a designer label intended to dignify the everyday denim of popular fiction, but a reminder that such works receive very 'close reading' from those who buy or borrow them. So, for example, the readers of novels published by Mills & Boon or Silhouette not only value the individual style and themes of their 'favourite authors', but report their findings back to the companies' monitoring service. Thus, if the essays collected here concentrate on the formal structures of the written text rather than the social structures in which those texts are produced and read, then at least they resist patronizing generalizations about the reading habits of those (unlike ourselves) who live and read outside the academy.

When we came to make the selection of essays for inclusion in this book we lighted fairly quickly upon about twenty real possibilities out of the 120 or so articles that had appeared in *Literature and History* since 1975. Those twenty essays included discussion of texts as diverse as *Frankenstein, The Beggar's Opera, Pickwick Papers* and *Ginx's Baby*. What made these (and not others) appropriate for a book on popular fictions was that the texts they dealt with were, by and large, all widely read, seen or sold; and this fact itself opens up questions of literary and historical placing which cut off the retreat into the immobility of standard literary criticism. The point of this book, however, is not rigidly to re(de)fine once more the term 'popular fiction', but to see what happens when proven best-selling fictions are placed within the dialectic of Literature-and-History.

However, to go back for a moment to the inception of the journal in 1975: we had then no clear-cut, neatly worked-out or theorized notion of what that dialectic was or might be. But we did have certain starting points, and they remain important starting points for this book. We recognized that works of literature were historically located, and that within what was called History (i.e. what was studied as History in schools and higher education) literature as a form of consciousness probably deserved much greater prominence. We subscribed, then, to the hardly earth-shattering view that literature was produced and consumed in a material world which was itself shaped by a complex mix of economic, political, social, cultural and intellectual forces; we wished, in other words, to stress the concrete materiality of literature. But we wished to do this by not then arguing that literature was a mere *reflection* of the historical forces shaping society. Literature, as we saw it, was part and parcel of how societies are formed and changed; it had, for us at least, some dynamic of its own. Or, to put it another way round,

History needed literature not as some kind of creative affirmation of what we already knew, but as an active and integral part of reaching an understanding of past societies and their relation to the present.

This, then, represented, and represents, a point of departure. It is no more than that because, once confronted, the problems proliferate. But there is one vital difference between 1975 and now, and this book bears testimony to it: many of these problems have at least been engaged. One that has become important to us is why, as we have already implied, one piece of literature is seen as 'great' whilst others are assigned the labels 'lesser', 'minor', 'popular', or are indeed considered so inferior as to be not worth mentioning at all. On its own, the question 'what makes novel X better than novel Y?' represents no challenge to traditional literary criticism. Indeed, the theoretical assumptions and methodology of that criticism are designed precisely to ask, and resolve, such a question. But once shift the theoretical foundation that underpins the 'major'/'minor' divide, and not only does a whole new range of literature become available to us, but new ways of looking at the relationship between literature and society also emerge. For example, they allow us to explore a specific definition of a 'popular fiction' which we have already touched on: one that presupposes a large readership or audience for it in its own day. To take an example from this book: once Edward Jenkins's *Ginx's Baby* does not have to be judged on a scale of 'literary greatness', then some pressing questions about Jenkins's contemporary popularity can begin to be taken seriously. The problem that this in its turn raises is: how do we relate Jenkins's work to his society; how do we *read* it historically?

Once the procedures of conventional literary criticism have been shown to be problematical, they clearly cannot be deployed in an innocent or unselfconscious way. *Meaning* in such works has to be found by reference to other criteria. This is not to say that literary critical skills prove totally inappropriate. The question of how to 'read' such works must involve detailed reference to the written text as well as to the wider society and discourses within which it is located. But the essays in this book clearly indicate that when we address best-selling authors, those skills have to be combined with a variety of strategies in which 'the literary' can be made to meet 'history' and vice versa in order to search out meaning. The essays on Mrs Oliphant, Edward Jenkins, Geoffrey Household, Daphne du Maurier and Philip Gibbs, for example, all dismiss the 'history-as-context-for-the-study-of-fiction' approach, and seek instead to weave together the text, the genre and the specific history of the period. And all these essays create specifically different 'histories' in order to answer the question why those books were a popular 'good read' in their own day.

Two things stand out here. The first is the difficulty that some (though not all) of these popular fictions present to the modern reader. They are not easy reading. But then not many present-day readers can escape into an effortless reading of George Eliot or Henry James. The equivalent difficulty, say, of late nineteenth-century 'popular' texts results from historical changes in language and narrative form rather than from a confirmation of any elitist distinction between 'ephemera' and 'classics'. The second point is that the histories of 'popular fictions' have to be constructed; that is, their histories cannot be taken from standard secondary works on the history of their period. Hence not only are those works rediscovered and examined, but in the process the history of the period is itself reappraised. The reason for this is obvious: if a piece of popular fiction is both difficult to read and not subject to the conventional criteria of 'literary merit', then how to read its 'meanings' has to be extracted more deliberately from the ideological, social and political matrix that encloses and, in large measure, produces it. We are not saying, however, that the history comes first and the text is then applied to that history; rather that the text itself forms part of that history – part, in other words, of the attempt to understand forms of consciousness and the articulation of ideas in a past society. Michael Denning's essay on John Gay's *The Beggar's Opera*, while also introducing popular theatre into the book, illustrates this point. It is not simply that the *contemporary* meaning of *The Beggar's Opera* has to be sought within the specific history of the period, but that Gay's work constitutes a dynamic part of that history, helping both to articulate the tensions and contradictions within society and, in giving them popular expression, to heighten their significance as part of contemporary consciousness. To write about popular fictions is to write history.

Indeed, to write about any kind of literature should lead to the crucial recognition that it is inevitably implicated in the process of history. So, to write about 'Literature' is also to write history. But popular fictions are not some trivial exhibit waiting to be discovered and mined by historians whose respect for 'great literature' persuades them that they should leave the task of re-reading the traditional texts to their literary colleagues: they, too, have specific formal structures which need equally careful analysis. Only when we reject the notion of 'popular fiction' as topical content and 'literature' as timeless form can we begin properly to interpret its historical significance. That is why it is important to avoid a dismissive critical condescension in the use of terms like 'formula' and 'stereotype'. If the twelve romance novels written by Charlotte Lamb in 1985 follow a familiar narrative formula, then part of their familiarity comes from their conscious inheritance of narrative structures found in Emily or Charlotte Brontë. This is not a question of one 'unique' original being converted into the facsimiles of mass production: there are eccentric best-sellers and formulaic classics. The readers of Charlotte Lamb do indeed have a comforting idea of how her novels will end; but there are not many surprises, either, on the final pages of Jane Austen.

But the arbitrary distinction between popular fiction and literature is even more problematical. Why, for example, are some pieces of fiction which were popular in their own day still apparently popular in the late twentieth century? Why are some popular fictions also rated as 'great literature'? The answers provided by the essays in this book point us in some interesting directions. First, we need to recognize that a piece of fiction is produced not just once, but time and again for each succeeding generation, and that it is 'read' differently by different generations, each making its own sense of the text for its own purposes. Second, these texts are constantly reproduced in other ways: turned into films, TV plays, radio dramas and so on. A work of popular fiction can then literally take on a multitude of forms, be given a multitude of historically specific 'meanings', and thus become one work of many popular fictions. Hence, as the essay on the 1944 film version of Shakespeare's *Henry V* shows, what is already constituted as part of England's 'great literary tradition' can be used quite consciously as part of a patriotic, morale-boosting, war effort; thereby re-creating Shakespeare as popular fiction, while at the same time allowing audiences of the day to see that their national identity ('Englishness') is something shaped by, and understood through, the work of a literary titan like Shakespeare.

What the film of *Henry V* also suggests is the extent to which conscious efforts are constantly made to popularize 'great literature'. In the second half of the twentieth century, by such devices as the 'classic serial', television has further enhanced this popularization. In one sense, therefore, the 'great tradition' has been strengthened by means of turning novels and plays into modern 'popular fictions'. But equally, as the activities of the Virago publishing house show, the notion of an exclusive canon can be subverted by simply calling every novel published a 'modern classic'. This may be merely a canny publisher's decision to promote a new evaluation of work previously ignored or unsold, but anti-hierarchical effects are equally achieved by less direct political mechanisms. The BBC Drama Department has a continuing investment in the national icon of Charles Dickens, so that an adaptation of, say, *Bleak House* can be used to prove that the BBC still brings 'culture to the masses'; that it can do so 'artistically'; and that it can also make 'culture' a commercial success. Yet it takes the BBC a full-page advertisement in the 'quality' national press to construct an arbitrary tradition in which *Tender is the Night* becomes the *natural* sequel to Dennis Potter's re-creation of the Jazz Age in *Pennies from Heaven*.

Similarly, for every popularization of an 'A-level' certified classic, there is the reverse process whereby a steady middle-brow fiction such as Paul Scott's *Raj* trilogy is converted into a classic to be adorned by the Dames of the British stage and sold to Mobil's Masterpiece Theatre. And here Granada proves its own fitness to make great literature speak to each age and generation. The fact that this literature does so 'speak', of course, largely depends on the way in which it is *made* to speak to its audience, on the way it is given 'relevance' and modern popular appeal. These notions of relevance and popularity can appear to be arbitrary. Why decide, for example, that 1983 should be the 'Year of India'? The explanation must be that such a decision is bound up inextricably with perceptions of proven public taste – the success, for instance, of Attenborough's *Gandhi* two years earlier – so that in 1983 India comes to be represented on our screens by Paul Scott, E.M. Forster and M.M. Kaye, author of *The Far Pavilions*. In the end, though, what television and film have done is to create a fusion of 'great' and 'minor' literature very much within the realm of 'the popular'. Despite this process, perhaps ironically, 'great literature' does not lose out. Its status seems, on the contrary, to be enhanced. Indeed, we might suggest that the very survival of that ideological concept 'the great tradition' depends as much upon its artefacts being transformed into contemporary popular entertainment, as upon their appearance on A-level and degree syllabuses.

A play's or novel's popularity can, therefore, be re-created time and again. But the creation of that popularity involves aiming a fiction at a specific audience – or market. The musical version of *Oliver Twist*, first as theatre then as film, does not seek exactly the same audience as the BBC TV serialization. The success of one may help to increase the popular audience for the other, but in no sense are popular fictions directed towards, or consumed by, an undifferentiated mass audience. Clearly we need to know more about its composition, and Kate Flint's essay recognizes the importance of the nature of the audience in accounting for the success of popular fictions.[3] But despite such honourable exceptions, this is one area with which *Literature and History* has not been able to deal. What does emerge in many of the essays collected here, however, is that popular fictions are made not simply by audience response, but, more importantly, by the determined efforts of some authors, film-makers and publishers: some, that is to say, who so consciously gear their books, films or plays to what they believe or know to be popular, who have such a heightened sense of market, demand and 'taste', that they must know what they are 'creating' is, in fact, a *product*. Most fiction is of course a product in the sense that it is written or made to be sold and marketed, but one characteristic of 'popular' fiction must be that *its* relationship to the market, *its* place in the socio-economic relations of production, is different from that of 'non-popular' fiction.

Two essays deal with this issue, though in significantly different ways. Kathy MacDermott points to the early eighteenth-century relationship between writing and the market as a key moment in the creation of the concept 'literature', and thus to the imminent dichotomy between 'high culture' and 'low culture'. Norman Feltes highlights the way in which Dickens, who is now considered to have written 'serious' fiction, was consciously involved, not simply in writing a best-seller, but in producing a *commodity*. What these two essays jointly challenge is the myth that 'great literature' is produced by those whose creative genius drives them unerringly on, and 'popular fictions' by those whose only real concern is market demand. Deliberately conceived popular fictions may, indeed, be seen by their producers first and foremost as commodities; but the relationship between *all* fictions and the market – its nature and composition, and how the commodity is produced for it – must be a crucial consideration in any full discussion of literature, popular or otherwise.

This leads on to another set of questions neatly highlighted by Paul O'Flinn's essay on *Frankenstein*.[4] It illustrates, first, an earlier point: that popular fiction is continuously reproduced, until, in the case of *Frankenstein*, one text has become a multitude of popular fictions. Second, it asks why and how some popular fictions stay 'popular' from one generation to the next (*Dracula* and *Sherlock Holmes* spring to mind here, as well as *Frankenstein*), other than by their elevation to canonic literature. Third, it asks how far the re-creation of popular fictions involves their transmission more widely within people's everyday lives – as O'Flinn says: 'Versions of the monster glare out from chewing-gum wrappers and crisp bags . . . [while] in the USA he forged a chain of restaurants.' *Frankenstein* forces us to recognize, therefore, that some popular fictions have virtually nothing to do with their authorial text. What do the scores of Frankenstein films in the twentieth century have to do with Mary Shelley's original? Indeed, is her text, apart from supplying a name and a basic idea, at all relevant to an investigation of the 'Frankenstein' phenomenon in twentieth-century mass entertainment? Feminist critics such as Ellen Moers may have established Mary Shelley's creation of an enduring myth for a widely varied audience, but there is a vast gulf between a writer's – or director's – knowledge and use of an original source and an audience's perception of something called 'Frankenstein'. This is not to make an elitist distinction between intellectual respect for, and popular indifference to, the 'original text' (after all, Mrs Gaskell was capable of the now hackneyed confusion between monster and creator). But while an audience may have to have some kind of recognition of Shakespeare as England's 'greatest poet' to be attracted to the film of *Henry V*, no such knowledge of Mary Shelley attracts audiences to the latest Frankenstein film. It is not Mary Shelley that matters, but a consciousness of numerous previous films. The question thus becomes: how is this *Frankenstein* kept alive as a popular piece of modern fiction? And much the same might be asked of *Dracula* or Sherlock Holmes. What we must note is that a complex set of ideas and expectations surround à name, and so enable some variation on the theme to be constantly reproduced – even, in the case of Sherlock Holmes, to the point where a television company can make a series 'based on' the original Conan Doyle stories. But such a series is only possible, in effect, because of a whole legacy of previous fictionalizations of 'Holmes' which have little to do with the original.

With some popular fictions, then, it is possible to work and rework a particular motif within a given set of audience expectations, so that, in the case of film, people can 'know' what they are seeing before they have seen it, or, with format books such as Mills & Boon romances, to 'know' what they are going to read before they have read them. But that knowledge comes from practised viewing and reading which, in themselves, contribute to the successful formula: Hollywood films are pre-viewed and re-edited until they coincide with 'the audience's' expectations; Mills & Boon elaborately test their readers' responses to variations in the traditional ingredients of their romances. Such an emphasis on the complicated reciprocal relation between consumer and product may seem to come uncomfortably close to praising the democracy of the market, but we need to take that risk if we are to avoid a functionalist sociology which insists upon mechanically reading off ideological effects from the formulae ossified in a 'lesser tradition' of popular fiction. 'Formula' and 'genre' *are* important to the study of popular fiction, but not because these notions serve to distinguish it from 'Literature', rather because they draw attention to the ways in which readers go about their reading. As Janice Radway has established in *Reading the Romance*, there is a real gain in moving our attention from the solitary text 'taken in isolation, to the complex social event of reading'.[5] But the present essays are written in the main by academics trained in the formal close reading of texts rather than in the ethnographic skills which inform *Reading the Romance*. *Literature and History*, predictably, has not received many investigations into what can be called the sociologies of taste or pleasure. This does not mean that the readings published in the journal merely celebrate the arcane textual mysteries of 'popular' discourses. It is because many works of popular fiction are seemingly 'easy to read' that so much interesting work can be done in tracing the historical processes of reproduction and revaluation. A best-seller can provide an enjoyably slick surface from which we can skid away from the fixities of literary typology to the freedom of historical and cultural change.

And yet the cry may still go up that what distinguishes 'Literature' from popular fiction is that 'great art' stimulates and enhances our imagination, our understanding, our intellect, whereas most popular fictions subdue, deaden or deny them. So, the argument might run, the intellectual challenge of reading Richardson's *Pamela* proves far more demanding, and therefore rewarding, than that involved in reading Jackie Collins's *The Bitch*. But for many people in the late twentieth century *Pamela* is scarcely readable, while *The Bitch* presents an 'easy read'. Is this, then, still to say that, having acquired the status of 'great art', *Pamela* speaks now more meaningfully than *The Bitch*? What *we* want to deny is the factitious distinction between 'high' and 'low' culture, the boundary between them being so frayed by constant movement that its only use now is to mark the ideological motives of those who insist that it still provides a necessary function. Those who read or scrutinize Dickens as a novelist secure within the canon (if not 'the great tradition'), and ignore his simultaneous appearance on TV at Sunday tea-time, are substituting a previously freeze-dried version of the past for the dynamics of historical process. A properly *historical* reading of Dickens, or any other writer, has to recognize these seismic shifts – movements which make any Richter-like measurement of 'popular' and 'classic' fiction futile or partisan.

If we need any further proof, we can simply turn to the essay on Angela Carter. Patricia Duncker discusses Carter's very particular use of that most popular genre, the fairy story; and, of course, Carter's work has already been turned into film. But, intriguingly, the back cover of the King Penguin edition of Carter's *The Bloody Chamber* promotes the book in this way: 'In tales that glitter and haunt – strange nuggets from a writer whose wayward pen spills forth stylish, erotic, nightmarish jewels of prose – the old fairy stories live and breathe again'; and goes on to quote Robert Coover's opinion that it is 'a classic of short fiction, literally aglow with lyrical intensity, comic ingenuity'. Indeed, this promotion neatly sums up the dilemma: how do you market a contemporary writer like Angela Carter? Of what literary tradition should she be *made* a member? The blurb touches both the potentially 'classic' nature of her writing, as well as the potentially 'popular' – the erotically gothic. But it is not just Penguin's dilemma; it is ours too. Can we locate her writing within 'popular fiction', and how does it affect our definitions of that term if we do? One thing is clear: Carter's work refuses any inclination we may have to measure and define popular fictions over against 'serious' literature. If we once deny any such discriminations, then *all* writing, theatre or filmmaking has to be understood and studied in a different set of terms. And if these terms contain the notions of the author's sense of his or her 'market', of audience and audience expectations, of writing/film/theatre as product or commodity, and of the specific historical location of that product, then we may have a better chance of understanding the place of *the cultural* within the social formation and, within *that*, what we might mean by 'popular fictions'. In the end, however, the ultimate issue is not a better understanding of the 'popular fictions' themselves, but what they tell us of the constitution of culture – in particular *popular* culture – and of cultural politics.

Finally, it is also important to recognize that the cultural politics and theory which inform the essays collected here have their *own* history. All appeared as articles in *Literature and History* some time between 1979 and 1984, and they are marked by the particular history of political and intellectual debate that pervaded the 1970s and early 1980s. One significant effect of this on the journal's editors was our recognition that it was not enough passively to reflect the current arguments. We concluded that we should actively encourage contributions to the debate. So these essays did not appear in the journal by accident, and neither is it a coincidence that the earliest date of publication of any of them was 1979.

In 1979 *Literature and History* became more explicitly interested in theory than it had been previously. It was, ironically perhaps, a strange moment for this to happen, and the strangeness of the moment affected the character of the journal's theoretical offerings. 1978 had seen the publication of E.P. Thompson's *The Poverty of Theory*, his call to History to act as the last bastion of defence against Theory: a Theory that had (only on the left, of course) already greatly influenced literary studies. The following year saw the issues raised by *The Poverty of Theory* turned into a moment, a very theatrical moment, of high drama. At the Ruskin College History Workshop that autumn, in the packed arena of a disused church, to the delight of many and the embarrassment of some, Edward Thompson again attacked theory. The politics of this are significant. Addressed as it was to cheering (socialist) historians, the attack encouraged them not simply to be wary of theory, but to deny it an important place in historical studies. Moreover, there was nothing fortuitous in the fact that the person attacked that night was Richard Johnson of the Centre for Contemporary Cultural Studies, himself a historian. There was, it seemed to some of us, a markedly reactionary tenor to the whole performance. The Centre had done a great deal in the 1970s to stress the importance of theory, but by the late 1970s it, and Richard Johnson in his own work, had already begun to explore new ways of applying the 1970s 'moment of Theory' to intellectual debate and academic research.[6] By 1979 'Theory', as an autonomous and abstruse field of study (a latter-day scholasticism?), was already giving ground to new forms of *empirical* work. What the debates of the 1970s had taught us was that such work could not return to an innocent *empiricism*: an empiricism which, in literary studies for example, simply centred on 'the text itself', or even 'the text in its social context'. We needed to utilize theory, but to take it beyond its self-referential exclusiveness and its resistance to direct engagement with material problems. What we learned, however, from

that dramatic moment at Ruskin College was that this intellectual and political shift in the use of theory would be easier to
achieve in literary studies than in history, since an influential
group of socialist historians seemed to be refusing history any
part (except outright resistance) in the debate about the uses of
theory. In addition, there was a larger context in which this
'moment' occurred: the impact of Thatcherism on left politics,
plus the urgent need to understand the popularity of such a
destructive political regime and to discover how the left could
counter it. *Literature and History*, then, as a 'radical' journal was
set a problem: how to respond both to the debate about 'Theory'
and to developments in national politics?

What we have called 'the moment of Theory' in the 1970s had
been, for the most part, a peculiarly introverted left political
affair. But if this theory was to be utilized, it had to engage with
the existing *loci* and practices of most literary and historical
studies. It had to recognize that they occur, by and large, in the
classroom; that these disciplines have an institutional form; and
that within the institutions of education radical notions of what
constitutes 'literature' and 'history' are in conflict with the
traditional constitution of these subjects. The 'Literature
Teaching Politics' network had been addressing this problem
since 1979, but it was also one that *Literature and History* could not
ignore. Indeed, since 1979 the journal has tried to marry theory
to the more immediate demands of *teaching* literature and
history in higher education. We recognized, in other words, that
there was little point in *theoretically* deconstructing the status of,
say, Jane Austen, when Jane Austen continued to be required
reading on the curriculum of most, if not all, English degrees.
But that by no means implied that we thought theory was
pointless. Rather it meant that *Literature and History* had to find,
first, theoretically-informed articles on established texts and
authors and, second, articles which shifted the debate from canonic texts and authors towards other forms of writing. Hence
our special interest in 'popular fictions'. For what that interest
signals is not an appropriation of the latest intellectual fad, but
a way of re-thinking – *and of teaching* – Literature-and-History.

What this book should demonstrate, therefore, is that the
study of popular fictions helps to reformulate conceptions of
'Literature' and of literary criticism. Certainly, it represents

something of what *Literature and History* has been trying to achieve, at least since 1979: a way of forging the relationship between 'writing, history and ideology'. These essays display theoretical work which is – no longer paradoxically – preoccupied with particular texts, authors or genres, and materially specific issues such as the processes of production and reproduction. And yet, as the inclusion of Tony Bennett's essay shows, this in no way denies the validity of work concerned to define 'popular fictions' in more general theoretical terms. All the essays argue that to continue to teach 'Literature' as if it comprises only the 'great texts' is to play *Hamlet* without the Prince (or even *Dracula* without the Count). The study of popular fictions calls History back on to the stage as a crucial participant in reformulating a relationship between fictional production and society. This book, then, represents a contribution to an intellectual debate and to a political struggle, because it aims to place popular fictions, as a dynamic element of the socio-cultural formation, on the curriculum. It aims to legitimize the critical study of *all* forms of writing. And it aims to make Literature without History, and History without Literature, intellectually and educationally unthinkable.

Notes

1 Janet Batsleer, Tony Davies, Rebecca O'Rourke and Chris Weedon, *Rewriting English* (Methuen, London 1985), p. 2.
2 Tony Bennett, 'Marxism and popular fiction', *Literature and History*, vol. 7:2 (Autumn 1981), p. 151. An edited version of this essay appears later in this book.
3 See also on this topic the important essay by Darko Suvin, 'The social addressees of Victorian fiction', *Literature and History*, vol. 8:1 (Spring 1982).
4 Paul O'Flinn, 'Production and reproduction: the case of *Frankenstein*', *Literature and History*, vol. 9:2 (Autumn 1983), pp. 200–1. An edited version of this essay appears later in this book.
5 Janice A. Radway, *Reading the Romance: Women, Patriarchy and Popular Literature* (University of North Carolina Press, Chapel Hill, NC, 1984), p. 8.
6 See, for example, Richard Johnson's essays in John Clarke, Chas Critcher and Richard Johnson (eds), *Working Class Culture: Studies in History and Theory* (Hutchinson, London 1979).

2
Literature and the Grub Street myth
KATHY MACDERMOTT

In scientific and philosophical reasoning the words, concepts and categories are 'instruments' of knowledge. But in political, ideological and philosophical struggle the words are also explosives, tranquillizers, poisons. Occasionally, the whole class struggle may be summed up in the struggle for one word against another word. Certain words struggle against themselves as enemies. Other words are the site of an *ambiguity*: the stake in a decisive but undecided battle.[1]

Behind this essay lies Althusser's argument that at different historical moments strategic words can become the site of a struggle between competing ideologies. I don't intend to deal directly with Althusser here, beyond accepting the fairly obvious premise that certain strategic words do control whole areas of discourse, and that whatever group can control the meaning of the word 'literature', for example, will also be able to control most or all discourse about poems and plays and novels. This has not always been the case. The word 'literature', that is, has not always isolated a particular category of reading and incorporated qualitative judgements about that category. It was not, in fact, until the eighteenth century that 'literary' came to mean something different from simply 'literate'. The ideological struggle which eventually issued in the new, improved and spiritualized meaning of the word 'literature' was historically conditioned, the result of a change in the circumstances of literary production. These circumstances – technological, political and social – conditioned the rise of the urban popular press in the context of a culture which remained largely rural and patrician. Under such circumstances the emergence of crucial redefinitions and newly discriminatory terms might be expected as part of a process of putting the specifically historical phenomenon in its ideological place, or determining an ideological place for it. This process of dehistoricization, I will be arguing, was largely organized through the mythology of Grub Street. Considered as dehistoricization, it cuts across that other process, fully described by Pat Rogers, whereby history connived with the major Augustan satirists to make an empirical state directly metaphoric for a spiritual state. What is at issue here is the transposition of a series of social and economic changes into a set of mythological constants which image contradiction as if it were continuity, and cultural bias as if it were natural verity. These mythological constants, their historical sources and their effects on meaning are the subject of this essay.

Raymond Williams is largely responsible for isolating the shift in meaning of the word 'literature' and locating it in relation to the rise of the popular press:

the first certain signs of a general change of meaning are from C18. **Literary** was extended beyond its equivalence to **literate**: probably first in the general sense of well-read but from mC18 to refer to the practice and profession of writing: 'literary merit' (Goldsmith, 1759); 'literary reputation' (Johnson, 1773). This appears to be closely connected with the heightened self-consciousness of the profession of authorship, in the period of transition from patronage to the bookselling market. Where Johnson had used **literature** in the sense of being highly literate in his *Life of Milton*, in his *Life of Cowley* he wrote, in the newly objective sense: 'an author whose pregnancy of imagination and elegance of language have deservedly set him high in the ranks of literature'. Yet **literature** and **literary**, in these new senses, still referred to the whole body of books and writings; or if distinction was made it was made in terms of falling below the level of polite learning rather than of particular kinds of writing.[2]

Williams simply asserts the appearance of a close connection between the shift in meaning of the word 'literature' and 'the period of transition from patronage to the bookselling market'. An account of the history of usage cannot press its conclusions much further than appearance. But if we cease to regard Williams's 'connection' syntagmatically – as a matter of historical coincidence – and begin to regard it paradigmatically – as part of a mythological structure – the appearance of a close connection becomes the fact of a formal analogy. That is, the division of 'literature' into 'learning' on one hand and (objectively) 'writing' on the other is analogous to the eighteenth-century distinction between the author-literatus ('man of genius') and the hack, the verbal mechanic, the mere producer of texts. In both these cases the distinction swings on the recognition of 'literature' as a form of production. This production Tom Brown, parodying Dryden's literary cataloguing, distinguished as either 'labour of the brain' or 'trouble of the fingers'.[3] We have already four terms in a cluster of associated antitheses which articulate the finished Grub Street myth, namely: literature-as-learning/literature-as-writing, genius/mechanism, brain/fingers, author/hack.

Like the word 'literature' (in its 'writing' sense) the word 'hack' (in its literary sense) is an eighteenth-century construction. The *Dictionary of Cant* (1699) notes the extension of the word into the semantic arena of the literary: '*Hacks* or Hackneys, hirelings. *Hackney-whores*, Common Prostitutes. *Hackney-Horses*, to be let to any body. *Hackney-Scriblers*, Poor Hirelings Mercenary Writers.'[4] The concept 'hack' is simpler than the new denotation of 'literature', and the simpler term certainly came into use earlier. But it is arguable that whatever the order of their introduction both usages were developed in order to fill the appropriate semantic/intellectual spaces in the antithetical cluster: that is, they supply bearers for pre-existing precipitates of meaning organized through a format of paired opposites. The opposition genius/mechanism is the only one of the four cited which was already embedded in the language and therefore capable of determining the associated semantic spaces in the antithetical cluster. Genius/mechanism is undoubtedly a crucial eighteenth-century opposition, dear to the authors of *The Art of Sinking in Poetry* and *A Tale of a Tub*. [. . .]

But even if the genius/mechanism antithesis can be viewed as holding a determining position among the antitheses organizing the Grub Street myth, there remains the question of how it was in its turn determined. What, that is, were the historical circumstances which raised to prominence a particular pair of semantically opposed terms which had always been available in discourse? Genius/mechanism, when associated with the process of literary production (via author/hack), is, after all, only a psychological metaphor. 'Genius' mystifies a literary process; 'mechanism' reifies it; neither does more than *illustrate* a dichotomy already perceived to govern the process of literary production. This dichotomy does not originate in psychological metaphor but rather in a second, economic and historical pair of causes in the process of literary production. Isolated by Goldsmith, this second pair constitutes 'that fatal revolution whereby . . . booksellers, instead of the great, become the patrons and paymasters of men of genius'. The opposition patron/bookseller is neither built into discourse like genius/mechanism nor constructed out of discourse like the new uses of the words 'hack' and 'literature'. It is not a natural or metaphoric but a historical and cultural opposition; it is the point in the Grub Street myth at which paradigm and syntagm cross: the point at which history is (re)produced as myth. It is this process of dehistoricization which I would like to turn to next.

In their book *The Sociology of Literature*, Laurenson and Swingewood argue that the move from a system of patronage to a system of commercial profit-making was neither a specifically eighteenth-century phenomenon nor as sudden as is implied by Goldsmith's use of the word 'revolution'. Instead, they trace a process of commercial sponsorship of writing beginning around 1600 and involving a gradual increase in the publication of trade manuals and, after 1688, an increase in political patronage.[5] But despite Laurenson and Swingewood's historical date, it is still the case that in (re)constructing its received version of events the eighteenth-century press took upon itself responsibility for the rise of commercialism by compressing a gradual process into a veritable and 'fatal revolution'. This it managed to do so convincingly as to have Ian Watt observing the growth of publishing-related technology and trade after the incorporation of the White Paper Makers in 1686, as well as studying an analogous expansion in the social prestige of the booksellers themselves, which issued in no fewer than five Lord Mayors of London during the eighteenth century. No doubt Watt is isolating significant points at the eighteenth-century end of Laurenson and Swingewood's broader historical process. But the fact remains that his attention was directed to the eighteenth-century end of the time scale by what he calls the 'Augustan View' of bookselling, a view whose ideological function was to reconstruct a technological, economic and social change within a patrician hegemony.

This crisis of literary patronage was only a symptom on one level of a wider social and economic crisis of paternalism which confronted the eighteenth-century gentry. A 'crisis' more likely to disturb than actually to threaten, it developed as a result of a number of changes in traditional patterns of employment, which in effect loosened the direct dependence of the labour force upon the gentry. E.P. Thompson considers these employment patterns in detail, and argues that the problem which they cumulatively posed for eighteenth-century paternalism was characteristically addressed by emphasizing cultural rather than economic or physical displays of power:

> A great deal of the gentry's appropriation of the labor value of the poor was mediated by their tenantry, by trade or taxation. . . . [Thus] ruling class control in the eighteenth century was located primarily in a cultural hegemony, and only secondarily in an expression of economic or physical (military) power. . . . To define control in terms of cultural hegemony is not to give up attempts at analysis, but to prepare for analysis at the points at which it should be made: into the images of power and authority, the popular mentalities of subordination.[6]

In short, then, the eighteenth century 'managed' the crisis of paternalism by dividing its functions into specifically economic and cultural spheres and conducting the cultural spheres directly while increasingly allowing the economic sphere to be visibly conducted by middlemen. Not a strategy but an adaptation, the ideological potency of this broad hegemonic response is apparent in T.S. Eliot's argument 250 years later that the aristocracy must be artificially preserved as a sort of cultural bloodbank. The problems posed to paternalism by the rise of the popular press, then, were (1) that it threatened to conflate cultural and economic spheres by making visible the relation between the cultural artefact and economic process, and (2) that it also threatened the cultural hegemony of the gentry by inserting a middle term between (high) patrician culture and (low) folk culture. Since the crisis of patronage was simply one level of the crisis of paternalism, it is not surprising to find it being treated in the same way: isolated from its historical context and imaged in terms of the opposition high/low. And just as the opposition paternal/filial is naturalized and removed from conflict by villainizing the middleman, so the opposition author/hack is naturalized and removed from conflict by villainizing the literary middleman: the bookseller.

Ian Watt notes that in the 'Augustan View' there is 'something of a special literary tradition in which the bookseller figures as a comic villain'. Watt adduces the works of Pope, Savage, David Hume, Dr Johnson, Goldsmith and Fielding in support of his argument, to which one might add the works of such significant hacks as Tom Brown, Ned Ward and John Dunton. 'Why', Watt concludes, 'do booksellers loom so large on the literary scene?'[7] One very possible answer is that the economic villainy of the middleman-bookseller is crucial to the mythology of Grub Street because it naturalizes the oppositions cited above by regrouping them under the heading art/commerce. Vilification is in the first place a special function of dehistoricization: in fact, the resources of biography have uncovered the remains of many 'booksellers [who] were knowing and conversible with whom, for the sake of bookish knowledge, the greatest wits were pleased to converse'. Their shops served the eighteenth century as 'a plentiful and perpetual emporium of learned authors' to which 'the learned gladly resorted'.[8] Dryden's bookseller Jacob Tonson, whether for his financial or his intellectual improvement, cultivated the society of the Kit-Kat Club; and even John Dunton (as bookseller) had Sir William Temple among his contributors. Many booksellers led sober, discreet lives, devoted to the Commonwealth of Learning and prospering as a result of their devotion.[9] After all, five became Lord Mayors of London. Nevertheless, the generic figure of the bookseller comes down to us – not from biography but from myth – as 'a little too cunning to be honest, and too miserly to be generous; [one who] loves nothing more than his money, and hates nothing more than to part with it'.[10] Of course Grub Street specialized in vilification, but Watt registers a common impression when he isolates vilification of the book-seller as a 'special literary tradition'.

In fact, the dehistoricization of the bookseller was a process largely underwritten by the historical bookseller. Take, for example, the case of Abel Roper, one of Tom Brown's book-sellers, who composed a version of the bookseller–hack relationship for use as a preface to one of Brown's works. Brown, it seems, had failed to supply a proper preface, and Roper employed the relevant space to speculate on the reasons behind Brown's latest exhibition of irresponsibility:

> What? says the Reader . . . has the fumes of a long debauch raised such Fogs about his Brains, that nothing could be pumpt from his Poets Fingers? [Note again the Brains/ Fingers opposition.] No, Gentlemen, he is retired into the Country with some yellow and white Chips of the *Tower*, and now looks as much above a Book seller, as a P— Councellor above a Porter. . . . This is an Epidemical disease among some Scribblers, who have no Wit to sell, while they have Money to spend or can be trusted; but when they are reduced to a low ebb, they'll sneak, fawn, and cringe, like a Dog.[11]

The bookseller and the hack, it appears, are eternally at odds: one solid, the other dissipated; one knowing his place, the other without a place, running with both the hare and the hounds; one knowing the value of money, the other periodically reducing himself to penury; one a man of orderly and business-like method, the other given to energetic fits of work and debauch. This is Roper's version of himself vs. Brown, and what it does is to release Brown from complicity in the whole chain of trades-man-like connotators set in motion by the presence of the bookseller. Brown is not solid, reliable, secure, predictable, systematic, businesslike. Though he may well be reliant on booksellers when 'reduced to a low ebb', Brown is defined in opposition to Roper, and in general the image of the poverty-stricken hack is defined against the image of the miserly and affluent bookseller. In this way the opposition takes the form of an explanation: the nature of the bookseller *accounts for* the nature of the hack: 'a poet that, for want of wit and sense, ran mad for want of victuals' did so at least partly by courtesy of 'a bookseller in this City . . . that has got an estate by starving authors'. Writers whose 'Learning . . . lies very often in as little Room as their *Honesty*' required booksellers less credulous than unwilling to meet the terms of the learned. The hack whose imagination was wholly taken up with *'How much a sheet'*[12] required a bookseller who, confounding quality and quantity, made it worth a poet's while to turn libeller, scandalmonger or satirist in abundant prose. A hack writing to order required a bookseller sedulously sniffing the wind before venturing an edition, like Jacob Tonson beating down the price of *Paradise Lost* with the observation that the times 'were not propitious to blank verse upon a sacred subject'. The image of the hack which is thus 'accounted for' by the image of the bookseller is of someone who would undoubtedly like to make a profit, is quite capable of betraying his art and his morals in order to make a profit, but who nevertheless never will make a profit – simply by virtue of being the sort of person who would choose a profession as unsubstantial and fly-by-night as writing (as opposed, for example, to bookselling). The nature of the literary beast simply is not commercial:

> But alas! after all, when I see an Ingenious Man set up for a mere Poet, and steer his course through Life, towards that Point of the Compass, I give him up as one *prick'd down by Fate, for misery and misfortune*. 'Tis something unaccountable, but one wo'd incline to think there's some indispensable Law, whereby Poverty and Disappointment are entail'd upon Poets.[13]

The image of the bookseller–hack relationship, then, displaces the cultural contradiction art/commerce which was embodied in the rise of the popular press and distributes the terms of that contradiction between the hack (art) and the bookseller (commerce). The hack may be a considerably degraded version of Sidney's Poet, but to recognize his degradation is at the same time necessarily to recognize his essential continuity with an established tradition of literary production.

Thus the vilification of the bookseller sponsors a 'continuous-but-debased' version of both the writer and (it follows) the literary work. Whereas – the argument runs – the patron's pocket was at the service of his taste, the bookseller's taste was at the service of his pocket. And everything, as Dryden pointed out, followed from that. Setting the case of the 'Art' of translation, he argued that

> [In England] *Booksellers* are the undertakers of Works of this nature, and they are Persons more devoted to their own Gain, than the Publick Honour. They are very parsimonious in regarding the wretched Scribblers they employ; and care not how the Business is done, so that it be but done. They live by selling Titles, not Books. . . . While Translations are thus at the disposal of the *Booksellers*, and have no better Judges, or Rewarders of the Performance, it is impossible, that we should make any Progress, in an Art so very useful to an enquiring People.[14]

Booksellers, that is, by their very ('parsimonious') natures, sponsor inferior versions of those 'undertakings' which used to be sponsored by 'better Judges, or Rewarders of the Performance' – namely, the traditional patron. Thus questions of the difference between the patrician and the popular press are only able to address that difference in terms of (unfortunate) deviations from the pre-established patrician norm. But if the patron/bookseller opposition makes possible the reading high (culture)/low (culture) throughout the antithetical cluster, the reading itself is nevertheless organized into narrative and (re-) produced as myth through a series of specifically and traditionally literary conversions or conventions. Two of these are crucial as well as easily inferred from the antitheses which specifically sponsor them: 'instrument of knowledge'/'object of commerce' and ancient/modern.

The pair in quotation marks comes courtesy of Dr Johnson and is a generalized version of the most common literary convention organizing the Grub Street myth: reductive wit. Reductive wit crops up most commonly in descriptions of Grub Street modes of production (the genius/mechanism pairing raised earlier) and of the products themselves, as is suggested by Johnson's pairing. Reductive accounts of composition consist in providing (low) mechanical-physical analogues for (high) spiritual-intellectual processes, and are perhaps best represented by the Lagadan 'Project for improving speculative Knowledge by practical and mechanical Operations', and Pope's literary cold in the head:

> it were great cruelty and injustice, if all such Authors as cannot write in the other [high] way were prohibited from writing at all. Against this I draw an argument from what seems to me an undoubted physical maxim, That Poetry is a natural or morbid Secretion from the Brain. As I would not suddenly stop a cold in the head, or dry up my neighbour's Issue, I would as little hinder him from necessary writing.[15]

Reductive accounts of each other's literary productions were a provocative speciality among hacks and consisted in pressing the analogy governing the act of composition into an analogy governing the thing composed. Generalizing, for example, from the 'flux of speech' and deficiency in retention that forced hacks to 'break words entirely for their ease', Grub Street wits arrived at the objective correlative for their literary distastes with 'Bum-fodder' and 'tail timber'. [. . .] More interesting modes of reduction operate by translating spiritual and literary effects into their nearest physical and medical equivalents. If poetry is meant to calm the unruly passions and purge the soul from fear and pity, Grub Street poetry acts as an infallible soporific or emetic. What is of interest in this latter form of reductive wit is its indirect citation of traditional uses of poetry. Seen in this light it appears as a crude form of the more sophisticated literary convention which helped to organize the Grub Street myth, namely the mock heroic.

The antithesis governing mock heroic is of course ancient/ modern. The ancient/modern debate as conducted in the Augustan age has been extensively documented and discussed by literary historians and historians of ideas, most notably R.F. Jones. It is, however, possible to view it outside an exclusively literary context by considering it as (yet another) case of dehistoricization and polarization. The basis of such an argument is supplied by E.P. Thompson:

> There were the rulers and the ruled, the high and the low people, persons of substance and of independent estate and

the loose and disorderly sort. In between, where the professional and middle classes, and the substantial yeomanry, should have been, relations of clientage and dependency were so strong that, at least until the 1760s, these groups appear to offer little deflection of the essential polarities. . . . This is a world of patricians and of plebs; it is no accident that the rulers turned back to ancient Rome for a model of their own sociological order.[16]

When the Augustan age imaged itself, it did so through polarity; when it placed a cultural value on polarity, it invoked ancient Rome; when it engaged in the ancient/modern debate, it drew Grub Street into line with the dominant cultural ideology. Ancient/modern, patron/bookseller, author/hack: in each case the second term signifies an analogy with high/low, original/degraded. But the oppositions also issued in a comparison of ancient and modern mythologies. The vehicle of the comparison was the mock heroic and the result was the elaboration of a full Grub Street mythology. The development of both the mock heroic comparison and the Grub Street mythology is caught at a half-way point in William King's modern answer to Lucian's *Dialogues of the Dead*. The dialogue in question is between the ancient and mythical figure of Hercules and the modern and generic figure of the butcher:

> *Hercules*. Did I not cleanse the *Augean* Stables, and conquer the Bull of *Marathon*?
> *Butcher*. And have I not stav'd and tail'd at the *Bankside* when the stoutest He would not venture; was it not I that when Tom Dove broke loose, and drove the Mob before him, took him by the Ring, and led him back to the Stake, with the universal Shouts of the Company? Besides, I question whether you ever saw a Bull-dog . . .
> *Hercules*. You enrage me! Now by the Gods I have taken the *Thermodoontiack* belt from the Princess *Thalestris*.
> *Butcher*. Hold a little, good Sir, I have flung down the belt in *Moorfields*, when never a *Lincolns-Inn-fields* Wrestler durst encounter me.[17]

'I find you will have the last word,' observes Hercules, accepting finally that classical stature will always fall short of modern pretension. Comic inflation of this sort figures prominently in the repertoire of Grub Street tactics, whence it was applied to generic figures and selected individuals and places, all of which were in due course bloated into types and archetypes definitely 'below' the classic models but (by the same token) answering to them. What has the bull of Marathon to do with Tom Dove or the '*Thermodoontiack* belt' with the belt at Moorfields? Partly they supply the ancient/modern debate with a mock heroic conclusion; partly, they supply hard-pressed hacks with a comic shorthand for innumerable *Trips*, *Spies*, *Journeys to* and *Letters from* the metropolitan readership. The Grub Street myth must in fact have offered itself to the hacks as a largely practical matter, as recyclable as the Homeric myths and considerably more appealing to a general readership with its topographies (Wills', Bedlam, Covent Garden, Moorfields, Smithfield, Newgate, Grub Street itself), archetypes (the beau, the Quaker, the 'cit', the bookseller, the hack), heroes (Sir Richard Blackmore, Dr Busby, George Fox, Titus Oates, Isaac Newton) and adventures (on the river, at the gaming house, in the brothel).

Through the agency of mock heroic and reductive wit, the relation high culture/popular culture was naturalized as comic inversion and extended into the coherent narrative of myth. This process of (re)production was managed largely by the hacks themselves, who incorporated the myth of the popular press (Grub Street, booksellers, hacks) into the myth of popular culture (topography, archetypes, heroes) and thus in effect closed the ideological circle. From as early as 'Macflecknoe', and often in a dialogue with the major satirists of the time, the writers of Grub Street located their own work largely in relation to and on the terms set by the dominant literary culture. The influence of this hegemonic conditioning on concepts of culture, literature and the function of literary criticism has been fundamental. In the first place, the qualitative distinction high/low directs critical attention away from popular writing – as if the distinction itself could be presumed, and as if it could be presumed to constitute the inner nature, essence, ideal core both of literature in general and the particular literary work. The Grub Street myth mystifies both the text and the act of reading, removing both from their actual historical situations with the assistance of a concept of literature which is itself dehistoricized.

Notes

1 Louis Althusser, 'Philosophy as a revolutionary weapon', in *Lenin and Philosophy and Other Essays*, trans. Ben Brewster (Monthly Review Press, New York 1971), p. 21.

2 Raymond Williams, *Keywords* (Croom Helm, London 1976), p. 152.

3 Thomas Brown, *The Late Converts Exposed: Or The Reasons of Mr. Bays's Changing His Religion* (London 1690), p. 23.

4 B.E., *A New Dictionary of the Terms Ancient and Modern of the Canting Crew* (London 1699).

5 See D. Laurenson and A. Swingewood, *The Sociology of Literature* (MacGibbon & Kee, London 1971), pp. 108, 111.

6 E.P. Thompson, 'Patrician society, plebeian culture', *Journal of Social History*, VII (1974), pp. 389, 387.

7 Ian Watt, 'Publishers and sinners: the Augustan view', *Studies in Bibliography*, XII (1952), p. 3.

8 Leona Rostenberg, *Literary, Political, Scientific, Religious and Legal Publishing, Printing and Bookselling in England, 1551–1700* (Burt Franklin, New York 1965), II, p. 286.

9 See, for example, Rostenberg's accounts of John Martyn and Robert Scott.

10 Edward Ward, *The London Spy*, ed. Arthur L. Hayward (Cassell, London 1927), pp. 75–6.

11 Abel Roper, 'The bookseller to the reader', preface to Thomas Brown, *A Collection of Miscellany Poems, Letters, &c.* (London 1699), n.p.

12 Thomas Brown, *Amusements Serious and Comical and Other Works*, ed. Arthur L. Hayward (George Routledge & Sons, London 1937), p. 27; Ward, *London Spy*; p. 13; John Dunton, *The Life and Errors of John Dunton Late Citizen of London* (London 1705), p. 11.

13 Dunton, *Life and Errors*, p. 243.

14 John Dryden, 'The life of Lucian', *The Works of Lucian, Translated from the Greek, by several Eminent Hands* (London 1711), pp. 56–7.

15 Alexander Pope, 'Peri Bathos: or, the art of sinking in poetry', in *Alexander Pope, Selected Poetry and Prose*, ed. William K. Wimsatt (Holt Rinehart, New York 1951), p. 311.

16 Thompson, 'Patrician society, plebeian culture', p. 395.

17 William King, 'Dialogues of the dead relating to the present controversy concerning the epistles of Philaris', in *Miscellanies in Prose and Verse* (London 1705), pp. 287–8.

3

Beggars and thieves:
The Beggar's Opera as crime drama
MICHAEL DENNING

The Beggar's Opera is too familiar a play. We know it before we read it, in part because of the Brecht/Weill adaptation. Popular songs have made Macheath and Polly Peachum well-known figures. But even when we read *The Beggar's Opera* it seems familiar; the device of comparing statesmen to criminals is a contemporary device; and given the fortunes of the word 'impeach', we have little difficulty substituting Nixon for Walpole. Francis Ford Coppola's *The Godfather* is a recent version of the rich figure of organized crime. Literary critics aid in this familiarization; to take one example, William Empson reads the *Opera* as a proto-romantic work, embodying the 'cult of independence', and foreshadowing the modern romanticization of criminals: he compares Macheath to a Chicago tough (of the 1920s and 1930s).[1] Given this familiarity, I think it is important to insist on the historicity of the work, a play of the English 1720s, and to see it as a condensation, a figuration, of contradictions within that society. Such a defamiliarization could restore to this drama its ability to provide an imagination of historical transformation to our supermarket culture.

The obvious place to begin in situating the work would be to uncover what is being satirized, that which is not on the surface of the play, to pull Walpole and the fashion of the Italian opera out from historical oblivion. But I would like to begin at the familiar surface, not with the object of satire but with the vehicle

by which it is satirized: Gay's choice of thieves and highway-
men. It seems a natural device to us; perhaps we need to
estrange it. Frank Chandler, in his comprehensive history of
rogue literature, tells us that satire enters the English literature
of roguery with Gay and Fielding.[2] And E.P. Thompson writes
that 'it was in these years that the comparison of statesmanship
with criminality became common coinage'.[3] On the other hand,
we know that Walpole was satirized in other ways: as a philis-
tine who could not recognize true poetry; and as a quack doctor
unable to cure a sick nation.[4] The choice of the criminal is
something new in the 1720s. In this essay I will begin with a look
at the figure of Jonathan Wild, the basis for both Gay's and
Fielding's satires; will then look at the institution of hanging;
and finally will consider the struggles over the law in the early
eighteenth century. My three main anchors are: Empson's
essay on the *Opera*; the work of the Warwick Centre for Social
History; and the work of Michel Foucault on punishment.[5]

The ideology of the gang

We can take an odd misreading of *The Beggar's Opera* as a place
to begin. Gerald Howson, author of the definitive biography of
Jonathan Wild, writes that after his death

> Jonathan Wild had become a symbol rather than a remem-
> bered historical person. . . . In *The Beggar's Opera*, John Gay
> had tried to show that 'Peachum' and 'Lockit' . . . were really
> pillars of the underworld; but his point was missed, for
> politicians saw the play only as an attack on themselves, and
> critics attacked the play because it showed criminals in a
> humorous and sympathetic light.

It is difficult to see how the *Opera* could be taken as an exposé of
the underworld in the manner of a 'true-to-life' Mafia paper-
back; one thinks the politicians and critics have seen at least
something of the play. But the vehicle of the play is the
underworld and the popular figure of Jonathan Wild, so it is
worth investigating this further. Jonathan Wild was, Howson
tells us, 'the subject of more "Accounts", "Narratives" and
"Lives" than any other criminal of the 18th century'.[6] So we are
involved in a double displacement, requiring two explanations:

why is Wild so central to the popular imagination, and is he a representative figure? And how does Gay transform the myth of Wild, and what does that transformation mean?

What is the character of crime in the 1720s? J.M. Beattie, in an account of crime in England from 1660 to 1800, quotes a pamphlet written against Wild which speaks of 'the general complaint of the taverns, the coffeehouses, the shop-keepers and others, that their customers are afraid when it is dark to come to their houses and shops for fear . . . that they may be blinded, knocked down, cut or stabbed'. Beattie adds that 'such comments can be found at other times, of course, but there seems to be a particular concentration of concern in the 1720s in newspapers, in the correspondence of those engaged in judicial administration, and in the masses of contemporary accounts of crime, including, in Defoe's novels, the first fictional accounts of criminal life'.[7] And E.P. Thompson has written that 'if that unsatisfactory term "crime wave" could ever be used with conviction, it might possibly be applied to the early 1720s'.[8] However, Douglas Hay writes that 'it appears as if it is not just a matter of "crime" enlarging but equally of a property-conscious oligarchy redefining, through its legislative power, activities, use-rights in common or woods, perquisites in industry, as thefts and offences'.[9] It was a time when capital punishment was being extended to more and more crimes, crimes not between people but against property. The Black Act of 1723 added some fifty offences, mostly poaching rabbits and fish and hunting deer, to the death penalty. Locke had written that 'government has no other end but the preservation of property',[10] and the Whig government was pursuing that end with a vengeance. This, together with the suspension of *habeas corpus* because of the revelations of Jacobite conspiracies in 1722, and the financial disorder following the South Sea Bubble in 1720 (in which Gay lost money), led to a repressive state in the 1720s (which Whig historians term 'the establishment of political stability'). It is against this background that the career and celebrity of Jonathan Wild is to be seen.

Wild was not a highwayman or thief. He maintained himself as a respectable Londoner working as a thief-taker and a restorer of lost property. As thief-taker, he captured criminals and brought them to prison, collecting the rewards. As a restorer of lost property, he maintained offices in the Old Bailey and enabled people who had had property stolen to retrieve it. He had agents throughout southern England. In the process he destroyed four London gangs; the Privy Council consulted him over ways to combat crime. These activities were welcomed and applauded by the community; Wild even petitioned to become a Freeman of London, and thereby to gain a sort of official recognition for his position. Since there was no regular police force, the thief-taking system was, Howson tells us, 'the most effective and least expensive way of keeping crime under control'.[11] The revelations after his fall that Wild, far from preventing crime, was the organizer of the largest crime net-work in London, were shocking. The thief-taking had been a means of establishing his reputation and controlling his sub-ordinates; at his trial he published a list of those petty criminals he had sent to the gallows. The lost property office had not only arranged the return of property but had planned the robbery of it.

A number of pamphlets were written on Wild, narrating his life and system; I want to look briefly at the one written by Daniel Defoe shortly after Wild's execution in 1725. Defoe, who claims to have gone to Wild's lost property office to enquire about a sword he had had stolen, emphasizes the 'business' side of Wild:

> He openly kept his Compting House, or Office, like a Man of Business, and had his Books to enter every thing in with the utmost Exactness and Regularity . . . he took none of your Money for restoring your Goods neither did he restore you any Goods; you gave him Money indeed for his Trouble in enquiring out the Thief, and for using his Interest by awing or perswading to get your stolen Goods sent you back.

But Defoe's disbelief is not directed to Wild but to his society, including himself, for tolerating, even applauding, what could not have been that surprising:

> He was now Master of his Trade, Poor and Rich flock'd to him. . . . How infatuate were the People of this Nation all the while? Did they consider, that at the very time that they treated this Person with such a Confidence, as if he had been

appointed to the Trade? He had, perhaps, the very Goods in his keeping, waiting the Advertisement for the Reward; and that, perhaps, they had been stolen with that very Intention?

Defoe also points out that the crowd at Tyburn, contrary to their usual compassion for the condemned, hurled 'curses and execrations' at Wild, and that there was 'not one pitying Eye to be seen'. This is in marked contrast to the hero of another of Defoe's criminal biographies, Jack Sheppard. Sheppard was a thief who was betrayed by Wild and then gained fame and sympathy by a series of extraordinary escapes, which Defoe narrates. His small size and Cockney wit made him the antithesis of Wild in the popular imagination, the boy who was first seduced to crime by, depending on the story, either a woman, Edgworth Bess, or Wild himself, and was betrayed by the two together. Defoe has Sheppard denounce thief-takers and the practice of impeaching; it hurts the 'Reputation of the British Thievery'.[12] Empson is wrong when he says Gay split Wild into Peachum and Macheath, into villain and hero. Rather, Gay used the popular opposition of Wild and Sheppard; when Fielding fuses Sheppard and Wild in his character of Jonathan Wild, the meaning, as we shall see, slips again.

The most important aspect of Defoe's Wild pamphlet is its rejection of satire. Attacking the comic and satiric versions of Wild's life, he says: 'The following Tract does not indeed make a Jest of his Story as they do, or present his History, which indeed is a tragedy of itself, in the stile of Mockery and Redicule, but in a Method agreeable to the Fact.'[13] Defoe maintains this moral tone a few years later when he comments on the portrayal of rogues: 'We take pains to puff 'em up in their villainy, and thieves are set out in so amiable a light in *The Beggar's Opera* that it has taught them to value themselves on their profession, rather than to be asham'd of it.'

But satire held sway; its ambivalence may be seen in that it begins with Wild's own pamphlet, *An Answer to a Late Insolent Libel*, published in 1718, satirizing the attack on thief-takers made by Charles Hitchens in an earlier pamphlet. Wild replies to a basically accurate account of his own illegal activities with ridicule and innuendo, and indeed wins the paper war, going on to consolidate his organization. After Wild's execution, there were satiric lives and an *Advice to His Successors*. But more serious satire arose by the coincidence of the exposure and execution of Wild and the impeachment of the Earl of Macclesfield, the Lord Chancellor, for bribery in 1725. The opposition journalist Nathaniel Mist first elaborated the Wild–Walpole analogy in 1725, and Swift is supposed (though I don't see any evidence of it) to have first dubbed Wild 'The Great'.[14]

Before going on to Gay's satire, the question remains: was Jonathan Wild a representative figure, and what does his infamy signify? E.P. Thompson, in his study of the Black Act, deals with the question of whether the Blacks were a 'gang'; he says that the category of 'gang' or the twentieth-century criminological term, 'subculture', can be applied to some criminal activity in London, like that around Wild, which was professionalized and institutionalized; but that 'in the 18th century it is probable that only a fraction of those who were caught up in the law – or who were hanged and transported – belonged to this professionalized sector'. 'What is at issue', he goes on to say, 'is not whether there were any such gangs (there were) but the universality with which the authorities applied the term to any association of people, from a benefit society to a group of kin to a Fagin's den which fell outside the law.'[15] And though Thompson does not mention it, it may be significant that in 1726 an Act was passed prohibiting combinations of workers.[16] That neither the Waltham Blacks nor King John, a Robin Hood figure, had any such celebrity as Wild leads to the conclusion that the accounts of Wild, whether realistic or romantic, whether fictions or histories, are less representations of England in the 1720s, even of the underworld, than embodiments of a powerful ideology of the 'gang' – seeing ideology not as a system of ideas or a false consciousness, but as a sort of narrative which creates an imaginary relationship for the individual to the collective world. Gay, by taking up the Wild story, stages not the 'cult of independence' but this ideology of the gang.

How does Gay structure his version of Jonathan Wild? The basic opposition among the characters is that between Macheath and Peachum. There are a number of semantic contraries by which we can express this: youth/age, prodigality/miserliness, escape/imprisonment, aristocrat/bourgeois, eros/money. To take the last contrary, we see this clearly made when

Macheath's review of the 'ladies' (2:4) parallels Peachum's earlier review of his gang (1:3). But it is a mark of the interdependence of the contraries that the characters define their own passion in the terms of their opposites. So Macheath says that 'money is not so strong a cordial' as women (2:3), compares his parting with Polly to the parting of a miser and a shilling (1:13), and says that 'a man who loves money might as well be contented with one guinea, as I with one woman' (2:3). For Peachum and Lockit, on the other hand, love, sex and marriage are forms of money: 'a handsome wench in our way of business is as profitable as at the bar of a Temple coffee-house' (1:4); Mrs Peachum says 'I am very sensible, husband, that Captain Macheath is worth money' (1:9); the estate of widowhood is seen as the intention of all marriage articles; and Lockit says to Lucy of Macheath's escape: 'Perhaps you have made a better bargain with him than I could have done – How much, my good girl?' (3:1). The interdependence of contraries is also evident in the inverted opposition between Polly/Lucy and Jenny Diver (like Peachum and Lockit, Polly and Lucy are identical; Lucy is more accurate than she intends when she says 'Then our cases, my dear Polly, are exactly alike. Both of us indeed have been too fond' (3:8)). Whereas Polly and Lucy are shopkeepers' daughters who in part reject their mercenary education for the romance of love and the imitation of the gentry, Jenny is the one of the 'fine ladies' who is thoroughly on Peachum's side: it is said of her that she acts 'as if money were her only pleasure. Now that is a command of the passions uncommon in a woman' (2:4). And she has a bourgeois scorn for the gaming table: 'cards and dice are only fit for cowardly cheats'.

This economy of contraries is attenuated by certain categories that encompass both contraries, and by an imbalance of power between the contraries. In the first case, it is clear that though there are two types of rogues, all are rogues; that though there are two types of predators, all are predators; and that whatever their pleasure, sex and money are not far apart in all minds. In the second case, there is a clear inequality of power between Macheath and Peachum. Lockit and Peachum, being good accountants, know their mutual interest; Peachum says 'for you know we have it in our power to hang each other' (2:10). For Macheath that knowledge is the product of the education of the play. Early in the play he says that 'business cannot go on without' Peachum, that he is a 'necessary agent', and that 'the moment we break loose from him, our gang is ruin'd' (2:2). But by the end, in what Empson sees as the only straight line in the play, Macheath says of Peachum and Lockit: 'their lives are as much in your power, as yours are in theirs . . . Tis my last request – Bring those villains to the gallows before you, and I am satisfied' (3:14). But one is not really convinced; Gay cannot hang his villain.

The detailing of these oppositions is little more than descriptive. But if meaning is created by difference, something may be gained by seeing how they differ from another telling of the Wild tale. So I will turn briefly to Henry Fielding's novel of 1743, *Jonathan Wild*. First of all, Fielding's Wild is, as I have said earlier, a mixture of the figures of Wild and Jack Sheppard or, in other words, of Peachum and Macheath. Fielding's Wild is a thief-taker, employing other hands to steal for him and impeaching them when it is profitable. He has a gang which we are told is regularized and organized; there is a brief account of the office for the return of stolen goods. But one feels that these are used because they are given in the life of the real Wild; they are not the sources of the narrative energy. Indeed the novel plays down the organized gang and the business aspects of Wild. When Fielding's Wild divides mankind into 'those that use their own hands, and those who employ the hands of others', he undercuts this by dividing the second group into 'those who employ hands for the use of the community in which they live' (by whom he means 'the yeoman, the manufacturer, the merchant, and perhaps the gentlemen'), and 'those who employ hands merely for their own use' (he lists conquerors, statesmen, and thieves).[17] Fielding's Wild is not a shopkeeper; he is closer to rogue than thief-taker, courting and abducting women, picking pockets, aiding and encouraging escapes from justice, gambling at cards and dice; he is an aristocratic man of fashion, a beau. So the aspects of Gay's villain are played down, and those of Gay's hero become villainous. This is emphasized in that whereas Gay's victims are themselves rogues, Fielding's victims are innocent. The Heartfrees and their apprentice, Friendly, are good-natured and generous; their peaceful existence is destroyed by the intrusion of Wild. They are the good bourgeois family that Peachum's family parodies: at the end the faithful apprentice marries the daughter and becomes a partner in the successful business. Placed on the grid of the *Opera*, this would be something like Filch marrying Polly.

Fielding's novel turns the contradictions of the Wild story as written by Gay into a bourgeois morality play much like the original criminal pamphlets. We are given the vicarious thrill in the life of the aristocratic villain (since the Heartfrees are neither very exciting nor very convincing) and are then gratified to see the villain brought to justice (Fielding's Wild, like the real Wild but unlike Gay's Peachum, is hanged). That this is, despite its satire on Walpole (who was no longer in power when this was published in 1743; there is evidence that Fielding suppressed the novel in return for money earlier), a Whiggish tale is seen by the dominant oppositions of liberty/tyranny and law/lawlessness, neither of which is to be found in Gay. This is also, I think, a real expression of the 'cult of independence', not by glorifying the criminal, as the romantics were to do, but by exploring the paradoxes and dangers of the new individualism.

To return to *The Beggar's Opera*: in the staging of the ideology of the gang, the moral problem of the play becomes a political one. For the gang is not just a party, a conspiracy, a set of evil individuals; it is the new system, the mercantile commercial capitalism. E.P. Thompson writes that

> Political life in England in the 1720s had something of the sick quality of a 'banana republic'. This is a recognized phase of commercial capitalism when predators fight for the spoils of power and have not yet agreed to submit to rational or bureaucratic rules and forms. Each politician, by nepotism, interest and purchase, gathered around him a following of loyal dependents.[18]

Gay senses the power of this system; this is why his heroes are not outside it. Macheath is part of the gang; the aristocracy and court are no longer an alternative to the money of the City but a parasite on it. They are all part of a system where 'money is the true fuller's earth for reputation' (1:9). Money has no origin, no smell; it doesn't distinguish between a thief, a shopkeeper or a gentleman. And this is why Gay cannot hang Peachum. No one has that power except Lockit, and these two are beginning to evolve rational and bureaucratic rules between themselves. But just choosing thieves as heroes and making businessmen thieves is a challenge to the contemporary deification of property. When Mrs Peachum says to her husband, 'You know, my dear, I never meddle in matters of death', it is clear that death and business are one for Gay.

How does Gay come to do this? Surely not in the way of this essay, from a reflection on the meaning of contemporary myths of criminality. [. . .] It may be that Gay's own financial losses in the South Sea Bubble turned him against the merchant capitalism of his day; and it may simply be the revenge of a disappointed office-seeker. But I think it may well have been derived from a reflection on the position of the writer in the early eighteenth century: a beggar dependent on the patronage of a government which under Walpole veered away from previous support of men of letters (of all parties). Without that, he had to turn, like Macheath, to the taste of the town.

The theatre of Tyburn

One critic has written of the play's 'particular double view of the world as both horrifying and ridiculous' and of 'the general lightheartedness of the play as a whole, lightheartedness which persists, paradoxically, despite the bitterness, the intense cynicism reiterated by the ending'.[19] And surely the difficulty with the first part of this essay is that, by concentrating on Macheath's last request to his gang to bring Peachum to the gallows, it misses the lightheartedness of the play, which is clearly the dominant tone. Can a historical reading of *The Beggar's Opera* give any account of this lightheartedness?

One could begin with the comic form of the play which generates much of its lightheartedness, subsuming somewhat its satiric qualities. But I will begin with hanging, ostensibly one of the more horrifying aspects of the eighteenth century. Peter Linebaugh writes of hanging: 'Indeed so often is it, as a symbol of all that is bestial, violent and brutal in 18th-century society, counterposed to the architecture, taste, music and literature of genteel civilization that it has lost whatever accurate connotations it once may have had and has now entered the ranks of the historical cliché'.[20]

Empson rightly latches on to the plays on the word 'hanging', seeing it as a 'covert metaphor for true love'.[21] But the uses of hanging seem to add to the comedy as well. Despite the battle over the hanging of Macheath, hanging is usually seen as preferable to the given state of things. Obviously Peachum and Lockit want Macheath hanged, and he wants them hanged. But, in addition, Mrs Peachum had rather seen Polly hanged than married (1:8); the parents (Peachum and Lockit) feel that widowhood by hanging is a desirable state (1:10); and Polly's duty to her parents obliges her to hang Macheath (1:10). Macheath would rather be hanged than suffer the furies of the whores (2:3), and rather than be faced with six wives (3:15). Lucy is willing to be hanged for revenge on Polly (3:7), and would rather see Macheath hanged than in the arms of another (2:15). Both Polly and Lucy would like to see Macheath hanged for revenge at one point (2:13); at another point they would both be hanged with him (3:15). The beggar would like to hang the whole cast. Surely some of the lightheartedness of the play comes from this universal desire to 'be hanged'.

This lightheartedness about hanging is rooted in the poetry of popular speech. Looking at the slang and the canting dictionaries that record the speech of the eighteenth-century London poor, Peter Linebaugh concludes that 'the speech of the labouring class described the hanging with irreverence, humour, and defiance'. He then catalogues the metaphors for hanging: 'To hang, like a dance, was "to swing", to "dance the Paddington frisk", "to morris". It was "to go west", "to ride up Holborn Hill", to "dangle in the Sheriff's picture frame", "to cry cockles" . . . Awe, majesty and dread were riddled to their proper meaning, death by hanging.'[22]

One of the most powerful conceits in the play juxtaposes hangings and weddings. When Macheath says to Polly, 'whenever you are talking of marriage, I am thinking of hanging' (2:13), it recalls Polly's early romantic vision of Macheath in the cart being brought to the gallows (1:12). Indeed the play itself, all about hanging, is written, the beggar says, to celebrate a wedding. Empson speaks of the song where the marriage knot and the hangman's knot are linked as the play's 'metaphysical poetry'.[23] But this is less a strikingly original conceit than a reworking of the hanging custom of the 'gallows wedding'.

Linebaugh, in his account of hanging customs and super-
stitions, documents the connection between hangings and weddings in speech – 'to be "noozed" in canting talk meant either to
be hanged or to be married'; and in journalistic simile – Defoe is
quoted as writing that criminals 'go to [their] execution as neat
and trim as if they were going to a Wedding'. He comments also
on the actual marriage-like practices at hangings.[24]

One conclusion to be drawn from this historicizing of Gay's
figures is that a more adequate object of study for the critic of
narrative and figurative language is what Foucault would call a
'discursive formation', the general economy of a body of discourses, not in terms of *Zeitgeist* (not to reinstitute a history of
ideas) but in terms of its characteristic tropes, figures and
narrative structures, treating that formation to a certain degree
anonymously. Without attempting that here, one might use it to
situate Gay's poetic practice within that field, if only sketchily.
Gay, for example, does not use the canting vocabulary used by
Grub Street productions; his position within the genteel literary
system prevents that. But the figure of the gallows wedding and
the irreverent, lighthearted uses of hanging are central to the
play and to its subsequent popularity. One begins to glimpse
the contradictions in the play: on the one hand an aristocratic
debunking of the middle-class, moralizing sentimental comedy
(the Italian opera may have been the direct target because it
heightened the artificiality of sentimental comedy – they reign
together); on the other hand in its ballads and its rhetoric a play
not only 'about' the people, but 'by' the people.

Hanging creates the comedy of the play not only through its
use as word or figure but through its nature as spectacle. The
passage where Polly envisions Macheath in the cart to Tyburn
strikes us as a bit macabre; but we have not seen such a
spectacle; the processions from Newgate to Tyburn were abol-
ished in 1783. Michel Foucault has argued that this was not a
quantitative development of less cruelty and more humanity in
punishment; it is a qualitative rupture between two very different notions of punishment. He says that 'we must rid ourselves
of the illusion that penalty is above all a means of reducing
crime'.[25] It is rather a symbolic action with political, religious
and ideological connotations.

The end of the procession, of the public execution, of judicial torture, was the end of punishment regarded as a spectacle. In Gay's time, executions were theatrical events: work stopped, thieves worked, taverns were full. It was a public death. Foucault writes of 'the insatiable curiosity that drove spectators to the scaffold to witness the spectacle of sufferings truly endured; there one could decipher crime and innocence, the past and the future, the here below and the eternal'. In this performance the main character, Foucault says, was the people. 'The people claimed the right to observe the execution and to see who was being executed.'[26] And the atmosphere around the execution was often one of a carnival. The hanging day was announced by the ringing of church bells; hawkers sold the broadside ballads, the criminal biographies like those Defoe wrote, and the pamphlets of the last speech of the condemned; people paid to see the condemned in his cell; the procession to Tyburn was along the most heavily travelled roads in London. A contemporary observer wrote: 'no solemn procession, it was just the contrary; it was a low-lived black-guard merrymaking'.[27] In England, unlike the France Foucault writes about, trials were also public, and Howson says that 'as far as the Old Bailey was concerned, "theatre" is less a metaphor than a literal description'.[28] The rituals of court, the trumpets and the guards, the sermons and sentences pronounced by the judge, combined to make it a spectacle that people came from all around to witness. As E.P. Thompson writes: 'The hegemony of the 18th-century gentry and aristocracy was expressed, above all, not in military force, not in the mystifications of a priesthood or the press, not even in economic coercion, but in the rituals in the study of the Justices of the Peace, in the quarter-sessions, in the pomp of Assizes and in the theatre of Tyburn.'[29]

The analogy between the theatre and the gallows, particularly in its carnival aspect, may help account for the incongruity that a play so largely about hanging could be so comic. But there is one place where the connection is taken as more than a metaphor: about 1700, 'it was remarked that the last time a party had torn down the stage in the city it had set up a scaffold in the court'.[30] And if anything seems more foreign to a modern sensibility than the spectacle of hanging, it is the moral attack on the stage. How do we understand the attacks by Jeremy Collier? Can we suspend our own sentiments and see them not

as 'irrational' or 'puritan' absurdities, but as the coding of a
political struggle over a social institution, to be compared with,
for example, the 'moral' attacks on modernism of a Lukács or a
Winters. For it is the same Hanoverian Whigs who established
the ascendency of the gallows who, with moral arguments (and
political purposes), established the Licensing Act of 1737 in
order to control the theatre more closely. Indeed *The Beggar's
Opera*, which mocks the majesty of the gallows, was attacked on
moral, not political, grounds. And the performance of Gay's
sequel *Polly* was suppressed.

It was also from the reforming wing of the Whigs that the
move to take the spectacle (but not the hanging) out of hanging
arose in the eighteenth century. Foucault writes that 'it was
evident that the great spectacle of punishment ran the risk of
being rejected by the very people to whom it was addressed . . .
the reformers of the eighteenth and nineteenth centuries were
not to forget that, in the last resort, the executions did not, in
fact, frighten the people'.[31] Indeed there were cases of the crowd
rejecting the sentence and saving the condemned, and of riots
occurring on execution day. To conclude I will note that both
Defoe and Fielding wanted to end aspects of the hanging
spectacle, with Fielding using a significant image: 'a Murder
behind the Scenes, if the Poet knows how to manage it, will effect
the Audience with greater Terror than if it was acted before
their Eyes'.[32] Is Gay's spectacle a defence not only of the stage
but of the spectacle of hanging?

Justice: poetical and . . .

To return to some early questions: why is this 'cult of crime and
roguery' so important? Why is this spectacle of the scaffold so
important? How does Gay produce (in the sense of producing
a play) these figures? Why is *The Beggar's Opera* the most
performed piece of the eighteenth century?[33]

Douglas Hay gives us part of the answer: 'the ideology of the
ruling oligarchy, which places a supreme value upon property,
finds its visible and material embodiment above all in the
ideology and practice of the law. Tyburn Tree, as William Blake
well understood, stood at the heart of this ideology; and its
ceremonies were at the heart of the popular culture also.'[34] I

have looked at the ideology of the gang and at the treatment of hanging in Gay, both of which are part of this ideology of the law. I have suggested that certain contradictions fissure the play; I have not yet shown that. In this final section, I will look at the escapes in the play, so as to return to two of Empson's points in order to make more explicit Gay's contradictory production of this ideology. Empson's points are: first, his claim that 'the essential process behind the *Opera* [is] a resolution of heroic and pastoral into a cult of independence'; and second, his claim that the *Opera* is an 'art-form that not merely evades but breaks through [the class system], that makes the classes feel part of a larger unity or simply at home with each other'.

There are three escapes in the play, one at the end of each act, and they definitely establish Macheath as a Jack Sheppard, the escape artist. In the first two escapes, it is Polly and Lucy, respectively, who enable Macheath to avoid the law, and they do it out of love. In the third case it is the taste of the town that helps Macheath escape the gallows and poetical justice, perhaps also out of love. It is an over-determined ending: poetical justice would have him hanged; the generic and 'un-natural' laws of sentimental comedy and opera would have him saved; the taste of the town would have him saved; 'realism' would have him executed. Or would it? It is a curious fact about the eighteenth-century legal system that the increasing exten-sion of the death penalty to offences against property coincided with a more frequent use of the pardon and reprieve. More death sentences led to pardons than to hangings.[35] The eight-eenth-century legal system was, as Hay says, a combination of majesty, justice and mercy, and part of the resistance to the rationalization of the legal code was the immense power created by the royal prerogative to pardon; majesty exercised power as much in pardoning as in executing, and the former was more useful in maintaining the consent and acquiescence of the governed.

There is a struggle in *The Beggar's Opera* between two types of law, the one represented by the reprieve, the other by poetical justice. It corresponds to the struggle over the rationalization of the law, and to the struggle between two meanings of property: on the one hand the common rights and customary perquisites, and on the other the enclosures and the absolute ownership of property. I have already cited Hay's comment that the rise in crime is in part accounted for by this redefinition of customary rights to use woods and commons as offences. In the play these two types of law also correspond to two types of honour. First, there is the law and honour of Peachum who says 'a lawyer is an honest employment, so is mine' (1:1). His is a law of counting and contracts, of preying on one's neighbours. Lockit, in a scene which parallels Peachum's opening scene, says that 'of all the animals of prey, man is the only sociable one' (3:2). Theirs is a law of self-interest, and one can understand, even admit, their self-assessment as men of honour (the meaning of honour as 'to honour, that is, pay, a bill' has its first usage, according to the *OED*, in 1706; surely that is Peachum's honour). When Peachum says that 'we encourage those who betray their friends' (2:10), he does not see himself as betraying anyone. He says that Macheath would understand: 'the captain knows, that as tis his employment to rob, so tis ours to take robbers; every man to his business' (1:10). But as a code implies a transgression, so the meaning of betrayal is love, as Polly and Lucy discover when they betray their fathers.

The other law, the other honour, is that of the gang and Macheath. Macheath is surprised that a member of the gang should betray him; we know that Jenny did not betray Macheath and it enforces our sense of the honour of the gang. It is a law not of counting but of extravagance, of personal favours. So after Lockit's song comparing men with pikes, preying on their friends, Macheath sings a lament about the erosive effect of money on friendship (3:4). Macheath gives away money, and tells Matt not to rob the 'fellow with a brown coat with a narrow gold binding'; 'he's a good honest kind of fellow, and one of us' (3:4). The betrayal implied in this code of honour is mercenary; so Macheath's betrayal of Polly and Lucy for other women is an extravagance within that code.

The escapes that end each act are ruled by the law of custom, not contract; it is against any economy for them to be allowed; they all come from love, rather like the benevolent king's pardon. The reprieve in particular should be looked at. Fielding has a reprieve in *Jonathan Wild* but it is not extravagant: first of all it reprieves a totally innocent man; second, a clear reason is given for it. As the narrator says:

lest our reprieve should seem to resemble that in the *Beggar's Opera*, I shall endeavour to show [the reader] that this incident, which is undoubtedly true, is at least as natural as delightful; for we assure him we would rather have suffered half mankind to be hanged than have saved one contrary to the strictest rules of writing and probability.[36]

Beggars and thieves are not bound by contract, but by paternalism, customs, ancient rights, a discretionary system of law. The new system of Peachum would replace these rights with counting, with a rationalized law, indeed with the bourgeois morality that triumphs in Fielding's comic morality play in prose. So far from being a resolution into a proto-romantic cult of independence and individualism, it is a defence of English custom (and here we see how the *Opera* might be seen as an affirmation of both the pardon *and* the spectacle of hanging).

The great strength of *The Beggar's Opera* is that this defence is not one of genteel English custom but manages to make an odd union of the aristocracy and the people. And here we are faced with Empson's other comment, that the play breaks through the class system and creates a greater unity. Though I think this is the overall effect of the play (and another part of its continuing popularity), it seems slightly more complicated than Empson puts it. For in my account of the royal pardon, the reader may have noted a slip: the reprieve in the *Opera* is not a royal one at all; it is granted by the 'rabble', the 'taste of the town'. It is a very artificial representation of the riots at hangings that both Foucault and Hay tell us the authorities feared, when the 'rabble' would take justice into their hands and reverse the sentence. The spectacle of hanging, the display of the power and authority of the state, could also become the occasion for rebellion against that authority. Certainly Gay did not intend, as Brecht did, that the play should lead the audience to revolution; but as a corollary to Empson's idea of the play creating class unity, I will cite a suggestive comment by Foucault:

Perhaps we should see this literature of crime, which proliferated around a few exemplary figures [Foucault's footnote cites Wild and Sheppard as well as French examples], neither as a spontaneous form of 'popular expression', nor as a concerted programme of propaganda and moralization from above; it was the locus in which two investments of penal practice met – a sort of battleground around the crime, its punishment and its memory.[37]

The Beggar's Opera is one such locus of contrary investments, of party satire, popular speech, fashionable opera, and two codes of law and honour. And this is why it does not have a proper happy ending, why the hero is not really moral, why the unity is incomplete. The comedy seems a straightforward youth vs. age plot; however, it is curiously inverted. For the new system, the growing, thriving commercial capitalism, is figured as the parents, and the children act out the part of an impotent and parasitic aristocracy, now more and more aligning itself with the money-lenders (who Macheath advises robbing: 3:4). The aristocracy may be a figure for total villainy, as in Fielding, but it is difficult in the eighteenth century for even Gay, a hanger-on of the aristocracy, to create a real hero from it. Macheath and Polly cannot win – without the artificial intervention of the rabble.

Notes

1 William Empson, 'The Beggar's Opera', *Some Versions of Pastoral* (1935; New Directions, New York 1974).

2 Frank Chandler, *The Literature of Roguery*, 2 vols (1907; Burt Franklin, New York 1958).

3 E.P. Thompson, *Whigs and Hunters* (Pantheon, New York 1975), pp. 216–17.

4 Bertrand Goldgar, *Walpole and the Wits* (University of Nebraska Press, Lincoln, Nebr. 1976), pp. 218, 58.

5 Empson, 'The Beggars Opera'; Thompson, *Whigs and Hunters*; Douglas Hay, Peter Linebaugh, John G. Rule, E.P. Thompson and Cal Winslow, *Albion's Fatal Tree* (Pantheon, New York 1975); Michel Foucault, *Discipline and Punish* (1975), trans. A. Sheridan (Allen Lane, London 1977).

6 Gerald Howson, *Thief-Taker General* (Hutchinson, London 1970), pp. 284, 280.

7 J.M. Beattie, 'The pattern of crime in England: 1660–1800', *Past and Present*, 62 (1974), p. 72.

8 Thompson, *Whigs and Hunters*, p. 196.

9 Douglas Hay, 'Preface', in Hay *et al.*, *Albion's Fatal Tree*, p. 13.

10 Douglas Hay, 'Property, authority, and the criminal law', in Hay *et al.*, *Albion's Fatal Tree*, p. 18.

11 Howson, *Thief-Taker General*, p. 42. Most of the details of Wild's career come from Howson.

12 Daniel Defoe, *Selected Poetry and Prose*, ed. M.F. Shugrue (Holt, Rinehart & Winston, New York 1968), pp. 228, 255, 290, 291, 293, 307.

13 ibid., p. 271.

14 Howson (*Thief-Taker General*) states this on p. 6. The account of the various pamphlets is ibid., pp. 100–12.

15 Thompson, *Whigs and Hunters*, pp. 191, 194.

16 Christopher Hill, *Reformation to Industrial Revolution* (Weidenfeld & Nicolson, London 1967), p. 179.

17 Henry Fielding, *Jonathan Wild* (1754; New American Library, New York 1961), pp. 65–6.

18 Thompson, *Whigs and Hunters*, p. 197.

19 Patricia M. Spacks, *John Gay* (Twayne, Boston, Mass. 1965), p. 157.

20 Peter Linebaugh, 'The Tyburn riot against the surgeons', in Hay *et al.*, *Albion's Fatal Tree*, p. 68.

21 Empson, 'The Beggar's Opera', pp. 223–8.

22 Linebaugh, in Hay *et al.*, *Albion's Fatal Tree*, p. 66.

23 Empson, 'The Beggar's Opera', p. 224.

24 Linebaugh, in Hay *et al.*, *Albion's Fatal Tree*, pp. 111–15.

25 Foucault, *Discipline and Punish*, p. 24.

26 ibid., pp. 40, 57–8.

27 Linebaugh, in Hay *et al.*, *Albion's Fatal Tree*, p. 68. The details of hanging day are from Linebaugh's essay.

28 Howson, *Thief-Taker General*, p. 27.

29 Thompson, *Whigs and Hunters*, p. 262.

30 Joseph Wood Krutch, *Comedy and Conscience after the Restoration* (1924; Columbia University Press, New York 1969), p. 92.

31 Foucault, *Discipline and Punish*, p. 63.

32 Quoted in Linebaugh, in Hay *et al.*, *Albion's Fatal Tree*, p. 68.

33 William Schultz, *Gay's 'Beggar's Opera'* (Yale University Press, New Haven 1923).

34 Hay, in Hay *et al.*, *Albion's Fatal Tree*, p. 13.

35 ibid., p. 23.

36 Fielding, *Jonathan Wild*, p. 177.

37 Foucault, *Discipline and Punish*, p. 67.

4

The moment of *Pickwick*, or the production of a commodity text
NORMAN FELTES

'More than *Childe Harold* or Waverley, more than *Adam Bede* or *The Heir of Redclyffe* . . . , *Pickwick* was the most sensational triumph in nineteenth-century publishing.' George Ford's discussion of the reviews, Richard Altick's study of circulation figures, John Butt and Kathleen Tillotson's account of Dickens at work transforming the shilling, serialized issue, all point to the uniqueness of Dickens's first triumph.[1] All of these are 'pioneer' explorations of various empirical facts surrounding the appearance of *Pickwick Papers* and so, focused on those sorts of specific information, none can attempt an explanation of the event. A literary historian would need to read these accounts, the stories of the publication of *Pickwick*, symptomatically, or dialectically, to explain the historical event and its significance, and that is what I shall attempt here. The general outline of the story of the publication of *Pickwick Papers* is well-known: in early 1836 the new firm of Chapman & Hall planned with the popular illustrator Robert Seymour for a series of sporting prints in shilling numbers, and they invited the young journalist, Charles Dickens, whose recently collected *Sketches By Boz* had had a moderate success, to write the accompanying text. Dickens joined the enterprise as an ambitious, opinionated junior partner, differing from the start with Seymour about the precedence of illustration over letterpress, and over the proposed rural setting and the 'sporting' interests of the Pickwickians.

Seymour, who was harried by personal worries, committed suicide just as the second number was being published, new illustrators were sought and Hablot K. Brown (Phiz) was hired; Dickens was left the dominant partner. His ideas for the Pickwickians quickly prevailed; in the fourth number he introduced into the story Sam Weller, who was especially applauded in the *Literary Gazette*, which reprinted Sam's monologues. Before the year was out Dickens was 'the most widely-read author in England', with the instalments of *Pickwick* selling 40,000 copies each month – a success 'unprecedented in the history of literature'.[2]

That is one version of the standard account of the circumstances surrounding the publication of *Pickwick Papers*. Literary historians may differ over specific details and their significance – the relation of Seymour's depression to his differences with Dickens, the precise level of *Pickwick's* initial success or the influence on that success of the intervention of Jerdan, the editor of the *Literary Gazette*.[3] But the implications of their conclusions are generally in agreement: the publication of *Pickwick Papers* marks the explosion of Dickens's 'genius' upon the literary world. A series of accidents permitted that genius to flower and its comic essence to be discerned and encouraged early, so that *Pickwick Papers* might reach its inevitable and waiting audience: 'Dickens and his publishers', writes Patten, 'discovered the potential of serial publication virtually by accident', and Ford suggests that the appearance of *Pickwick* coincided with a 'shift of taste'.[4] Only occasionally does one find literary historians glancing towards historical explanations for the accidents or for Dickens's 'genius'. Patten, for example, speaking of serialization, remarks that 'what forces made that format suddenly possible, and how the changes in publishing converged in 1836 and were connected by two shrewd, courageous, and lucky booksellers with the one man who could write letterpress for *all* the people, needs to be understood more fully than it has been so far'.[5] And Steven Marcus draws an 'only partly fanciful' analogy between the language of *Pickwick* and 'the take-off into self-sustained growth' of the Victorian economy, noting that a critic might work out elsewhere 'the mediations that would provide it with substance'.[6] What I shall attempt here is not at all fanciful, risking perhaps more 'banging the field-piece' than 'twanging the lyre'.[7] I shall say nothing of 'genius', luck or the shrewdness of Chapman & Hall, since those things, as I've mentioned, are thoroughly discussed elsewhere. Instead, I want to look at those historical processes which such discussions necessarily ignore, processes which shaped and determined the material production of *Pickwick Papers*. For the publication of *Pickwick* took place within a determinate sub-ensemble of emerging industrial capitalism, the production of written texts. Indeed *Pickwick Papers* marks the transition (the 'explosion' or 'take-off') from the petty-commodity production of books to industrial capitalist production of texts, and these are the changes which need to be understood more fully. We also need to understand the ways in which the literary text, *Pickwick Papers*, 'bears the impress of its historical mode of production', how it 'encodes within itself its own ideology of how, by whom and for whom it was produced';[8] this understanding is also, finally, part of my project.

We need not spend long on the transformation in the general mode of production which took place in Britain from 1750 to 1850, from simple or petty-commodity production to industrial capitalism; I want merely to note some general forms of that transformation. As Hindess and Hirst point out: 'It is not wage-labour and commodity production as such which define capitalism but the production and extraction of surplus-value as the dominant mode of appropriation of surplus-labour'.[9] What defines precisely the capitalist mode of production is not a *specific form of ownership* of the means of production (that began around the sixteenth century) but a *specific form of control* over the labour process so as to produce surplus value.[10] These changes in the forces and relations of production slowly produced a very different market; as E.J. Hobsbawm describes the market of petty-commodity production:

> the available and prospective market – and it is the market which determines what a businessman produces – consists of the rich, who require luxury goods in small quantities, but with a high profit margin per sale, and the poor, who – if they are in the market economy at all, and do not produce their own consumer goods domestically or locally – have little money, are unaccustomed to novelties and suspicious of

them, unwilling to consume standardized products and may not even be concentrated in cities or accessible to national manufacturers.

Industrial capitalism changed the market by 'enabling production – within certain limits – to expand its own markets, if not actually to create them';[11] this was achieved through its characteristic control over the labour process. The usual accounts of publishing in the early nineteenth century, reluctant to speak of 'modes of production', present rather a formless picture of publishing practice. Louis James alludes vaguely to 'the feverish publishing activity that took place in the 1830s, and to a lesser extent in the previous decade', while another writer describes the discovery of 'wove' paper, of new paper-making materials, and the invention of a paper-making machine and of the iron printing press as simply a 'graphic confluence' around 1800.[12] But the transformation of the general mode of production necessarily determined the forces and relations in the subordinate sector of book production in particular ways, and it is these mediations, these changes in the social relations of production in a particular place at a particular time, that I want primarily to address, reinterpreting 'the rise of the publisher', the rise of the 'professional author', and the status of the 'literary text'.

For the formula 'the rise of the publisher' obscures the complexity of the historical changes in book production at the beginning of the nineteenth century. So does the word 'bibliomania' which, while clearly gesturing towards the material effects of general economic change (speculation, etc.), is conventionally used simply to describe the frantic activity in the rare book trade during the Napoleonic Wars which allowed booksellers to 'rise' as 'publishers': 'Fortunes could be and were made in the antiquarian book trade, allowing many men [to] amass the capital to set up as publishers, where there were still greater profits to be made'.[13] The early years of the nineteenth century marked 'a significant change in the function and spirit of publishing', a 'turn towards specialization', as booksellers and publishers became less and less 'involved in each other's spheres'.[14] These changes produced 'a firm which wholesales its own books but does not wholesale anybody else's – the firm

which organizes the production of a book, and then sells it direct
to retailers all over the British Isles'. Such a firm organized its
market in the country by means of the literary reviews, commercial travellers, prospectuses and catalogues, and these were, of
course, dependent on the development of paved roads, fast
coaches, canals and, eventually, railways. From the 1760s,
provincial banks had begun to appear and London publishers
could replace cumbersome arrangements of personal ac-
quaintance and trust with impersonal financial facilities.[15]
But the organization of the market for books was only an
extension of the organization of the production of books, the
control of production, of which 'the publisher' was the specific
form.

The 'professionalization' of the writer may be seen as part
of the same transformation of the relations of production,
although again an understanding of the relationship is
smothered by the free-enterprise epithet. For to posit a simple
contrast between 'aristocratic patronage and amateurism' on
the one hand, and 'professional writers' on the other,[16] is to
make it impossible to see a transition from the forms of petty-
commodity book production to those of a mature capitalism.
That Byron and Scott had their doubts about authorship as a
profession did not affect the historical change in writers' relationships to the literary mode of production, any more than did
Dickens's unprecedented earnings, however much those may
have helped make fiction writing 'as professionally respectable
as the law, medicine or the civil service'. The ideology of free
enterprise, in particular the notion of the 'profession', necessarily overlooks the new relationship of the writer to the new
structures of publishing. When Constable, the publisher, in-
sisted that every contributor to the *Edinburgh* was obliged to
accept 'a worthy wage', he may have, ideologically, 'made the
first move to dignify professional authorship by erasing the
distinction between the gentleman amateur and the workaday
writer and by cancelling the line between the Grub Street hack
and the genius',[17] but he certainly was recognizing, on the
economic level, the place of the writer, genius or hack, in the
relations of capitalist literary production, universalizing their
labour-power rather than levelling up or down. The conventional accounts do not recognize the vulnerability of the writer

in these new relations of production; dazzled by Dickens's £93,000 legacy, they can speak only of an author's new 'independence' and 'complete unaccountability', of how the 'autonomous novelist', 'his own man', 'unfettered', communicates 'the artist's awareness of his own power and the prime responsibility of looking after it'.[18] Only this last phrase seems to acknowledge the precariousness of the writer's new position within the publishers' new structures for controlling the production of books. While the condition of early nineteenth-century writers never could decline to that of their wretched contemporaries, the hand-loom weavers, nevertheless Marx's comment on the weavers' predicament in the face of the new relations of industrial production is illuminating. Marx called attention to 'the character of independence from and the estrangement towards the worker, which the capitalist mode of production gives to the conditions of labour and the product of labour'; 'free labour = latent pauperism', Marx wrote, and the writers' new professionalism concealed just such latencies.[19] If, in the late eighteenth century, 'to a large extent the professional writer was the employee of the bookseller',[20] with the 'rise of the publisher' in the early nineteenth century, this dependency was changed and deepened. The writer, genius or hack, presented himself to the publisher, as did any other worker in the capitalist mode of production, as 'the owner of nothing but his labour-power',[21] and so he needed, as a 'professional', to be 'skilled and militant' in the face of the publishers' new forms of 'trade cooperation' and the new 'sense of exclusiveness in trade affairs'.[22] And the object of this new, necessary militancy was to be the literary text, newly defined as a commodity, newly available as the locus of surplus value.

John Sutherland says of publishing in the early decades of the nineteenth century that 'it was not the book which was cheapened but the reading of it'.[23] His distinction is that between a *book* and a *text*, precisely the distinction which had been made in the statutory law during the preceding century in the struggle over copyright, over the right to property in a text. Augustine Birrell described this long process as a controversy as to whether authors had a right to their published works 'as *property* or as *privilege*'; for previously the author's right to his text had only been recognized in the common law, and 'copyright' had signified only a stationer's sole right to print and sell copies. 'Property in literature was the right to make copies – not the right of authorship', and copyright was like 'a perpetual lease of personal property ... for one specific purpose, that of publishing'.[25] It was only with the Statute of Anne (1709) that 'the author in his own right appears on the scene'[26] and, more to our point, the rights to the 'incorporeal property' in a work begin to be defined and established in statutory law. Whereas the Statute of Anne revoked the author's common law 'perpetual' copyright and limited the initial period of copyright to fourteen years, the author 'could, for the first time, own the copyright of his work himself'. Indeed, the statutory copyright to 'this amorphous property which increases so with technological progress' was now available to the author merely because it was now available to anyone; 'the author could own the copyright only by virtue of the fact that anyone was now eligible to hold copyright'.[27] This, I believe, is the significant historical point: with the Statute of Anne and the series of legal struggles and decisions culminating in the judgment in the Donaldson case in 1774, what had been a 'continuing inchoate property' was redefined so that it might become a commodity like any other. As one historian puts it, 'if the publisher is to profit, he must be able to acquire from the author an exclusive right – and so must the author be able to grant it', and so copyright came to be defined in law as 'a monopoly of a work, rather than the basis of the monopoly of the book trade'.[28] For the first time in statutory law there came to exist a property right in the text itself and that right was alienable. This was 'precisely the kind of property', as C.B. Macpherson has shown, 'that was required by a full capitalist market society': 'a man's own labour, as well as capital and land, was made so much a private exclusive property as to be alienable, i.e., marketable'.[29]

A 'commodity-text' is such a text, produced in the new capitalist mode of production, produced in struggle by the new 'professional' author within the new structures of control over the publishing process. These forms are, again, obscured in discussions, for example, of the kinds of agreements over the rights of their texts that writers signed with their publishers.[30] For what is at issue is not a straightforward matter of wages, royalties or profits, as might be the case in a petty-commodity

mode of production,[31] but rather the production of surplus
value in a text, permitting high profits, and often high payments
to the author. The term 'commodity-text' thus indicates the text
whose form, in Pierre Macherey's words, 'is not an initial datum,
but a product, at the point where several lines of necessity con-
verge'.[32] Not a 'structure' but a 'structuration',[33] a commodity-
text is indeed 'a differential network, a fabric of traces referring
endlessly to something other than itself, to other differential
traces',[34] if we understand the traces to refer to the forces and
relations of its production. The change in the understanding of
copyright made it possible to imagine a commodity-text, just as
the new forces and relations determined the limits of its possibility. Most importantly, the 'fabric' of the commodity-text is
'traced' by the mass bourgeois audience, for, while 'specific
literary works are determined by the history of literary production from which they receive the means of their own realization',
so also 'readers are made by what makes the book': 'the book
does not produce its readers by some mysterious power; the
conditions that determine the production of the book also
determine the forms of its communication. These two modifications are simultaneous and reciprocal.'[35] The commodity-text
of the capitalist literary mode of production produces its readers
by interpellating, that is, by addressing and engaging an infinity
of bourgeois subjects, 'traced' in the text. These are the necessi-
ties determining the commodity-text, 'the real diversity of
elements which gave it substance'.[36] It realizes its surplus value
in the ensemble of relations which structure its production and
by its interpellation of a mass bourgeois audience; the concept commodity-text permits us to think of these processes as
'simultaneous and reciprocal'.

I shall return to my analysis of the historical processes, but I
would first like briefly to describe more precisely in Marxist
terms how the commodity-text may be thought, by placing its
production in relation to the general capitalist mode of production. The capitalist mode is characterized generally, as Gareth
Stedman Jones says, 'by a specific form of control over the
labour process'. And so in the labour (or 'creative') process of
producing a commodity-text the specific form of control is series
production. Whether the commodity-text is to take the particu-

lar form of a series of books, a magazine serial or a part-issue novel, series production, by allowing the bourgeois audience's ideological engagement to be sensed and expanded, allows as well the extraction of ever greater surplus value from the very production (or 'creative') process itself. The series writer in the capitalist mode, however the task may be perceived ideologically, must produce or discover in each successive book, or instalment or part, that 'virtually limitless multiplication' of ideological 'inventions and combinations and configurations' which interpellate by constituting the bourgeois subject. This is not to be confused with writing to a 'formula', for the audience we are describing is not 'there', but rather always/already there. Whereas a formula novel takes its value from something reduced and mechanical and prior to its production, a commodity-text takes its value from the labour power ('imagination') expended in the very process of interpellation. Nor, on the other hand, does the simple category, 'best seller', necessarily contain the concept commodity-text; 'best seller' simply indicates value accrued through distribution and exchange, rather than through the production process. The commodity-text, again, is produced by a writer within a determinate capitalist mode, a structure of specific means and relations of production, in which the series provides the distinctive form of control, and in which the profits are made by the ever more inevitable interpellation of a mass bourgeois audience.

Free-enterprise assumptions have shaped most accounts of the audience for books, implying that readers are brought together by their 'reading habit' or their 'appetite for fiction' into 'the market-place', where the publisher tempts them with his wares. Or entrepreneurial publishers are said to have behaved as if they stood on a peak in Darien, 'beholding for the first time a vast sea of common readers'.[37] But two recent articles by Scott Bennett allow us to analyse 'the take-off period for the mass reading market'[38] from the point of view of production, to see the audience as being made by what makes the book, rather than waiting to be 'beheld'. Bennett analyses first the publishing project of John Murray's Family Library from 1829 to 1834, and he makes very clear the impossibility within the forms of petty-commodity book production – whose available and prospective market, as Hobsbawm says, 'consists of the rich, who require luxury goods in small quantities, but with a high profit margin per sale' – even to 'behold' what might constitute a mass audience. Murray, at the time London's most respected publisher, introduced the Family Library as both an 'early venture in the cheapening of books' and an 'effort to publish across class lines at a time when class divisions were newly felt to be threatening the fabric of national life'. The Family Library experiment was thus a publisher at once trying to create an audience and trying 'to speak to the common reader in such a way as to heal the fundamental divisions created by the emerging industrial order'. The experiment failed because 'Murray was unable to translate the publishing practices of the market in which he had first established himself into the market for the common reader'; blocked in this way from producing a commodity-text by the forms of petty-commodity book production, Murray was equally, necessarily, unable to imagine how a text might interpellate a mass audience. His basic tactic was 'to apply a brand name to a series of books and to rely on the general reputation of that name, as well as the individual books, to sell the series'. At the same time his conservative political purpose was 'to shape social attitudes through the use of literacy', to make his series 'a vehicle for reuniting a dangerously divided society'.[39] But neither his organization of production nor his conception of the text itself was adequate to the production of a commodity-text.

The project of the Society for the Diffusion of Useful Knowledge, however, as Bennett describes it, was radically different, marking 'revolutions in thought' about the production of books and the relation to the audience. The SDUK, in conjunction with Charles Knight, combined the 'conscious and innovative design' of sharply increasing the number of copies printed of its non-fictional publications to achieve a dramatically lower unit cost, and the idea of publishing serially, that is, to control the production process so as to lessen the attendant risks. At the same time the SDUK, unlike John Murray, approached 'the issues of the day' indirectly: 'as it matured in its purposes [the SDUK] was looking for a common ground in ideas and interests'. Bennett suggests rightly that 'the emergence of mass markets should stand alongside the emergence of class consciousness in our estimation of the new, most socially potent forces of the period'. And since, as he says, 'mass markets can exist only where widely shared interests or values exist or can be created', he explores the efforts of the SDUK to discover the common ground, that 'common feeling, however partial it may be, in the day-to-day lives of the individuals who make up that market'. What his study reveals is a stage in the structuration of the new mode of literary production, as Knight and the SDUK strive towards the possibility of a commodity-text. Their failure to achieve that 'take-off' is less important historically than the fact that their project permitted 'the clear emergence of fiction as the most saleable commodity on the market',[40] for this conjuncture of capitalist control of the process of production with the emergence of the possibility of a commodity-text is the moment of transition into the specifically capitalist literary mode of production, just as it is (by no accident) the moment of *Pickwick*.

For *Pickwick Papers*, produced in the capitalist mode of production and drawing forth a mass bourgeois audience, was the first commodity-text.[41] The production of *Pickwick* was, again, a complex process of structuration, and preoccupation with questions of genre and sources again blocks perception of what Patten calls 'the relationship in that novel of process to end'.[42] While it has been claimed that *Pickwick* was 'a highly derivative work . . . another example of a familiar and well-loved genre', or that the forerunners in *Pickwick's* format 'are found in two very different types of part-issue common in the eighteenth and early nineteenth century',[43] the process by which it was produced, its literary mode of production, was original, as we can see by examining its specific historical determinations: Chapman & Hall can be recognized as the new publishers of industrial capitalism, just as Dickens can be seen as a free, professional writer, and their mutual antagonistic struggle to produce a commodity-text analysed as a whole process. *Pickwick Papers* was unique in Dickens's work 'in being *begun* in response to an external demand';[44] as Patten puts it, it 'originated in the minds of others'. Moreover, because of the structures of capitalist publishing and because of prior discussions with Seymour, several crucial decisions had already been made when Dickens was recruited: 'subject, relation of author to illustrator, publisher and format' were all pre-determined.[45] The publishers' position in the enterprise was determined, of course, by their ownership of the means of production, but the other decisions affected those relations by which they would control the production process. The plan to publish in serial form was undoubtedly the most crucial of these, for here an original combination of factors was being explored. For only in the late 1830s, that is, with the publication of *Pickwick Papers*, was the monthly part established as a method of publishing new fiction. *Pickwick* differed from its predecessors in 'one simple and all important feature': 'Chapman & Hall had *Pickwick* designed from the first as [one-shilling] parts with a view to subsequent consolidation in volumes'.[46] Whereas Chapman & Hall (and Seymour) might have been thinking at first in terms of 'yet another serial publication wedding hack letterpress to humorous plates', that is, still thinking in terms of petty-commodity production, the particular relations of production which they and Dickens were to struggle over produced something qualitatively different from earlier serial publications. *Pickwick Papers* became something more than 'piecemeal publishing', which had merely made it 'easy, for middle- and lower-class Englishmen to buy and read books';[47] *Pickwick's* relations of production, its format and its literary form, constituted the very commodity-text which could reach, as it produced, a mass audience.

From the very beginning Dickens struggled with Chapman & Hall, and with the unfortunate Seymour, for control of the work process. There were disagreements, as we have seen, over the setting and over the balance of illustrations and text, and Seymour's views prevailed for the first few numbers.[48] In any form of serial publication, an author 'ran the risk of subservience to editorial policy',[49] but in the uncertainties following Seymour's death, Dickens was able to take charge and to argue successfully for increasing the monthly letterpress from twenty-four to thirty-two pages while decreasing the number of illustrations from four to two; thereafter, says Patten, 'the author dictated all subjects and reviewed all designs, withholding approval until every detail satisfied him'.[50] This did not mean that the struggle to produce a commodity-text was over, with the publishers raising Dickens's rate of payment and eventually presenting him with a £500 bonus.[51] Chapman & Hall had bought Dickens's intellectual labour power for nineteen months, divided into monthly intervals; the forms of control, initially imposed by capital and adjusted in the ways we have seen, determined that the 'monthly something'[52] should be a discrete, illustrated written text of a determinate length, produced regularly, and to be collected, complete, in a stated time. These details constituted the ideological form of the commodity-text: that each part was discrete, not a segment of a larger serial issue, allowed a focused, potent ideological apparatus; furthermore, the length of each written part demanded the development of setting, action and characters 'in richer detail and . . . somewhat greater roundness than hitherto'.[53] Steven Marcus describes in another way the ideological effect of this aspect of the form of the text; the language of *Pickwick*, he says, 'becomes capable of a constant, rapid, and virtually limitless multiplication of its own effects and forms in new inventions and combinations and configurations'.[54] The expansion of the letterpress, while perhaps not 'virtually limitless', nonetheless produced just such an ideological effect of plenitude. Moreover, the ideological experience of *Pickwick* was to be regular and prolonged; as Dickens said in his announcement at the conclusion of Part 10, 'we shall keep perpetually going on beginning again, regularly',[55] and there was produced in this way 'a close relation between author and reader', 'the effect of contact', 'a sense of long familiar association'.[56] But the association was at the same time moving towards a promised and predictable close. Being more than just an indeterminate number of sketches, *Pickwick* anticipates its end, 'discovers its shape',[57] and moves towards becoming 'a true whole, in which individual segments are subordinated to the totality of collective integration and collective affirmation'.[58] Mr Pickwick's 'only' question, 'where shall we go next' (p. 578), is thus tempered by anticipation of the close, 'in about twenty numbers'.[59] These specific elements of the form of the commodity-text, determined as we have seen by the mode of production, themselves interpellate the multitude of bourgeois readers, allowing to each his own shilling number, prolonging while measuring the months of shared intimacy, and accumulating eventually into 'that beloved Victorian thing, "a cheap luxury"'.[60]

The ideologically shaped commodity-text had, as well, specific ideological content, achieved, again, in the struggles over its

production. For example, the initial proposal from Chapman &
Hall had been for 'a book illustrative of manners and life in the
Country',[61] and the Advertisement in the *Athenaeum* had promised travels over 'the whole surface of Middlesex, a part of
Surrey, a portion of Essex, and several square miles of Kent',
penetrating even 'to the very borders of Wales in the height of
summer'.[62] But Mr Pickwick never makes it to 'the fairs,
regattas and market-days that were some of his original destina-
tions', as Duane De Vries notes; 'instead, he keeps returning to
London'.[63] Or, more precisely, in the fourth number Mr Pickwick returns to London, and from that point on, he was never
really to leave it. This change from the original plan is crucial to
the ideological content of *Pickwick Papers* because, as F.S.
Schwarzbach points out, 'as soon as Mr Pickwick set foot again
on the paving stones of a London Street, *Pickwick Papers* sprang
to life almost as if by magic'. The 'magic', we may add, is simply
the ideological potential of that setting, for, as Schwarzbach
mentions, 'modern life is city life'.[64] More specifically, ever
since the industrial revolution the 'urban realm' has become
'the locus for the controlled reproduction of the social relations
of capitalism',[65] and *Pickwick Papers* is that process on the
ideological level, its urban setting being one device interpellating the bourgeois subject of these social relations. The introduction into the story of that 'living embodiment of London life',[66]
Sam Weller, in the fourth number presents a yet more complex
ideological element. Terry Eagleton has called attention to the
'corporatist forms assumed by bourgeois ideology' from the
mid-nineteenth century onwards,[67] and I would suggest that
the introduction of Sam Weller into *Pickwick Papers* and his
relationship with Mr Pickwick is an early instance of corporatist
ideology. It is not just that '*Pickwick* cut safely across party
lines', or that 'all classes, in fact, read "Boz"',[68] but that 'the
affectionate communion' among Mr Pickwick, Sam and Tony
Weller produces a determinate ideological effect by becoming
'the novel's principal focus of interest' and by celebrating 'the
virtues of simplicity, innocence and directness in the relations of
men'. The portrayal of such a relationship between master and
servant in 1836 (whatever its origin in Dickens's own experience) was a clearly ideological reading of 'the revolution in
public manners that took place in both the lower and middle

classes during the eighteenth and the first quarter of the nineteenth centuries'.[69] Thus the significance of the relationship between Mr Pickwick and Sam lies less in its simple reproduction of the relationship between Don Quixote and Sancho Panza, than in its representation of an aspect of early Victorian England's way of seeing itself. For the implied parallel between Mr Pickwick and Don Quixote (which 'many readers must have detected'[70]), *together with* the difference in class and historical period, interpellate that specifically bourgeois Victorian sense of self. Acknowledging differences of status while blurring class antagonism, Pickwick's relationship with Sam incorporates that Pickwickian benevolence, which is 'not so much *the matter of how* an individual preserves his better nature and finer instincts in a largely hostile or indifferent environment as *the assertion that* an individual can preserve his humanity under those circumstances'.[71]

Finally, the gradual transformation, in the first five numbers, of the narration of *Pickwick* produces/is an effect of the ideological structuration of the commodity-text. This change has been noted often; Patten speaks, for example, of the alteration 'from detached irony at Chatham to sympathetic identification in the Fleet and subsequently', and J. Hillis Miller's account might serve as a last example of the ways in which *Pickwick Papers* interpellates its mass audience:

Bit by bit the distance and objectivity, with which the narrator at first watched Pickwick with ironic amusement, is replaced by sympathy and belief. This progressive destruction of a dry comic tone and its replacement by warmth and sympathy is, one might say, the hidden drama of the novel. What had been an interior play in which Dickens watched without sympathy another part of himself invent and enact the role of Pickwick becomes the mysterious attraction and domination of the author or narrator by his own creation. The narrator becomes fascinated by Pickwick, and, in the end, the narrator (and the reader) are wholly within the charmed circle of warmth and benevolence which derives from Pickwick and transforms everything around him. The reader and narrator, then, become believers in Pickwick, and, tempted to remain forever within his safe enclosure, we leave him reluctantly.[72]

Here Miller, like Steven Marcus commenting on the virtually limitless multiplication of *Pickwick*'s language, presents us with an ideological reading of the ideological effect of the text, his own prose measuring the process of interpellation, from 'the narrator at first', through 'the narrator (and the reader)' and 'the reader and narrator', to 'we'. It remains to us outsiders simply to put a name, again, to that 'charmed circle' of 'believers'.

Marcus comments that 'Dickens was in no position to understand discursively what it was that he had done' in *Pickwick Papers*.[73] 'Of course', he might well have added, as there was no such position available to anyone in 1836. Much of what Dickens had done in *Pickwick Papers* was beyond his understanding because it was out of his hands, produced by a set of forces and production relations whose historical determinations I have attempted to trace. What these structures (and Dickens) produced was a commodity-text with a determinate form, itself producing ideology, and the commodity-text, form and ideology, creating the wild and widespread enthusiasm of a mass bourgeois audience. 'Whatever work is, in fact, produced', writes Edward Said, 'is haunted by antecedence, difference, sameness and the future'.[74] I have tried to re-cast descriptions such as this in materialist terms: the 'hauntings', for *Pickwick Papers*, were not only 'antecedent' genres but an obsolete literary mode of production; the 'sameness' and 'difference' imposed themselves in the struggle to establish the new. 'The future', too, evokes no idealist form, but rather the historical form of the commodity-text. For the future, the new literary mode of production determined by the developing structures of Victorian capitalism, lay just there, in the ever more self-conscious, ever more assured exploitation of the surplus value of commodity-texts.

Notes

1 George H. Ford, *Dickens and His Readers: Aspects of Novel Criticism Since 1836* (Norton, New York 1965), p. 6; Richard D. Altick, *The English Common Reader: A Social History of the Mass Reading Public, 1800–1900* (University of Chicago Press, Chicago 1957), pp. 383–6; John Butt and Kathleen Tillotson, *Dickens at Work* (Methuen, London 1957), pp. 63–75.

2 J. Don Vann, 'The early success of *Pickwick*', *Pubishing History*, 2 (1977), p. 51; Robert L. Patten, *Charles Dickens and His Publishers* (Oxford University Press, Oxford 1978), p. 45.

3 See Ford, *Dickens and His Readers*, pp. 5–6; Vann, 'The early success of *Pickwick*', pp. 53, 51.

4 Patten, *Dickens and His Publishers*, p. 46; Ford, *Dickens and His Readers*, p. 12.

5 Patten, *Dickens and His Publishers*, p. 46.

6 Steven Marcus, 'Language into structure: *Pickwick* revisited', *Daedalus*, 101 (1972), pp. 189, 202, n.4.

7 Charles Dickens, *The Posthumous Papers of the Pickwick Club*, ed. Robert L. Patten (Penguin, Harmondsworth 1972), p. 79; '*Pickwick Papers*' will refer to this edition, and subsequent page references will be incorporated into my text.

8 Terry Eagleton, *Criticism and Ideology* (Verso, London 1976), p. 48.

9 Barry Hindess and Paul Q. Hirst, *Pre-Capitalist Modes of Production* (Routledge & Kegan Paul, London 1975), pp. 304–5.

10 Gareth Stedman Jones, 'Class struggle and the industrial revolution', *New Left Review*, 90 (1975), p. 49; my italics.

11 E.J. Hobsbawm, *Industry and Empire* (Penguin, Harmondsworth 1969), pp. 40–1.

12 'Economic literature: the emergence of popular journalism', *Victorian Periodicals News Letter*, 14 (1971), p. 13; Leonard B. Schlosser, 'The graphic confluence of 1800', in *A Miscellany for Bibliophiles*, ed. George H. Fletcher (Grastorf and Lange, New York 1979), pp. 67–95.

13 Terry Belanger, 'From bookseller to publisher: changes in the London book trade, 1750–1850', in *Book Selling and Book Buying*, ed. Richard G. Landon (American Library Assn., Chicago 1978), p. 15.

14 Royal A. Gettmann, *A Victorian Publisher: A Study of the Bentley Papers* (Cambridge University Press, Cambridge 1960), p. 1; John A. Sutherland, *Victorian Novelists and Publishers* (Athlone Press, London 1976), p. 11.

15 Graham Pollard, 'The English market for printed books', *Publishing History*, 4 (1978), pp. 34, 37; Belanger, 'From bookseller to publisher', p. 12.

16 Patten, *Dickens and His Publishers*, p. 11.

17 Gettmann, *A Victorian Publisher*, pp. 5, 6; Sutherland, *Victorian Novelists and Publishers*, pp. 22, 23.

18 Sutherland, *Victorian Novelists and Publishers*, pp. 78, 80, 81; an exception, Jane P. Tompkins, outlines the changes which occur 'once authors become dependent for their means of support upon

the sales of their printed work': 'The reader in history: the changing shape of reader response', in *Reader-Response Criticism: From Formalism to Post-Structuralism*, ed. J.P. Tompkins (Johns Hopkins University Press, Baltimore 1980), p. 214.

19 Karl Marx, *Capital* (Penguin, Harmondsworth 1976), I, p. 558; *Grundrisse* (Penguin, Harmondsworth 1973), p. 735.

20 H.G. Aldis, 'Book production and distribution, 1625–1800', in *The Cambridge History of English Literature* (Cambridge University Press, Cambridge 1914), XI, p. 318.

21 Marx, *Capital*, I, p. 1017.

22 Sutherland, *Victorian Novelists and Publishers*, p. 96; James J. Barnes, *Free Trade in Books: A Study of the London Book Trade Since 1800* (Oxford University Press, Oxford 1964), pp. 2, 3.

23 Sutherland, *Victorian Novelists and Publishers*, p. 27.

24 Augustine Birrell, *Seven Lectures on the Law and History of Copyright in Books* (1899; Rothman, New York 1971), p. 10.

25 Philip Wittenberg, *The Protection and Marketing of Literary Property* (J. Messner, New York 1937), p. 20; Lyman Ray Patterson, *Copyright in Historical Perspective* (Vanderbilt University Press, Nashville 1968), p. 10.

26 Birrell, *Seven Lectures*, p. 93; see also Wittenberg, *Protection and Marketing*, pp. 22–3; Patterson, *Copyright*, p. 12; and Ian Parsons, 'Copyright and society', in *Essays in the History of Publishing in Celebration of the 250th Anniversary of the House of Longman, 1724–1974*, ed. Asa Briggs (Longman, London 1974), p. 39.

27 Wittenberg, *Protection and Marketing*, p. 11; Patterson, *Copyright*, p. 13; Wittenberg, *Protection and Marketing*, p. 7; Patterson, *Copyright*, p. 13.

28 Patterson, *Copyright*, p. 11; Wittenberg, *Protection and Marketing*, pp. 3–4; Patterson, *Copyright*, p. 16.

29 *Democratic Theory: Essays in Retrieval* (Oxford University Press, Oxford 1973), p. 130; see also C.B. Macpherson, *The Political Theory of Possessive Individualism* (Oxford University Press, Oxford 1962), pp. 215, 231. I owe this reference to Macpherson to Professor Pamela McCallum.

30 See, for example, Patten, *Dickens and His Publishers*, pp. 21–7.

31 Contrast Eagleton, *Criticism and Ideology*, p. 51; this discussion attempts to fill a perceived gap in Eagleton's 'Categories for a materialist criticism', ibid., ch. 2.

32 Pierre Macherey, *A Theory of Literary Production*, trans. Geoffrey Wall (Routledge & Kegan Paul, London 1978), p. 42.

33 Roland Barthes, *S/Z*, trans. Richard Miller (Hill & Wang, New York 1974), p. 20.

34 Jacques Derrida, 'Living on: border lines', in *Deconstruction and*

Criticism, ed. Harold Bloom (Seabury Press, New York 1979), p. 84.

35 Macherey, *A Theory of Literary Production*, pp. 53, 70; the 'forces of literary production determine and are overdetermined by the modes of literary distribution, exchange and consumption': Eagleton, *Criticism and Ideology*, p. 47.

36 Macherey, *A Theory of Literary Production*, p. 49.

37 Altick, *The English Common Reader*, pp. 260, 274; Sutherland, *Victorian Novelists and Publishers*, p. 11.

38 Scott Bennett, 'Revolutions in thought: serial publication and the mass market for reading', in *The Victorian Periodical Press: Samplings and Soundings*, ed. Joanne Shattock and Michael Wolff (Leicester University Press, Leicester 1982), p. 226.

39 Scott Bennett, 'John Murray's Family Library and the cheapening of books in early nineteenth century Britain', *Studies in Bibliography*, 29 (1976), pp. 140, 141, 161, 162.

40 Bennett, 'Revolutions in thought', pp. 242, 228, 248–51, 246.

41 'The fact was that Dickens' main audience, overwhelmingly the most numerous one, was the middle class'; Richard D. Altick, 'Varieties of readers' response: the case of *Dombey and Son*', *Yearbook of English Studies*, 10 (1980), p. 73; 'the general ideological profile [is] *bourgeois* rather than *popular* (plebian, democratic)'; Darko Suvin, 'The social addressees of Victorian fiction: a preliminary enquiry', *Literature and History*, 8 (1982), p. 26.

42 *Dickens and His Publishers*, p. 71; unfortunately the list of questions which Patten poses in his introduction works against seeing publication as the sort of 'process' I am trying to analyse.

43 Ford, *Dickens and His Readers*, p. 10; Kathleen Tillotson, *Novels of The Eighteen-Forties* (Oxford University Press, Oxford 1954) p. 26; Patten lists five kinds of 'early serial publications', *Dickens and His Publishers*, p. 46.

44 Butt and Tillotson, *Dickens at Work*, p. 66.

45 Patten, 'Introduction', *Pickwick Papers*, pp. 11, 12.

46 *Novels of the Eighteen-Forties*, p. 26; Sutherland, *Victorian Novelists and Publishers*, p. 21; see also the letter from Chapman & Hall to Dickens, 12 February 1836, proposing terms for *Pickwick Papers*, *The Letters of Charles Dickens*, ed. Madeline House and Graham Storey (Oxford University Press, Oxford 1965), I, Appendix C, p. 648.

47 Patten, *Dickens and His Publishers*, pp. 64, 46, 47.

48 Patten, 'Introduction', *Pickwick Papers*, pp. 12–13.

49 Tillotson, *Novels of the Eighteen-Forties*, p. 32.

50 Patten, 'Introduction', *Pickwick Papers*, pp. 15, 16.

51 Patten, *Dickens and His Publishers*, p. 69.

52 *Pickwick Papers*, Preface to the cheap edition, 1847, p. 44.

53 Duane De Vries, *Dickens' Apprentice Years: the Making of a Novelist* (Harvester Press, Brighton 1976), p. 143.

54 Marcus, 'Language into structure', p. 189.

55 *Pickwick Papers*, Appendix A, p. 903.

56 Tillotson, *Novels of the Eighteen-Forties*, p. 33.

57 Butt and Tillotson, *Dickens at Work*, p. 71.

58 Edward Said, *Beginnings: Intention and Method* (Basic Books, Baltimore 1975), p. 226.

59 *Pickwick Papers*, Appendix A, p. 900.

60 Sutherland, *Victorian Novelists and Publishers*, p. 22.

61 *Dickens Letters*, I, p. 648.

62 *Pickwick Papers*, Appendix A, p. 899.

63 De Vries, *Dickens' Apprentice Years*, p. 144.

64 F.S. Schwarzbach, *Dickens and the City* (Athlone Press, London 1979), pp. 44, 1.

65 David Harvey, 'Class-monopoly rent, finance capital and the urban revolution', *Regional Studies*, 8 (1974), p. 254.

66 Schwarzbach, *Dickens and the City*, p. 44.

67 *Criticism and Ideology*, pp. 110–11, n. 26.

68 Ford, *Dickens and His Readers*, pp. 8, 10.

69 Steven Marcus, *Dickens: From Pickwick to Dombey* (Simon & Schuster, New York 1965), pp. 31, 35, 28.

70 See Alexander Welsh, 'Waverly, Pickwick, and Don Quixote', *Nineteenth Century Fiction*, 22 (1967–8), pp. 19–20.

71 Steven V. Daniels, 'Pickwick and Dickens: stages of development', *Dickens Studies Annual*, 4 (1974), p. 77.

72 *Charles Dickens: The World of His Novels* (Harvard University Press, Cambridge, Mass. 1959), p. 34.

73 'Language into structure', p. 185.

74 *Beginnings*, p. 227.

5
History and 'literary value': *Adam Bede* and *Salem Chapel*
PETER BROOKER,
PAUL STIGANT
and PETER WIDDOWSON

Forward from Leavis

We are inevitably concerned, in approaching the question of 'value', with the relations between literature and ideology. The difficulties in comprehending this relationship are now commonly appreciated, but generally seen to reside in the effective elaboration of a theory of ideology. Both terms, however, are difficult, and the problems with the concept 'literature' are our more immediate point of entry into the discussion. The fact that 'literature' has been and still is used as a supposedly neutral descriptive category to designate types of printed work ought in itself to alert us to its radical lack of innocence. Through its long association with the criteria of 'taste', 'sensibility' and 'intelligence', its refined application to 'serious, imaginative' works, joined latterly in a 'tradition', which is presented as evincing a morally committed, but vaguely open and comprehensive attitude towards 'life', the concept 'literature' has evidently performed a heavily ideological function: nowhere so actively and extensively in this century in England as in the work of F.R. and Queenie Leavis.[1]

As Perry Anderson argued convincingly in the seminal essay

'Components of the national culture', Leavis and *Scrutiny* rushed to fill the vacuum, the 'absent centre', within British culture, created by the lack of a native classical sociology, or national Marxism, which would offer a totalizing theory of society.[2] 'With him', wrote Anderson, 'English literary criticism conceived the ambition to become the vaulting centre of "humane studies and of the university". English was "the chief of the humanities"', and here 'the notion of the totality found refuge in the least expected of studies'.[3] In the texts *New Bearings in English Poetry* (1932), *Revaluation* (1936) and *The Great Tradition* (1948) especially, Leavis altered the cartography of English literature, drawing in highways along which the teaching and reading of literature still travels. Informing his method was a zealous but circular empiricism which gave metaphysical and ethical value to 'life', synonymously with 'humane values', of which canonized literary works were the surviving evidence, and the English university, i.e. Cambridge, i.e. its antagonistic and exiled representative *Scrutiny*, was the sole defence. Though Leavis and *Scrutiny* intervened, as Terry Eagleton explains, as a progressive vanguard on behalf of the 'discipline' of literary studies so as to dislodge the amateurism of academic belles lettres, their position as a notional 'real' elite could only be sustained by a reactionary appeal to 'standards' or 'civilized values' or 'the university'.[4] Leavis's notoriously self-defining critical procedure, encapsulated in the phrase 'This is so, is it not?', depended on the existence of shared assumptions within an educated reading public. To acknowledge the non-existence of such a public and sustaining unified culture drew him to raise the myth of a receding, pre-industrial 'organic community' and drew with it, in Queenie Leavis's *Fiction and the Reading Public* (1932), the necessary argument for a cultural history which traced the increasing dilution of civilized standards in the face of commercialism, the mass literary market and the barbarism of the mass media.[5] In spite of Leavis's increasingly strident paranoia and reactionary assertion since the 1950s, he had already determined not only what poetry and novels are read but the terms of an epistemology and cultural history by which they are read. In particular he had, through *Scrutiny*, engaged with and routed the struggling Marxist literary theory of the 1930s. Of this Leavis wrote in the late retrospect to *Scrutiny*:

> We were anti-Marxist – necessarily so (we thought); an intelligent, that is a real, interest in literature implied a conception of it very different from any that a Marxist could expound and explain. Literature . . . mattered, it mattered crucially to civilization – of that we were sure. It mattered because it represented a human reality, an autonomy of the human spirit, for which economic determinism and reductive interpretation in terms of the class war left no room. Marxist fashion gave us the doctrinal challenge. But Marxism was a characteristic product of our 'capitalist' civilization. . . . The dialectic against which we had to vindicate literature and humane culture was that of the external or material civilization we lived in.[6]

In the resurgence of Marxist literary theory within recent years this doctrinal 'challenge' has been directly renewed, and as a consequence the stifling weight Leavis has borne upon criticism has been significantly eased. The studies by Eagleton and Lawford, for example, would suggest that the ideological function of the combined Leavisite enterprise has been adequately expounded and combated. In a general way this is true, but there remains the problem of how we read and 'value' particular works.[7] In answer we have felt in common the need for a full, specific materialist analysis which tests theoretical propositions against their object: literary works; and to this end have wanted to focus the problem of the relation of art to ideology and the question of 'value' on two novels: *Adam Bede*, which with George Eliot's work as a whole has had a received status within the literary canon, and Mrs Oliphant's *Salem Chapel*, a related work, but one which has been variously ignored or dismissed or patronized as a successful pot-boiler. We want, in examining these novels, both to explain the valuations placed upon them and, in locating them in the social and historical moment of their production, to propose alternative criteria of value.

For Leavis *Adam Bede* was 'not perfect', but a promise of perfection to come; in itself it could be seen as an 'illuminating case', a proof, in the remarkable series of influences Leavis detects upon it (Scott, Hawthorne, Aeschylus, Johnson,

Shakespeare and Wordsworth), 'that there is indeed an English literature'.[8] Leavis judges George Eliot and her novel as one; as displaying alike the co-ordinates of 'psychological interest', 'native intelligence', 'imaginative sympathy', 'intellectual culture' and 'creative memory'. Together these comprise a personal 'genius' which in its turn made her an 'incomparable', a 'scrupulously precise', sociologist and social historian, and her novel authentic social history. 'The historical value of *Adam Bede*', writes Leavis, 'lies in her novelist's creation of a past England – of a culture that has vanished with the triumph of industrialization'. 'English literature' and 'a past England' therefore become mutually supportive. For George Eliot to belong to the one (she is 'widely and deeply rooted in literature of the past') underwrites the social accuracy of her 'novelist's creation' of the other, where 'rootedness has very decidedly its advantages'. Leavis's ideological appropriation of the literary text is here then transparent. *Adam Bede* is made to subserve the concept of 'Literature' (evidenced in the most casual citation of 'touchstones' and influence, in an assumed continuity) at the same time as it subserves an inseparable nostalgia for a rural 'organic community'.

In this thinking Mrs Oliphant can only acquire 'value' in so far as she can be placed in the 'tradition', and so qualify as 'literature'. And this is precisely the case made by Queenie Leavis, not for *Salem Chapel*, which she glosses as an 'inferior' novel, 'wrecked on the rocks of a melodramatic plot halfway through', but for the novel *Miss Marjoribanks* which in its ironic and unsentimental tone and heroine is offered both as a consolidating link between Jane Austen and George Eliot's *Middlemarch*, and as 'social history' of a kind 'no historian could supply'.[9]

An assumption we might appear to share with Leavis and bourgeois criticism in what follows is that literary works are worth 'scrutiny'. Not, certainly, 'in themselves' by way of the naive empiricism of 'practical criticism', as verification of 'individual creativity' or of an 'imaginative tradition' or of 'humane values' – but in relation to their own and, in different ways, to our society. To this extent we attribute an initial 'value' to them. With this beginning, we wish to investigate the basis for a

criterion of value and for a discrimination between literary
works suggested in the three essays on art by Louis Althusser
and in Terry Eagleton's *Criticism and Ideology*.[10] The general
proposition which concerns us here, as it is presented most
explicitly in Althusser's 'Letter on Art', is that 'real' or 'authentic art' while 'bathed' in ideology, can, by virtue of its particular
aesthetic structures and modes of signification, attain an 'internal' and 'critical' distance from it, enabling us therefore to
'perceive' that ideology. 'Average or mediocre' works, as
Althusser parenthetically terms them, would appear by contrast to lack this 'internal distance', and to be indistinguishable
from ideology. (This would seem to be the case, where it has a
particular bearing upon our own examples, of the element of
melodrama which Althusser identifies in Bertolazzi's play *El
Nost Milan*.) Ideology, we assume in these formulations, is to be
understood as Althusser defines it elsewhere, as representing
'the imaginary relationship of individuals to their real conditions of existence'.[11]

The essays on art are significant and suggestive, and have
helped prompt our interest, in terms of critical procedure, in
features of structural asymmetry, in implicit or abstract contradictions, in points at which a dissenting voice is silenced or
breaks the surface, so as to interrupt or crease a novel's formal
coherence and so disclose its relation to ideology. We do not
mean, however, to offer the approach or findings of this paper as
a 'practical demonstration' of Althusser.[12] The essays on art
and Eagleton's discussion of aesthetic value are stimulating and
in some ways unparalleled, but carry also important residual
uncertainties which we would wish at least to draw attention to.
The first is the distinction, casually drawn by Althusser, and
endorsed with substantial elaboration but little serious qualification by Eagleton, between 'real' or 'authentic' art (or in
Eagleton 'major authors') and 'average or mediocre' works (in
Eagleton works of 'irretrievably minor status'), with informing
it an argument that the 'internal distance' (or 'tangential
relation') to ideology within art is a 'critical' (or 'alternative and
antagonistic') distance. Not the least troubling feature here is
the incipient circularity by which 'major' art is valued for the
'internal distantiation' by which it is defined. A second weakness appears in the relative lack in Althusser and the broad,

skeletal reference in Eagleton to the ideology and social relations which are specific to particular moments in history. We
would volunteer, as a necessary complication to these
questions, a more precise and materialist history than either
Althusser or Eagleton have undertaken in the above texts.

Adam Bede's realism: the limits of conviction

Adam Bede professes conviction in both senses of the word: of
being convinced, and of being convincing. It expresses a firm
belief in the view of the world it espouses, and it assumes its own
truthfulness in giving an account of the world so perceived. The
two senses – of perceiving and of recounting – are consequential,
and, in effect, imply a *total* comprehension of the world. The case
we wish to argue about *Adam Bede*, in terms of its 'value', is less
the *actual* partiality of such a self-professed totality, but more the
effects of that assumption. Certainly, *Adam Bede* reveals its
ideological location; it does, through tensions and moments of
uncertainty in the text, expose the contradictions within that
ideology; it may even achieve, in Althusser's terms, a 'critical
distance' from the ideology in which it is 'bathed', and so be
'authentic' rather than 'mediocre' art. But the question still
remains as to *how* that 'distance' which denotes 'authenticity' in
art (and, more particularly, in *Adam Bede*) is achieved – in
contradistinction to works which are 'mediocre' or 'average'.
What does *Adam Bede* have or do, to penetrate beyond the
circumscription of the world-view which informs it?

We would want to argue that the answer, in part, resides
precisely in the 'conviction' of the text. *Adam Bede* purports to be
describing a real world, to be addressing a material situation
and material issues. It proposes, to borrow Carlyle's terms, to
lay before us a 'solid Action', rather than the 'linear narrative' of
history;[13] a vertical section of life, bounded by time and place,
but as complete and as fully realized as the truthfulness of the
author will allow. [. . .] The world of the book, in other words, is
conceived as 'real' – that is, in terms of a particular conception
of reality (George Eliot's). But the very materiality of that
conception, realized as the world of the book, invokes other,
extra-textual, 'realities' which are implicit, but not directly
addressed, there. Or, to put it another way, a dialectic is

established between the 'realism' which results from the informing view of reality, and other conceptions of reality invoked by
the very solidity of realization that one view has received; a
dialectic between text and context, between 'realism' as an
ideological literary practice, and the real social relations which
that realism at once both suppresses, or explains away, and
implies in its solid specificity.

It is important to emphasize, however, that the possibility of
penetrating into this extra-textual space, or context, depends on
the degree of conviction the text itself assumes. It is this
assumption of 'truthfulness' which enables a material world to
be realized in specific and coherent structures. The 'world' of
Adam Bede is realistic in this sense and contains, for the most
part, a coherent positivist-humanist explanation of the action
and relations it proposes. It is, at one level, convincing, and is,
therefore, what might be described as a 'stable' text – by which
we mean that it is so adequately 'woven' (Lat. 'text') that it is
possible to define its relation to that which it is 'woven in with'
(Lat. 'context'). The contexts, in this sense, are an implicit
dimension of the text; if the text is inadequately 'woven' it is
likely to continuously forestall or withhold any perception of its
relation to its 'real' contexts. Hence, we might argue, it is an
'inauthentic' or 'mediocre' work. But no text will, of course, be
totally secure or 'stable'; indeed its 'conviction', as we noted
earlier, is itself the expression of the partiality of its world-view,
its ideology. Tensions, irresolutions, absences, 'creases' in the
text will reveal themselves because of it, and *Adam Bede* is no
exception. Nevertheless, without a large degree of stability,
such 'creases' will not be perceptible; the unstable text will be so
criss-crossed with them that the significance of any one crease in
relation to the whole will be unclear. We might, then, argue that
it is by way of the unstable moments in a largely stable text that
the 'real' relations, the contexts, are perceived; they are, to
continue the weaving analogy, the flaws in the texture of the
particular motif which lead the eye to the larger pattern. The
status of a text like *Adam Bede*, then, might be defined in terms of
the dialectic it establishes between its own reality and the reality
of the contexts it invokes.

We wish to discuss this dialectic [. . .] by way of noticing a
number of uncertainties in the novel's structures, in relation to a

set of three interrelated issues: the locating of the novel's action in the past; the presence of Methodism; and the significance of Dinah Morris as a woman to some degree emancipated by her work as an itinerant preacher. What we hope to indicate is that a novel like *Adam Bede* both encourages and demands empirical discussion of precise historical contexts, simultaneous with close analysis of its text; that material historical analysis helps to disclose the contexts the text invokes, and thus alters and reinforces our perceptions of the penetrating realism the novel attains.

[. . .] *Adam Bede* is a seemingly confident affirmation of bourgeois humanist ideology. By the end of the novel, the elements of egoism have been eradicated, Adam Bede has learnt sympathy through suffering, and has at the same time prospered – while Arthur Donnithorne, of the landed gentry, has not. In this sense, humanism is revealed as the ideology of a particular social and economic group (it is not insignificant that the character of Adam Bede was influenced by Samuel Smiles's 'Life' of George Stevenson). Furthermore, the novel posits a triumph for humanism over Methodism, an important element of that nonconformity in religion which Matthew Arnold, eight years later in *Culture and Anarchy*, was to characterize as 'Hebraism' – in contradistinction to the humanist 'Hellenism' – and which he saw as one of the most powerful forces opposed to 'Culture' in English social life: 'Look at the life imaged in such a newspaper as the *Non-conformist* – a life of jealousy of the Establishment, disputes, tea-meetings, openings of chapels, sermons; and then think of it as an ideal of a human life completing itself on all sides, and aspiring with all its organs after sweetness, light, and perfection!'[14] Hence the incorporation of Dinah into the humanist idyll of the last pages of *Adam Bede*.

[. . .] As we have noted, the novel is an instance of a partial world-view conceived as a totality, and in which realism assumes a consonance with reality. If we need an explanation for its immediate popularity (this second work by a largely unknown novelist had sold 3350 copies of the three-volume edition and 11,000 copies of the cheaper two-volume edition by the end of the year); for the enthusiastic response of someone like Mrs Carlyle who found herself 'in charity with the whole human race' at the end of it;[15] and for its retention in Leavis's phrase as a 'classic in itself',[16] then it surely lies in the text's ostensible *conviction* as fictional realism disguising its ideological commitment – *so long as* that ideology remains the domain within which it is read and understood. But it is precisely this conviction (the 'stability' of the text) which throws into relief both its own momentary uncertainties and the implied – and often de-stabilizing – contexts in which it is situated.

As an instance of this, let us first consider the most obvious 'moment' when the realism slips – Hetty's reprieve. The chapter entitled 'The last moment' is not only the shortest in the book, but is only one page long. The actual reprieve is contained in a single paragraph, which slips uneasily and self-consciously into the present tense; no further mention of it is made in the book and no explanation is given of how Arthur obtained the '*hard won*' reprieve (p. 438, our italics). (Hetty is transported and dies on her way home, as a single remark informs us in the last chapter.) It is a moment of melodrama, of fictive contrivance, which stands in stark relief to most of the rest of the book, and it seems to exude an embarrassed recognition of its own fictionality. George Eliot's realism gives way here, and draws attention to its contrivance by attempting to reduce it to nothing. How do we explain this fissure in the firm terrain of the novel? Why could Hetty not have been hanged, as the logic might suggest? Or failing that, why could there not have been fuller treatment of how and why Arthur wins a reprieve? The short answer is that the moral conception of the book has no room for such material: Hetty [. . .] has fulfilled her purpose in the moral schema and must be removed *hors de combat*. Hanging her would introduce into the moral universe of the book a note of barbarity (George Eliot has at the start of the chapter shuddered at 'the hideous symbol of a deliberately inflicted sudden death' (p. 437)) out of tune with social and moral humanism, and, perhaps more importantly, a recognition of public institutions and issues which could not be assimilated into the humanist pastoral of the novel. Much the same would be true of any extended explanation of Arthur's use of privilege and position in obtaining a reprieve; it would introduce a dimension of public affairs (especially, class influence) inimical to the world-view

George Eliot is propagating – let alone being a digression from the focus of the novel. Equally, to allow Hetty to remain in, or return to, England would raise questions about the social position of the 'fallen woman' and about prostitution (Hetty's possible, but precluded, destiny?) inimical to the domestic ideology which the end of the novel, with Dinah's marriage to Adam, seems to endorse, and which, in humanist terms, conceives of Love as 'the mother's yearning, that completest type of the life in another life which is the essence of real human love' (p. 409). The embarrassment of that short, fictive, moment, together with the dismissal of Hetty at the end, is, we would argue, a sublimated recognition of the exclusiveness of the novel's realism.

A larger and more general instance of exclusiveness, however, is the exclusion of George Eliot's own contemporary social world – by dint of setting the action sixty years in the past. Realist fiction invariably *does* deal with the past because, in purporting to 'tell things as they really are', it would be a contradiction in terms to deal with things that have not happened or could not happen. In setting the novel historically, then, George Eliot enhances the realism, the sense of a 'fixed' knowable community whose perimeters are delimited by written history which, in this case, is the novel itself. But also, in 'realizing' a static, moral (rather than primarily social), world-view, whose values – if the world-view is 'total' must hold good for any period, it is self-evident that the most appropriate social formation will be chosen: hence, the setting of *Adam Bede* in a small rural community at the end of the eighteenth century.[17] But this, of course, is geographical as well as historical; indeed, Hayslope and its environs constitute the *only* model of community in the novel. Snowfield, where Dinah works, is never described, and Adam only visits a cottage on the edge of the town and turns back; the scenes in Stoniton take place in Adam's room and Hetty's cell – neither of which is described – and Hetty's journey to Windsor and back is represented, characteristically, through the miasma of her own state of mind. It is as though a particular historical moment in a particular place has been sealed off as the world of the book. Certainly there are scattered references throughout the novel to the French wars, but these represent the attitudes of the Hayslopians to the wars, not an exploration of the bearing the wars may have on the community. Again, despite the ostensible interest in Methodism in the book, the only real presence of it is Dinah herself, whose idealism and independence are neutralized, and then reconstituted as realism and domesticity. Methodism, as a powerful religious and social movement, is, as it were, *excluded* by the presence of its sole representative. Now all these exclusions and elisions are, in a sense, accounted for, or explained away, by precisely the totalizing (and therefore limit-forming) realism of the novel: few Hayslopians *would* travel to Snowfield or Stoniton; villagers *were* trapped in their own locality all their lives; the wars *would* mean little, except in so far as they were good for prices, to men like Poyser and Craig; Methodism *did* make little headway in rich, rural areas; and so on. But it is also *because* of the solid realism of this small world that these absences are also presences – presences which invoke the larger contexts of their real historical materiality. And these 'contexts' conjure up questions and issues which the totalizing world-view has, in a sense, been at pains to exclude or suppress, and which threaten its totality and absolute 'conviction'.

If the world-view of *Adam Bede* is universal, i.e. valid for all times and places, why set the action sixty years in the past? Do the occasional moments which disclose the distance between the past and the present time of writing (the nostalgic passage on 'old leisure' (pp. 484–5); the tone of the whole 'Harvest supper' chapter which immediately follows this, or passages which idealize Adam as workman (pp. 163–4, 208–9) and the use of the aged Adam Bede in chapter XVII to idealize Irwine and criticize Mr Ryde) imply that the society of the 1850s is less susceptible to humanist ideology than Hayslope in 1800? Is the exclusion of urban, industrial communities – where, we gather, there is acute distress – an indication that such communities might respond more to the energy of Methodism and other forms of dissent, than to the harmony of bourgeois humanism? Is the minimization of the effects of the French wars – which keep prices up and exacerbate the distress of the urban poor – a recognition of a public domain impervious to humanist individualism? Is Methodism a force as easily converted to a 'religion of humanity', and assimilated into the community, as the treatment of Dinah would suggest? Early in the novel, the 'stranger' who leads the reader into Dinah 'preaching' is described as, *until then*, only knowing 'but two types of Methodist – the ecstatic and the bilious' (p. 33), forms which are not present in the novel in the person of Dinah. Equally, in the early chapter 'The Rector', Will Maskery (who never appears in person) is revealed as a very different type of Methodist, opposed to Irwine and the establishment, and a threat, certainly, to Joshua Rann and his kind. It is significant that George Eliot – via Irwine – knows that Irwine could raise (and pay) a mob to hunt Maskery out of the village. The fact that Irwine sensibly does not do so is part of George Eliot's case for humanism, but it does not erase *the fact* of Will Maskery's Methodism, and the threat it seems to offer to the established community. The world, and world-view, of *Adam Bede* we see can accommodate Dinah, whose sole presence excludes other more intractable forms of Methodism.

But this returns us to our original point: that it is Dinah's presence, realized in solid material form, which invokes the absent contexts. In contradistinction to Hetty, who occupies only 'fictional space' because she is conceived as a fiction, Dinah, because she is so realistic, creates around her extra-textual space. George Eliot's direct use of her sources – her aunt's story and Southey's *Life of Wesley* in particular – account for Dinah's sermons, speeches, dress and manner of speaking, and these, in fact, constitute the vast bulk of her depiction in the book. It is notable that Dinah has no 'character' in the conventional sense: there is, for instance (and in absolute contrast to Hetty), almost no direct exploration and transmission of her 'inner life'. And this is because her 'inner life' *is* Methodism; indeed everything about her is, as it were, 'explained' by Methodism. It is her 'realism', then, which precisely invokes the context which 'explains' her: the real, historical, development of Methodism which lies beyond the world of the book. It is in this way that extra-textual space develops around her, space predominantly occupied by Methodism, of course, but also – since she is an independent, and to some degree emancipated, young woman who is finally reassimilated into domesticity – occupied also perhaps by the intensifying debate on 'the Woman Question' in mid-Victorian society. [. . .]

Salem Chapel : melodrama and ideology

Salem Chapel forms one of seven works of fiction which comprised the Chronicles of Carlingford. Of these, three were long short stories ('The Executor', 'The Rector', 'The Doctor's Family') and four were novels (*Salem Chapel* 1863, *The Perpetual Curate* 1864, *Miss Marjoribanks* 1866 and *Phoebe, Junior* 1876). The series was conceived clearly out of economic necessity. Mrs Oliphant was in 1860 newly widowed, with three children and a dependent alcoholic brother; she held a lease on a London home she could not afford, and was in debt to the tune of £1000, most of it owed to her publisher Blackwoods. The idea of the series she offered to help pay off the debt. Of these *Salem Chapel* was the most commercially successful – 'it really went very near', she said, to making her 'one of the popularities of literature' and it enabled her to bargain with Blackwoods and to win from them £1500 for the next novel, *The Perpetual Curate*.

But if *Salem Chapel* was a commercial success, it was, in Mrs Oliphant's mind, as well as in the minds of contemporary reviewers, and those who have commented upon the book since, an artistic failure. The main objection in these responses has been to the incongruity of the novel's parts: its uneasy combination of the 'inner life of a dissenting congregation' which we are told in the one full-length study of Mrs Oliphant was 'the great attraction of that novel for Victorian readers' and the 'plot of a sensation novel' which has been thought 'unnecessary' and 'crudely melodramatic'.[18] This judgement is in itself significant, plainly informed as it is by organicist criteria which respect and confer artistic merit upon an achieved internal coherence. The apogee of such an aesthetic has of course been the intensive, totalizing, fictional world possible within the realist novel, a form which, as we see in George Eliot, lends its conviction to the reproduction of bourgeois hegemony. It is no surprise therefore that an objection to the broken surface of *Salem Chapel* should be accompanied by a superior regret for its 'crude' (or 'cheap', or 'low') melodrama. The Colbys, for example, who assume the main theme of the book is Arthur Vincent's 'keen sense of personal failure', write:

> Had Mrs Oliphant explored and developed the idea at leisure, she would certainly have produced a better book.

> Unfortunately she set out to write a best seller. More import-
> antly, from the point of view of her literary reputation, she
> succeeded. Artistically it is a failure. Her interesting hero
> becomes enmeshed in a crudely melodramatic plot almost
> totally obscuring the important issues of the book.[19]

The Colbys, like others, repeat the stock, largely unexamined,
response which views melodrama both culturally and artistically as inherently 'low'. It is not the case either that the novel
would, in this view, be redeemed if it were entirely and consistently melodramatic. If this were so the popular theatre of the
nineteenth century, and the 'sensation novels' of Lytton, Wilkie
Collins and Mrs Henry Wood, upon which Mrs Oliphant
draws, would have had a more openly acknowledged 'place'
than they do. Neither would the 'Great Tradition' have had to
struggle as it has done to accommodate Dickens. In Q.D.
Leavis's notorious early judgement, Dickens was guilty of
'crude emotional exercises', to the extent that only two of his
novels could be weighed as 'literature'.[20] In her discussion of
Mrs Oliphant, similarly, only one novel, the ironic, unmelo-
dramatic, anti-sentimental *Miss Marjoribanks*, can be accepted
as 'art', a stepping stone retrieved from the intervening slough
of popular fiction to see us safely across from Jane Austen to
George Eliot.[21] The popular best seller (melodrama) and 'art'
(realism), then, are, in this thinking, truly incongruous if not
inconceivable together, and Mrs Oliphant's *Salem Chapel* is in
'bad taste' and bound to fail in seeking to combine them. But the
offence the novel gives is not simply that it appeals, through
melodrama, to popular taste, although it may in part do this.
The fundamental, though unuttered, offence is that it exposes
the dependence of literature (all literature, including George
Eliot) on the literary market which is itself indifferent to formal
distinctions between literary modes. In the market, 'realism'
and 'melodrama' are of 'value' if they sell, and a novel is even
'better' if it can combine these modes and so combine markets.
What is incongruous and an embarrassment to bourgeois
aesthetics is compatible within, and an enrichment to, the
bourgeois literary market. The insistence on (surface) formal
artistic coherence, then, and the forced separation of artistic
from commercial success are ideological blinds designed to

conceal a (deep) compatibility of modes, one with the other, in the market where 'art' is sold.

In the response to melodrama the blind is drawn more rapidly (through reflex dismissal) because there is more to conceal. As Althusser comments on Marx's study of Eugène Sue's *Mystères de Paris*, 'it could not be more bluntly put that it was the bourgeoisie itself that invented for the people the popular myth of the melodrama, that proposed or imposed it (serials in the popular press, cheap "novels") just as it was the bourgeoisie that "gave" them night shelters, soup kitchens etc.'[22] This is perhaps to put it too bluntly, since it is difficult to accept that Victorian melodrama, given its evolution from diverse, often working-class or populist antecedents, is the 'invention' of the bourgeoisie, or that it is 'imposed' in any direct way. Like other cultural forms it occupies a place and function in the exercise of a consensual hegemony, which allows, within itself, for a degree of licensed subversion (the images, for example, in melodrama of the villainous gentleman or capitalist and heroic working man), though this is 'in the last instance' contained and controlled in the interests of the hegemonic class. But it is true, nevertheless, as Althusser suggests, that for melodrama to retain its ideological force as an accepted veneer on real conditions, its function had to be 'forgotten' by both its audience and those who would materially profit from it. Mrs Oliphant's *Salem Chapel* would give offence in this way not only because it contaminates 'art' with 'popular' taste, exposing their equal operation in the market, but because it threatens to bring 'popular taste', the orphan child, home to roost. The danger of melodrama and realism cohabiting in the same novel is that a blood relationship might in fact be revealed between them, and if it is one thing for the bourgeoisie to admit that 'art' exists within a market, it is quite another for it to admit to exploiting that market to its own advantage.

A discussion of *Salem Chapel*, then, must attempt to free itself of the ideological categories of bourgeois criticism. We do not wish to claim that Mrs Oliphant's novel has in fact a formal coherence which others have failed to see, and that it is therefore a neglected 'artistic success'. Nor do we wish to claim that, though lacking in 'art', *Salem Chapel* is of 'sociological interest' and that it may be read transparently as a text for ideology. The entire novel is 'art' in the most descriptive sense, in that it employs the structures and notations specific to realism and melodrama. It is the relation the novel contrives between those modes, we would argue, which, while it is designed to safeguard, in fact unlocks the work's ideological function. This relation is signalled conspicuously at the inception of the melodramatic ambience and plotting in chapter X, when the nonconformist minister Arthur Vincent is asked to speak at a tea-meeting given in celebration of a series of successful lectures on the Church and State. Vincent rises to warn the gathering of the 'dark sea of life that surged around them' beyond 'this little gaslighted perch', of 'that dark unknown existence that throbbed and echoed around: he bade them remember the dark night which enclosed that town of Carlingford'.[23] The speech is listened to with 'breathless interest' and Vincent, perceiving its effect, 'proceeded to deepen his colours and make bolder strokes of effect': 'His success was perfect; before he had concluded he had in imagination dismissed the harmless Salem people out of their very innocent recreation to the dark streets which thrilled round them – to the world of unknown life.' His hearers 'were startled, frightened, enchanted. If they had been witnessing a melodrama, they scarcely could have been more excited' (p. 82). Vincent works upon his audience, then, with the deep colours and bold effects of melodrama, to intimate a dark, hostile external world beyond known and lighted boundaries, and ends 'with the consciousness of having done his duty by Salem for this night at least' (ibid.). His duty has been to lecture them on the limits of their world and the constraints they would exercise over himself. From the beginning Vincent's idealism had been frustrated by the petty rivalries, the commonplace luxuries and suffocating domestic complacency of 'the shop-keeping Dissenterism' of Carlingford which threatened to convert the chapel from which he was to influence the world into 'a miserable scene of trade before his disenchanted eyes – a preaching shop where his success has to be measured by seat letting' (p. 38). At the tea-meeting Vincent can answer back, and can dismiss his petit-bourgeois deacons and congregation, 'in imagination', through the veiled devices of melodrama, into the 'dark streets' of an 'unknown life'. But he too, and from the beginning, has been presented as limited, 'well educated and enlightened according to his fashion', but 'entirely unacquainted with any world but that contracted one in which he had been brought up' (p. 4). In his ambition and 'ignorance of the real world', Vincent 'in imagination' saw himself admitted to the 'social pleasures of society', *naturally* believing that this was his 'natural place' (p. 5). When he encounters that world directly it appears in the persons of Mrs Hilyard and the Lady Dowager through the bold opposition of darkness and light which anticipate the novel's melodrama. He is invited to the Lady Dowager's breakfast party, and spends 'the days in a kind of dream' before he is admitted to 'the Bower of Bliss', the 'Eden Garden, where the woman of all women wandered among the flowers' (p. 55). But it is a 'fool's paradise'; society does not know him, and far from this being his natural place he discovers 'no link or connection existed between him and this little world of unknown people except herself' (p. 59). Vincent is prompted in his chagrin to make himself 'known', and embarks on the series of Church and State lectures, lambasting the Church's connections with 'worldly possessions, rank, dignities, power' (p. 61). Interestingly, he acts, as Mrs Oliphant indicates, out of a confusion of personal and class enmity: his state of mind quickened 'all the prejudices of his education' and gave 'individual force to all the hereditary limits of thought in which he had been born'; his cry is not only that of 'wounded self regard' but that of a man who 'had entered life at disadvantage, and chafed, without knowing it, at all the phalanx of orders and classes above him, standing close in order to prevent his entrance' (ibid.).

The society breakfast party is set in the novel against the chapel tea party, and both provoke an indirect attack on the failings of the worlds between which Vincent is caught. His class situation is ambiguous; he is in the employ of the petit-bourgeois chapel 'connection', but is removed from them by his upbringing, 'in painful gentility', and by the 'taste for good society' given him by his mother (p. 12). Hence the dream of paradise proffered through the 'heavenly vision' of the Lady Dowager. Stung by his exclusion from this 'privileged class', Vincent levels the armoury of his nonconformist training against its supporting structures of Church and State, to speak, in the understanding at least of his deacons, as the intellectual spokesman of the chapel community. Mrs Oliphant is concerned to show us, however, how on both occasions Vincent's sentiments and address are 'worked up'. He launches himself against Church and State in a delusion of personal conviction which evaporates at the close of the lecture series with a 'few words and smile' from Lady Western (p. 66). His realization that he has been motivated by personal envy serves Mrs Oliphant's purpose to expose what would be a class antagonism as limited and prejudiced. Class difference is subordinated in this way to what is offered as the 'reality' of romance convention. Later in his lecture to the Salem congregation, Vincent speaks again at a remove from his own real sentiments, with conscious 'humbug'. His satisfaction is that he has jolted his audience into a 'visionary uneasiness' which is akin to his own at the 'far-withdrawing perspective of gentility and aristocratic seclusion' (p. 70). The society world of aristocratic privilege to which Vincent aspires, by way of romance, is presented then in the novel as the paradoxical 'unknown, real world', and it is on the strength of his 'vision' of his natural place in this world, now denied him, that Vincent (and through him Mrs Oliphant) can admonish the petit-bourgeois nonconformist connection on its vulgar materialism and the 'limits of its thought'.

Once the reality of the chapel world has been undermined in this way the novel can *consistently* usher in its own 'real' world of 'Society' through the continued displacement of melodrama. The deep colours and bold strokes of effect of melodrama by which Vincent excites his congregation become (in the confines of the novel) 'real', as he retires to the vestry to overhear from the 'absolute darkness' outside the bitter and violent exchange between the gentleman villain Colonel Mildmay and his estranged and mysterious wife Mrs Hilyard. Vincent is immediately involved in Mrs Hilyard's intrigue to protect her daughter from Mildmay, and awakes the next morning to the 'spectacle of passionate life, full of evil and noble qualities – of guilt and suffering' beside which the controversy of Church and State has paled to nothing (p. 92). The subsequent melodramatic spectacle of the novel – Susan Vincent's abduction, Vincent's pursuit across country of Mildmay, the attempted murder of Mildmay by Mrs Hilyard, the shame and guilt attaching to Susan, her illness, recovery and reprieve, are here all set in train.

Melodrama then serves to introduce the 'unknown real' world of 'Society' into the novel in earnest. Vincent has exploited its effects to lift the blinkers and unsettle the complacency of his petit-bourgeois employers. So also does Mrs Oliphant exploit it (leaning, as the Colbys show, for inspiration and specific plot detail on the examples of Collins's *Woman in White* and Mrs Henry Wood's *East Lynne*) to display not only the logic of Vincent's infatuation but the pretensions and gullibility, in its 'painful gentility', of the Vincent family. As Vincent dreams of entry into 'Society' through marriage, so his mother and sister Susan are easily duped by the young Dowager's brother Mildmay posing as Mr Fordham. As Mrs Vincent writes of Mildmay's false proposal of marriage, the world beyond their 'strict household limits . . . expanded towards the widow's pen' (p. 39). The family then is exposed to its dream, and the effect is shattering: not because they are awoken to its illusory nature, but because the dream turns to nightmare, sundering the family apart and inducing shame, guilt, derangement and delirium in its members. The family in due time recovers and is in fact strengthened as the dream (and hence a version of 'reality') is reconstituted. Mildmay, true to form and to his instincts as a gentleman, absolves Susan of crime and shame. From a 'ruined' woman she is reclaimed 'intact' as a fit prospect for future marriage and, as the mother in proxy of the rescued Mildmay daughter, returned to her own mother. The outcome is for Mrs Vincent an example of the victory of innocence over evil and a vindication of God's justice, the fatherless women of the Vincent family finding in her restored faith a 'Father' in God (p. 337).

Arthur Vincent, the favourite but gullible brother and son, is reclaimed as the family's male more slowly and uncertainly. His pursuit of the villain Mildmay and the angel Lady Western incites his congregation to a vote of censure, and in spite of the efforts of his deacon Tozer to accommodate his gift for preaching and his distaste for his flock, Vincent resigns his office. But as Vincent rejects the proffered role within one world as petit-bourgeois intellectual, so he is rejected by the other – by way of Lady Western's marriage to her former lover and social equal, the real Mr Fordham. Vincent is cast into limbo, 'plunged into that world of life which the young man did not know' (p. 365). Too 'high' still for eminent Dissenting families, but hostile too in 'education and prejudice' to the Church, Vincent dreams of a surrogate marriage, 'A Church of the Future – an ideal corporation, grand and primitive, not yet realised, but surely *real* to become so one day – shone before his eyes' (ibid.). In the meantime, 'as was natural', he passes into literature, and the domain of public opinion, as the founder of the 'Philosophical Review' to fight out his battle 'in silence' in his 'neutral coloured household' (p. 366). Human voices and colour re-enter his life only with the return of his mother accompanied by the transformed Susan, and 'the other – ?', the girl Alice (the name also of Lady Western), who occupies at once the roles of daughter, sister and prospective wife. These two are 'apparitions' but yet 'visible tangible creatures and no dreams'; they are 'real creatures' but move with a 'fairy light-ness', transforming Vincent into 'an enchanted prince in a fairy tale' (pp. 366–8). His mother can look now to Vincent's return to preaching and the (unuttered) prospect of his marriage. The dream of romance then, which while a dream is insistently 'real' for the Vincents, is restored after the banished tribulations of melodrama's nightmare. At its centre is the presiding figure of the mother and through her the family, which has absorbed the 'other' – the innocent child of society. In prospect there is the sustaining vision of a future double incorporation; of church and chapel, and of a darkly incestuous marriage with Alice (and therefore 'Society') which will fulfil Vincent's social ambitions, while it further secures rather than endangers the family.

'The dream which is real' might serve, of course, as a blunt definition of ideology, of a 'foreign consciousness' which yet suffuses lived relations.[24] If it is unsettled by nightmare, it is nowhere in *Salem Chapel* unsettled by an awoken apprehension of 'real conditions'. The aristocratic society which the novel presents through the stereotypical figures and plotting of romance and melodrama as the 'real world' is clearly a token of its own 'limits of thought', and of its relation to ideology. The mid-Victorian period witnessed a crisis in hegemony coinciding with the mass production, marketing and reading of popular novels of which Mrs Oliphant's oeuvre is an exemplary instance.[25] Bourgeois domination, exercised through consent rather than coercion, acquired from the 1850s a stability which depended on the stabilization and diversification of the economy (in book production as elsewhere) and on the alliance of classes within the construction of a power bloc.[26] While the bourgeoisie consolidated its economic and industrial power within this bloc, the landowning aristocracy retained a place in government, the army and administration. Landowners, as Marx pointed out, were retained 'as the *aristocratic representatives* of the bourgeoisie, of the industrial and commercial middle class'.[27]

Mrs Oliphant's *Salem Chapel*, in presenting this 'representative' class as 'reality', in fact presents only a façade behind which lay the real conditions of bourgeois hegemony. It is not, as Roger Bromley claims generally for popular fiction, that the 'economic base' and the truth of capitalist relations are excluded from the novel,[28] since these appear in the relations the nonconformist 'connection' contracts with its employee, the minister. Capitalist relations are here rather 'transferred' from the bourgeoisie to the petit bourgeoisie. But the exclusion of the truly hegemonic class itself from *Salem Chapel* is a significant ideological closure and the novel works further, through the Vincent family, to achieve a freedom from the claims of economic necessity. In its final configuration the novel has shut out the world of trade and absorbed the innocent façade of 'Society', detaching the family and Vincent from any economic definition. It comes to settle, one might think, in an 'improved' paradigm of the petit bourgeoisie, centred in the mother and family, and purified of both exploitative aristocratic villainy and the vulgarity of money. In this sense *Salem Chapel* is 'critical' of the ruling class and of trade, but it achieves this criticism, significantly, only *within* ideology, through a blinkered partiality which can only be sustained by a confused insistence that Vincent's position is 'natural' and that the family's dreams can come true.

In these respects the novel would seem to bear particularly upon Mrs Oliphant's own situation. It is at the outset deeply imbued (as are her other novels) with her own strong belief in motherhood and her relations with 'weak' men: her husband (a failed painter), her brother (an alcoholic clergyman removed from his living) and her sons, all of whom were economically dependent on herself. What, in the resolution of the novel, she strives to imagine and project through the combined figures of Mrs Vincent and Arthur is a freedom for herself as mother and author from her own economic dependence on the literary market. Analogically, the Salem connection which judges sermons in terms of seat-letting is Blackwoods, the publishers, who judged Mrs Oliphant's fictions in terms of their commercial success. Her freedom from the economic determinants of her own existence as an author can, of course, only appear displaced in the dream of fiction, and what *Salem Chapel* itself secured her was not freedom, but the strength to bargain with Blackwoods for her next novel. The ideological closures of the book, then, while they speak to and on behalf of the petit bourgeoisie, relate in particular to ideology as it operates through the apparatus of literary production. The 'freedom' Mrs Oliphant achieves as a writer is internal to the literary market and its sustaining ideology; a stepping only from one sub-market into another by which she can retain at most the space that is opened by a cynical exploitation of the conventions of romance and melodrama which, as it were, write themselves according to formula. Vincent's self-removal and the 'success' of his address to the chapel tea-meeting are therefore Mrs Oliphant's own:

> Mr. Vincent perceived the effect of his eloquence . . . when he saw it, he awoke . . . to feel how unreal was the sentiment in his own breast which had produced this genuine feeling in others, and with a sudden amusement proceeded to deepen his colours and make bolder strokes of effect. His success was perfect. . . . Mr. Vincent was rather pleased with his success, although it was only a variety of 'humbug'.

(pp. 82–3)

This is the success and acknowledged humbug of the professional hack-writer. But just as Mrs Oliphant exposes Vincent's cynical use of melodrama to its 'reality' in the course of the novel, so her exploitation of its conventions to achieve a freedom 'in imagination' is contained and licensed by the reality of book publishing which can market and nullify her exploitation as internal to and, in fact, subserving its own ends. The constraints of trade and of money which the novel has sought internally to deny and free itself from are, ironically, all too triumphant.

Towards a conclusion

How then do we weigh *Salem Chapel* with *Adam Bede*? And what of Althusser's formulations with which we began on the distinction between 'authentic art' and 'average or mediocre' works and their relations to ideology? It is not altogether clear whether Althusser would describe 'average or mediocre' works as 'art', but it is clear to us that *Salem Chapel* in its use of the highly conventionalized artistic structures of romance and melodrama is both 'average' and 'art'. It would seem also that the function of romance and melodrama in the novel is to exert a specific and internally 'critical distance' on the realistically portrayed, petit-bourgeois world of the chapel community. Althusser, it would seem, attributes such an internal critical distance on ideology to 'authentic art' only, or to 'art' *per se*. We must, then, on our evidence refine these categories if we are to articulate the difference between our two novels. *Salem Chapel* in fact criticizes petit-bourgeois ideology in terms of ideology. Beneath its broken surface, by which it means to escape the world of trade and wage relations, it is ideologically one-dimensional. It escapes as in dream only to be returned to the workaday world where the economic constraints of the petit bourgeoisie it had fled are writ large in the literary market. Its 'critical distance' one might think is illusory, but it would be wrong to deny its presence. *Salem Chapel*'s weakness, in fact, and where it differs from *Adam Bede*, is that it does not engage 'internally', and even in spite of itself, with the real conditions of its time. It is only 'externally', in the position it occupies in the market place, that these are encountered. *Adam Bede*, while it works to subserve liberal humanist ideology, raises by its very self-conviction issues in mid-Victorian social relations, particularly concerning labour, class and the position of women, which are potentially subversive of that ideology. This subversion is most often oblique but it is also at certain moments quite conspicuous, and it is dealt with in different ways; sometimes knowingly accommodated, sometimes self-consciously parried or silenced. But *Adam Bede*, we would argue, has shown us in the process more *intrinsically* how ideology is reproduced (in this instance through the specific rhetoric of fictional realism) so as to persuade us of the explanatory power of ideology's *in fact* 'imaginary' account of real relations.

We have also, in discussing *Adam Bede*, referred repeatedly to its 'world view', and this term is useful in pointing a distinction between the two novels. Not, certainly, if it is understood to designate a true, total and coherent account of real relations, since it is none of these. A 'world view' is in fact the expression of a partial and limited consciousness, and is hence ideological, but it is ideology at its most persuasive and therefore most apparently coherent and totalizing. *Salem Chapel* does not have this appearance; it works upon its materials opportunistically so as to achieve a precarious, suspicious and unpersuasive coherence, although it does this, like *Adam Bede*, for ideological ends. A similar distinction between 'world view' and 'ideology' is drawn by Terry Eagleton in his discussion of *Jane Eyre* and *Wuthering Heights*.[29] There he argues also that the 'intensive totality' of *Wuthering Heights*'s world view forms the basis for a 'finer artistic achievement'. This is not our emphasis and, since it requires too limiting an acceptance of formal coherence as an artistic virtue, not the kind of conclusion we wish to reach. We would rather suggest the need for a criterion of value which accounts necessarily for the artistic, ideological and historical threads which weave a 'text' with its 'context'. By this means we will confer 'value' not simply, either, on those works which most nearly achieve formal coherence or those which are more transparently ideological, but on those whose cognizance is such that it opens the dialectic between the internal world a work presents and the historically precise 'real relations' in which it stands. On this reckoning *Adam Bede*, which argues for its world to the point where it is scarred by the debate, is a superior work to *Salem Chapel*, which does not know it is sealed in a debate of its own making.

Notes

1 Cf. the discussion in Raymond Williams, *Marxism and Literature* (Oxford University Press, Oxford 1977), pp. 45–74, and also Tony

92   Popular Fictions

Davies, 'Education, ideology and literature' in *Red Letters*, 7 (1977), pp. 4–15.

2 Perry Anderson, 'Components of the national culture' in *New Left Review*, 50 (1968), pp. 5–6, 50–6.

3 Ibid., p. 50.

4 Terry Eagleton, *Criticism and Ideology* (Verso, London 1978), pp. 14–15.

5 Cf. Paul Lawford, 'Conservative empiricism in literary theory: a scrutiny of the work of F.R. Leavis', *Red Letters*, 1 (1976), esp. pp. 13–14.

6 *Scrutiny – A Retrospect* (1963), p. 4. Quoted in Anderson, p. 54.

7 The more basic and prior question might appear to be 'why do we read literary works at all?' But this, and the significance of our relative enjoyment, discomfort, boredom or antipathy in what appears to be the 'natural' process of reading is not a topic we are able to address with any unity. We cannot fail, however, to acknowledge its brooding presence.

8 George Eliot, *Adam Bede* (Signet, New York 1961), foreword, pp. vii–xv (all the following page references in the text are to this edition); reprinted in Frank Leavis, *'Anna Karenina' and Other Essays* (Chatto, London 1967), pp. 49–58.

9 Introduction to *Miss Marjoribanks* (Chatto, London 1969), pp. 9–10.

10 Althusser's essays are 'The "Piccolo Teatro", Bertolazzi and Brecht' in *For Marx* (London, Allen Lane 1970), pp. 131–51; 'A letter on art' and 'Cremonini, painter of the abstract', in *Lenin and Philosophy and Other Essays* (New Left Books, London 1971), pp. 202–8, 209–20. The most directly relevant section of Eagleton's *Criticism and Ideology* is the chapter 'Marxism and aesthetic value', pp. 162–87.

11 *Lenin and Philosophy*, p. 153.

12 Even less do we mean to signal a tacit acceptance of the assumptions and full implications of Althusser's position(s).

13 Thomas Carlyle, 'On history' (1830), in *Selected Writings*, ed. Alan Shelston (Penguin, Harmondsworth 1971), p. 55.

14 Matthew Arnold, *Culture and Anarchy*, ed. J. Dover Wilson (1869; Cambridge University Press, Cambridge 1971), p. 58.

15 Quoted in Amy Cruse, *The Victorians and Their Books* (Allen & Unwin, London 1935), p. 278.

16 Eliot, *Adam Bede*, foreword, p. vii.

17 Cf. John Goode, *'Adam Bede'*, in *Critical Essays on George Eliot*, ed. B. Hardy (Routledge & Kegan Paul, London 1970), pp. 19–21, where he offers other reasons for George Eliot's need, in the attempt to write a 'natural history' of English life, to set the novel in the past.

18 Vinera and Vincent Colby, *The Equivocal Virtue: Mrs Oliphant and the Victorian Market Place* (Archon, London 1960), pp. 46, 49.
19 Ibid., p. 49.
20 Q.D. Leavis, *Fiction and the Reading Public* (1932; Chatto, London 1965), pp. 156, 158.
21 Introduction to *Miss Marjoribanks*, pp. 1–24.
22 Althusser, *For Marx*, p. 139.
23 Mrs Oliphant, *Salem Chapel*, in *Chronicles of Carlingford* (Blackwood, London 1897), pp. 81–2. All following page references in the text are to this edition.
24 Althusser, *For Marx*.
25 Cf. Roger Bromley, 'Natural boundaries: the social function of popular fiction', *Red Letters*, 7 (1977), p. 40.
26 Cf. Robert Gray, 'Bourgeois hegemony in Victorian Britain', in *Class, Hegemony and Party*, ed. Jon Bloomfield (Laurence & Wishart, London 1977), esp. pp. 76–7.
27 Karl Marx, *Surveys from Exile* (Allen Lane, London 1973), p. 259; quoted in Gray, 'Bourgeois hegemony', p. 77. Cf. also Antonio Gramsci, *Prison Notebooks* (Laurence & Wishart, London 1971), p. 83.
28 Bromley, 'Natural boundaries', p. 43 and *passim*.
29 T. Eagleton, *Myths of Power: A Marxist Study of the Brontës* (Macmillan, London 1974), pp. 97, 98.

6

What shall we do
with the starving baby? –
Edward Jenkins and *Ginx's Baby*
BRIAN MAIDMENT

The preface to the tenth thousand of Edward Jenkins's polemical novel about drunkenness, *The Devil's Chain* (1876), begins with a statement of perplexity about the novel's function, which is hardly expected from an experienced novelist whose first novel *Ginx's Baby* (1870) had just reached its thirty-sixth edition. 'One is rather at a loss to know what sort of a book one had written', Jenkins comments with a mixture of surprise and complaint. Yet not only Jenkins was unsure of what kind of book he had written, as the successive prefaces to his more famous *Ginx's Baby* suggest. In these prefaces, Jenkins prints or comments on repeated criticisms by others of his work, criticisms which clearly exemplify the way in which his works confused and confounded conventional expectations. To a large extent it is not Jenkins who is unsure of his role, but the reading public, and Jenkins's insecurity develops more out of hostile criticism than from any lack of confidence in his published work. The closeness of Jenkins's relationship with his readers is clearly established by his need to take their complaints seriously despite his enormous sales figures.

Jenkins's critics were mainly concerned with the need for factual accuracy in novels dealing with major social or political issues. In *The Devil's Chain* Jenkins characterizes his critics' demands in the following way: 'A good many objections have been taken to the construction and style of this story. It is said to have no "plot"; it is assailed for its unreality; and, finally, it is averred . . . to be "sensational" and "exaggerated".[1] Jenkins then proceeds to answer these points individually. Plot, he claims, is irrelevant to his purpose – 'I do not pretend that I have succeeded in making an artistic book' – because his object is to startle and inform rather than to satisfy. The unreality of his work is defended by again pointing to the dramatic need of the subject rather than its artistic coherence: 'is it not legitimate for one who is writing a parable to link together a series of dramatic scenes, each one of which is natural and probable?' Thus far Jenkins's response to his critics is both intelligent and effective. On the third issue, that of factual accuracy, Jenkins, while still replying with characteristic intelligence, reveals the insecurity of his position by showing the need to defend the absolute factual accuracy of his statements and the propriety of dealing with such shocking evidence as he provides in his book. He had already admitted earlier in his preface that factual accuracy need not be fundamental to the polemicist's method, and suggested that the need to publicize and shock was greater than the need to be totally faithful to documentary evidence. The preface to *Ginx's Baby* reveals similar insecurities and also provides another opportunity for Jenkins to air publicly the problems he had met in writing his own kind of novels:

> To those who have criticized the book in the modern fashion, the Author has only most gently to deprecate that they should have felt themselves constrained to make objections when they obviously had none to make. To take an instance: one not unkindly critic declares that the Author 'OFTEN mistakes invective for satire' – a remark so paradoxical as to require solution. The author is conscious of having deliberately used both invective and satire, but the error of confounding them he returns to the critic.[2]

Yet even when he is so evidently capable of dealing with his critics, Jenkins still exhibits his uncertainty in his need to include in his preface the documentary and factual sources of the evidence he uses in his fictional account of Westminster slum life in the 1860s. An immediate impression, then, on looking at Jenkins's novels is of his extraordinary self-consciousness and sensitivity to the limitations of naturalism as both a polemical and a literary technique. Yet in spite of this awareness, Jenkins still obviously feels the need to stand by the 'truth' of his evidence in the face of his critics. This sense of a dual purpose is necessary to an understanding of the whole genre of polemical fiction.

In using the word 'polemical' to describe a certain mode in Victorian literature, I am using an adjective never, so far as I know, used by the Victorians themselves. Polemical fiction draws on both propagandist and experimental modes. Propagandist fiction largely suspends consciousness of the audience as *readers* in order to persuade. In other words, the imperatives of content make attention to literary form seem almost indulgent. Experimental fiction, on the other hand, confronts the audience not as socially concerned individuals, but as *readers* whose moral sympathies are usually subsumed by their expectations of the genre. These two contrary concepts of the novel – the one seeing literary form as a 'vehicle' of ideas, and acknowledging the authority of content, and the other seeing the attack on genre or literary form as the necessary way of changing the social meaning of the novel – are contained in polemical writing in an attempt to change the ideas and beliefs of the *person* by first changing the *reader*. Whereas propagandist fiction attempts to change the reader's mind regardless of his or her expectations of being entertained or informed, and experimental fiction changes the status of the reader without full reference to the world outside the novel, polemical fiction attempts to alter the status of the reader in order to change his or her view of the outside world. By polemical writing, then, I mean a group of fictions and non-fictions of the 1850s and 1860s which use advanced formal experiments in this way in order to change social perceptions. Apart from Jenkins's novels I would include such books as William Gilbert's *De Profundis* (1866), the novels of James Greenwood, and, in a non-fictional mode, Arnold's *Friendship's Garland* and Ruskin's *Time and Tide*.

Accordingly, the two main impulses of the polemical novel become clear. The first is the drive towards naturalism, towards getting the facts right, in order to shock the complacency of readers and to enlarge their awareness of social or political problems. The intention of such realistic fictions is to work towards political change through a rational and convincing assessment of the available facts. Such naturalistic writing also has the crucial advantage of fulfilling the expectations of the reader who is familiar with the factual presentation of material in newspapers, government reports and similar non-fictional writing. Concrete and rational evidence is one way of suggesting a response. Yet this naturalistic technique is obviously not an effective literary method, being more suited to the pages of a Blue Book than to those of a sensational novel. Detailed factual description of the most precise and objective kind is more likely to repel than convince the reader, and the intelligent novelist is obviously quick to recognize this limitation. An important passage in George Eliot's essay 'On the natural history of German life' shows her awareness of the issue:

> our social novels profess to represent the people as they are, and the unreality of their representation is a grave evil. The greatest benefit we owe to the artist, whether painter, poet, or novelist, is the extension of our sympathies. Appeals founded on generalizations and statistics require a sympathy ready-made, a moral sentiment already in activity; but a picture of human life such as a great artist can give, surprises even the trivial and selfish into that attention to what is apart from themselves, which may be called the raw material of moral sentiment.[3]

Jenkins, too, recognizes that unadulterated information is use-less as a fictional mode, and this recognition is a major cause of the radical nature of his novels.

The second drive of the polemical novel is positively away from naturalism. If the reader is to be shocked by facts, s/he is also to be simultaneously surprised and confounded by radical fictional techniques. The exploitation of unconventional fictional forms and methods is a legitimate way of dislocating the reader from his or her conventional and possibly unshockable response to factual information. Thus the polemical writer has as one of his weapons the whole range of novelistic techniques. The more experimental the form of his novel, the more it outrages the expectations of his readers, then the more likely it is to make its political point, or, at least, the more likely it is to serve as the centre of widespread discussion. In other words the polemical novelist can deliberately arouse controversy not only

through the revelation of appalling facts but also through
flouting all fictional norms, through rejecting the easy answer
which George Eliot characterizes as 'a sympathy ready-made'.
Thus we find in the polemical novel consistently radical fictional strategies, often derived from eighteenth-century models,
which do not fulfil the expectations of contemporary readers but
which rather redefine those expectations. The novelist is assert-
ing his or her right to enforce the genre in which s/he can operate
most effectively. Jenkins clearly exploits this dual impulse in the
polemical novel in a radical and self-conscious way which
demands further consideration.

The son of a Wesleyan missionary, Jenkins was born and
educated in Canada and came to England to be called to the Bar
in 1864. *Ginx's Baby*, which was published in 1870, made
Jenkins a famous and controversial figure overnight. Thirty-six
editions were sold by 1876, and a photograph of a howling and
distressed infant by the famous studio photographer O.G.
Rejlander which was published under the same title sold 60,000
prints and 250,000 cartes in the late 1870s.[4] Doubtless the
success of the photograph in enlisting public interest helped to
keep *Ginx's Baby* in the centre of controversy, but more important for the attempt to study the role of the polemical novelist is
the *Dictionary of National Biography*'s laconic comment that *Ginx's
Baby* 'had its influence on the religious compromise in the
Education Act of 1870'. Any specific link between political
change and the polemical novel has major consequences in
assessing the significance of such novels. The *DNB* further
categorizes *Ginx's Baby* as a 'pathetic satire on the struggle of
rival sectarians for the religious education of a derelict child'.

When the fame of his first novel subsided, Jenkins began a
career as both politician and political journalist inside and
outside Parliament. His writing career was varied and ambitious, but he never had another major popular success. This
did not stop his novels remaining determinedly polemical.
Published in 1872, *Little Hodge* supported Joseph Arch's agitation on behalf of the agricultural labourer, and four years later
The Devil's Chain dealt with the social implications of drunkenness. The title of another work, *Glances at Inner England*, calls to
mind all the other propagandist titles used by polemical writers
to capture public attention – Mearns's 'Outcast London',

Booth's 'Darkest England', Jack London's 'Abyss', and Gissing's 'Nether World'. Certainly, there seems to be a decline into melodrama and hysteria in these later works, as well as an unwillingness to revalue the role of the novelist in his or her treatment of social evils, but even so Jenkins's novels form an interesting and valuable body of work, whatever their aesthetic limitations.

The story of *Ginx's Baby* is easily summarized. Ginx and his wife, who lived in Rosemary Street, Westminster, are introduced as the desperate parents of twelve children. Their 'home' is described in detail, and also the effects of the Westminster environment on decent, kindly and hard-working people, whose most obvious characteristic was political innocence. With many digressions to put forward his views on the failure of politicians to grasp the realities of life among the very poor (Ginx brings up his twelve children on 18 shillings a week) Jenkins describes Ginx, driven out of his senses by anxiety, attempting to drown his youngest baby. Interrupted in this by a parish officer, street debates on the desirability of birth control are accompanied by the 'translation' of Ginx's baby to the charity of 'the Home of the Sisters of Misery'. The misplaced sanctimony of the nuns and their wish to impose their values on Ginx's baby (they want to christen him 'Ambrosius') are mercilessly described, but a larger section of the narrative is taken up by a bitterly comic account of the protracted wrangling between the Sisters of Misery and the Protestant Detectoral Association for the guardianship of Ginx's baby. The real needs of the baby were of course soon abandoned for sectarian politics, and eventually Ginx's baby was found on a doorstep wrapped 'in the largest daily paper in the world'. A committee, funded by a public collection, was set up to administer Ginx's baby, but, the committee having spent all its money on administering and thus having none to spare to help the child, Ginx's baby again appeared on a doorstep, this time wrapped in sacking. The child's journeys through uncharitable England continued by way of the parish Guardians (who 'neglected nothing that could sap little Ginx's vitality, deaden his happiest instincts, derange moral action, cause hope to die within his infant breast almost as soon as it was born') to the casual benevolence of a politician too taken up with debating poverty to understand or alleviate it, and finally to the balustrades of Vauxhall Bridge. The narrative becomes tract, debate, indignant denunciation and picaresque tale by turns, but it is held together by Jenkins's consistent grasp of the appalling but nonetheless comic discrepancy between profession and action, between intention and fulfilment, in Victorian attitudes towards poverty.

Yet, of course, Jenkins is a novelist, and is himself open to the charge of debating rather than acting. How is he to avoid exposing the benevolent ineffectuality of his own moral position as a novelist? One important way of overcoming this failure is used by Jenkins and Dickens alike – humour. The polemical possibilities of humour are extremely important and wide-spread in the Victorian novel, and the advantages of writing in comic modes are suggested by Louis James in *Fiction for the Working Man* when James discusses the work of the illustrator C.J. Grant: 'Many of his drawings are well proportioned and full of character, honest in their boisterous portrayal of comic ugliness in people and setting. Although their comedy is based on physical deformity, violence and sordid surroundings, they are too objective to be morbid.'[5] What James stresses here is the way that the cartoonist (normally thought of as an exaggerator of reality) is in this case an intensifier of reality, who selects specific characteristics and treats them in an 'honest' and 'objective' way. The interest of the humour in the grotesque, the squalor, the dirt, is justified in the statement that it is too 'objective to be morbid'. This appeal to the ability of humorous modes to cut across differences of class-based attitudes, to unify response in laughter, is a crucial one in considering the suc-cess of Jenkins's novels. As James rightly points out, humour stresses individuality, the unique characteristics of even the poorest and most oppressed. It is a humanizing quality for both presenter and recipient, and it places the realities of Victorian slum life outside overt political attitudes into a world of comic, humane discriminations which make horror and deformity aspects of individuality, and causes of pity or affection. Given the assumption that humour is one possible way of avoiding the problems of idealization and patronage which beset the liberal novelist, it becomes necessary to examine the specific humorous modes adopted by Jenkins in his novels.

Ginx's Baby adopts a curiously elaborate, and even experimental, fictional technique derived substantially from eighteenth-century models. Just as Dickens had looked back on a tradition of the English picaresque novel of Hogarthian observation, love of the grotesque, and caricature to evolve a Gothic perception of social relationships, so Jenkins relies on the self-conscious, almost self-parodying, formal complexity of eighteenth-century fiction to express a simple social indignation. One further aspect of an earlier picaresque tradition which Jenkins adapts is that of the treatment of low-life characters not just as grotesque but also as self-reliant and resourceful within the limits of their social location. There is an obvious relationship in his writing between the Victorian vigour and directness of Jenkins's perceptions of governmental negligence and national indifference, and the choice of tortuous, complex and humorous ways of expressing this understanding. I think that this alliance of simplicity and complexity proceeds from a recognition of the dual aim of the polemical novel suggested above. By using an eighteenth-century picaresque mode in the 1870s, Jenkins was in one way fulfilling a set of novelistic conventions which had found popular acceptance in a long tradition running through Sterne and Smollett to Pierce Egan, the Newgate Novel and to Dickens. In one sense then Jenkins is working in a mode which, for all its apparent eccentricity, lack of obvious narrative structure, and self-consciousness, was widely known and appreciated by mid-Victorian readers. Furthermore, this mode was primarily a *comic* one which was not directly associated with didactic purpose or with social and political controversy. The manner of Jenkins's book is in part an appeal to acknowledged popular taste, to the wish to be entertained and amused, and his choice of what fifty years previously would have been called a 'low-life' subject in no way contradicts the reader's expectation of humour, drollery, grotesque deformity, and a seemingly cynical use of suffering for comic purposes. Indeed, among the suffering and deprived poor, humour is seen as a method of survival, of reducing the surrounding horror to conceivable proportions. For all its concern with the deformities and cruelties of poverty, the picaresque mode has as its centre a reassurance – a comic world view that states that the grotesque and outcast eccentric is in fact human, individual, and interesting, and that he or she lives in a world which, whatever its overt social conditions, allows him or her to express individuality outside the restrictions of conventional social behaviour.

Yet Jenkins's perceptions of poverty are obviously beyond such reassurances and indeed at odds with them. The choice of the picaresque mode, while creating such difficulties, also gives Jenkins the means of solving them. An essential element of the picaresque convention is that the novelist, while working within a comprehensible tradition, can also confront and challenge orthodox demands through the deliberate eccentricity which is as much a part of the tradition as a love of the grotesque. Jenkins depends very heavily on this part-comic, part-serious challenge to the expectations he arouses through his choice of a specific fictional convention in which to write *Ginx's Baby*. An obvious example is the use of typographical eccentricity in *Ginx's Baby* to make overtly controversial points, points which are only rendered acceptable to the reader by the startling and comic ways in which they are presented. In Part III of the novel, for example, two official notices are laid out on the page in proper poster fashion surrounded by a typographic border, a device which clearly points to the deliberately confusing nature of the 'official' language with its 'whereases' and 'wherefores', and accentuates the cold inhumanity of the contents of authenticated communications. In another chapter, the official questions to be asked by one of the innumerable charity committees concerned with Ginx's baby are laid out in minuted form, from 1a ('Wherewithal he should be fed and clothed') down to 2d, 1 and 2 ('Should he be further baptised? If so 1. Into what communion? 2. By what ceremonial?'). A few pages earlier the balance sheet of the 'charitable' committee is laid out in the traditional pattern of such documents, revealing more clearly in statistics than in words the smallness of the proportion of revenues that was actually spent in looking after Ginx's baby, and the size of the income which went on the self-propagating activities of the committee itself. Another chapter prints in italics a learned barrister's opinion about the legal position of Ginx's baby, an opinion which takes four pages full of recondite references to such reliable authorities as *Barnes* v. *Barnes* L.R. 1, P & D 463 to show that the barrister does not, after all, have any opinion at all in the matter. All these ironic points are made as much visually as intellectually, and the inhumanity of officialdom is revealed as clearly in its artefacts as in any other way. Furthermore, the book is given a surface of documentary authority. The technique will be familiar to readers of Ed McBain's detective novels, where official documents are reproduced for exactly the same dual purpose of authentication on the one hand and ironic contrast between feelings and responses and the official embodiment of such emotions on the other.

If typographical adventure is one comic technique authenticated by the picaresque mode, the shifting narrative persona is another. *Ginx's Baby* has generally a consistent narrative voice dependent on the sustained indignation of the narrator at the callousness of official treatment of a pauper child. Yet within this overall consistency, Jenkins is willing to tell his story through any technique that seems suitable. The most frequent alternative narrative that Jenkins creates depends on an extended and effective use of dramatized dialogue, arranged on the page like a play script. The characters in such dialogues stand for attitudes – a 'chorus' makes frequent appearances and represents the humane common sense of working people. A 'Philosopher', who stands for subtle but inhumane rationality, also appears in a dialogue which suggests Jenkins's considerable ability to dramatize and enliven even his most serious and didactic passages:

PHILOSOPHER. Well, I will go further and say you ought not to have married without a fair prospect of being able to provide for any contingent increase of family.
CHORUS. Laws a'mercy!
PHILOSOPHER (waxing warm). What right had you to marry a poor woman, and then both of you, with as little forethought as two – a – dogs, or other brutes – to produce between you such a multitudinous progeny –
GINX. Civil words, naabor; don't call my family hard names.
PHILOSOPHER. Then let me say, such a monstrous number of children as thirteen? You knew, as you said just now, that wages were wages and did not vary much. And yet you have gone on subdividing your resources by the increase of what must become degenerate offspring. (To the chorus) All you workpeople are doing it. Is it not time to think about these things and stop the indiscriminate production of human

beings, whose lives you cannot properly maintain? Ought you not to act more like reflective creatures and less like brutes? . . .

The philosopher had gone too far. There were some angry murmurs among the women and Ginx's face grew dark. . . . Before he could translate his thoughts into words or acts a shrewd-looking, curly-haired stonemason, who stood by with his tin on his arm, cut into the discussion.

STONEMASON. Your doctrines won't go down here, Mr. Philosopher. I've 'eard of them before. I'd just like to ask you what a man's to do and what a woman's to do if they don't marry: and if they do, how can you honestly hinder them from having any children?

The stonemason had rudely struck out the cardinal issues of the question.

(*Ginx's Baby*, pp. 35–8)

In a scene like this the evidence is manipulated, even contrived, to make it polemically effective. The narrative is sustained here by turning a fairly dull and static debate into a dramatic scenario in which the greater intellectual understanding and, rationally, the much more convincing arguments are overcome by a combination of the good-hearted but emotional views of the crowd and by the severe authorial comments that Jenkins himself contributes to the debate at a crucial moment. In humanizing and dramatizing the argument, Jenkins assures his own victory. The debate can, in fact, only be won dramatically and rhetorically, by deployment of sympathies rather than ideas. In pointing to the virtues of commonplace affections, Jenkins appeals to the emotions of his readers, and because their sympathies are directed towards the crowd and against the abusive and coldly rational 'philosopher', the discussion is won by the forces of unreason. The complex use of narrative structures to allow the author to make overt and seemingly objective judgements on characters of his own making is an important one for the polemical novel. The didactic or reformist writer defends himself from irritating his readers by his sententiousness and his didacticism through the enlivening and dramatizing of his arguments in the complexities of his story telling.

A further technique of Jenkins's arguing is his use of the physical appearance of his books as an element in his polemic.

The eighteenth-century practice of issuing books in paper wrappers to be bound to their owners' requirements precluded any use of covers or bindings for decorative effect. The growth of publishers' cloth binding styles in the first half of the nineteenth century gave authors and publishers the chance to use cover design to catch and hold public attention as well as to comment on the contents of the books inside the covers. It is interesting that many writers of polemical works, Carlyle and Ruskin among them, who used every available method of confronting and disconcerting their readers in their texts, shared a horror of ostentatious or memorable bindings for their books. Jenkins, like Dickens, very sensibly ignored any such fastidiousness, and those of his books which I have seen represent some of the most effective and attractive use of decorative cloth bindings which I have ever seen. [. . .] *Ginx's Baby* has in fact the most restrained binding of any of Jenkins's books, but the point I want to make here is that of the tremendous awareness which Jenkins possessed of all available ways of creating response in his audience, an awareness which stemmed from an extreme self-consciousness about the novel as an object and about the many-faceted relationship between book and reader.

One final area in which Jenkins adapts eighteenth-century humorous fictional strategies to his own purposes can be seen in his use of every available kind of space in his book for extraneous, witty, and amusing comment. The clever title of the book sets the tone – *Ginx's Baby: His Birth and Other Misfortunes* – and the brief preface is equally provocative and entertaining:

CRITIC – I have never read a more improbable story in my life.

AUTHOR – Notwithstanding, it may be true.

The dialogue form of some sections of the book is adumbrated here almost before the novel has begun. The argument begins with the cover, runs through the title page and preface, and is naturally expanded in the text. The awareness of the physical and visual possibilities of the book is thus carried to extreme, and extremely effective, lengths. Jenkins's use of chapter headings, too, is instructive. The book is divided into five main sections, 'What Ginx Did With Him', 'What Charity and Churches Did With Him', 'What the Parish Did With Him',

'What the Clubs and Politicians Did With Him' and the
ominously short final section 'What Ginx's Baby Did With
Himself'. Each of these main sections is further divided into
sub-sections with elaborate titles, which in themselves almost
form a continuous narrative parallel to and commenting on the
main text, much in the manner of a Bulwer Lytton novel. This
device was, of course, extensively used in the eighteenth-
century and early nineteenth-century novel, but Jenkins gives it
a further dimension by carrying the sub-section heading on the
top of every right-hand page as a headline, emphasized by two
parallel lines. Thus, fully conscious of the ironic proximity of the
headline 'Loving One Another', one reads on p. 97:

> The platform and the meeting were by the ears again. It was
> fiercely contended that only Evangelical Christians could
> have a place in such a work, and many of the nominees
> declared that they would not sit on a committee with –
> well, some curious epithets were used. The Unitarians and
> Quakers took their stand on the Catholic principles em-
> bodied in the amendment, and on the fact that Ginx's Baby
> had now 'become national Protestant property'.

It is possible, then, to isolate the major strengths and weak-
nesses which are available to the polemical novelist. The two
persistent failings of the polemical mode are, firstly, the failure
of direct, naturalistic description to convey the force of the
novelist's indignation, and, secondly, the silencing or distortion
of verifiable information about social conditions in an attempt
to find the compensations and rewards of working-class life.
The great strengths of the polemical novelist must lie in his
ability to find exciting, original, and usually humorous fictional
forms to embody his political message. Of course, many other
writers as well as Jenkins were extremely conscious of the
limitations of naturalistic description and the need for a precise
new vocabulary in order to express devastating and newly
realized social evils. Here is John Ruskin, writing as late as
1880, and expressing quite brilliantly the limitations of literary
expression in dealing with urban poverty:

> beauty has been in the world, since the world was made, and
> human language can make a shift, somehow, to give account
> of it, whereas the peculiar forces of devastation induced by

modern city life have only entered the world lately; and no existing terms of language known to me are enough to describe the forms of filth, and modes of ruin, that varied themselves along the course of Croxsted Lane.[6]

Yet, as I have already suggested, one constant demand the mid-Victorian readership made of its authors was that they should get the facts right, and describe with rigorous and fastidious fidelity. The prefaces to Jenkins's books show him responding very clearly to such demands, but the text of *Ginx's Baby* too contains many examples. Here is the important opening description of Ginx's 'home', and it is necessary to realize that at this time Ginx and his wife had twelve children:

> I shall be as particular as a valuer, and describe what I have seen. The family sleeping room measured 13 feet 6 inches by 14 feet. Opening out of this, and again on the landing of the third-floor, was their kitchen and sitting room; it was not quite so large as the other. This room contained a press, an old chest of drawers, a wooden box once used for navvy's tools, three chairs, a stool, and some cooking utensils. When, therefore, one little Ginx had curled himself up under a blanket on the box, and three more had slipped beneath a tattered piece of carpet under the table, there still remained five little bodies to be bedded. For them an old straw mattress, limp enough to be rolled up and thrust under the bed, was at night extended on the floor. With this, and a patchwork quilt, the five were left to pack themselves together as best they could. . . .
>
> Not to be described are the dinginess of the walls, the smokiness of the ceilings, the grimy windows, the heavy, ever-murky atmosphere of these rooms. They were 8 feet 6 inches in height, and any curious statist can calculate the number of cubic feet of air which they afforded to each person.
>
> The other side of the street was 14 feet distant. Behind, the backs of similar tenements came up black and cowering over the little yard of Number Five. . . . I have seen the yard; let me warn you, if you are fastidious, not to enter it.
>
> (*Ginx's Baby*, pp. 7–9)

The assurances of objectivity and the truth of empirical observation are constant here. The opening statement that 'I

shall be as particular as a valuer, and describe what I have seen'
is followed by the even more earnest 'I have seen the yard'.
These attempts to stress the author's integrity and truthfulness
are further underlined by the appeal to precise physical description with exact numerical measurements to convey the squalor
of Ginx's lodgings. Yet are such methods effective? Are the dry
facts enough? The reader does his or her best to visualize the
scene, but s/he clearly has no real imaginative grasp of the
emotional implications. And what is s/he to make of Jenkins's
own admission of failure – '*Not* to be described are the dinginess
of the walls, the smokiness of the ceilings, the grimy windows'
and so on. Jenkins is right – they are not to be described. There
is no vocabulary, no vivid descriptive technique, no graphic
representation, however faithful, that can convey the full horror
implied by these rooms. The retreat to statistics – 'They were 8
feet 6 inches in height' – is not helped by the appeal to 'any
curious statist' where again it is the failure to make the calculation which is stressed. I think that Jenkins's admission of
failure, his decision that conditions are 'not to be described' but
only implied, is a crucial one which reveals convincingly the
limitations of naturalism as a polemical and novelistic technique. Jenkins is not only afraid of offending proprieties here,
but also acknowledging that factual modes of description are
ultimately unconvincing. [. . .]

Nathaniel Hawthorne, in his significantly titled 'Outside
Glimpses of English Poverty', offers a parallel retreat from the
earnest honesty of an attempt to look truly and unflinchingly at
English slum life:

> Whatever the disadvantages of English climate, the only
> comfortable or wholesome part of life, for the city-poor, must
> be spent in the open air. The stifled and squalid rooms where
> they lie down at night, whole families and neighborhoods
> together, or sulkily elbow one another in the daytime, when a
> settled rain drives them within doors, are worse horrors than
> it is worthwhile (without a practical object in view) to admit
> into one's imagination. No wonder that they creep forth from
> the foul mystery of their interiors, stumble down from their
> garrets, or scramble up out of their cellars, on the upper step
> of which you may see the grimy housewife, before the shower
> is ended, letting the raindrops gutter down her visage.[7]

This is vivid and compassionate writing, and yet there are two significant modulations in Hawthorne's understanding of what he sees. The first is the acknowledgement that at a certain point he stops himself from looking any closer at what lies before him because he knows that the full horror of what he sees will disturb his mental equilibrium to no practical purpose. In other words, a moment arrives when the humane observer has to deny the honesty of his own observation in order to preserve himself from the chaos of his own ineffectuality. The second modulation is equally significant. Hawthorne finally concedes that the lives that go on inside the slums are 'mysteries' to him. There is no vocabulary, visual or linguistic, that is adequate to the task of conveying the reality of the scene. The observer is hindered not only by his ultimate lack of commitment to the honesty of what he sees but also by his lack of language – the failure of the fictional vocabulary to convey adequately 'forms of filth and modes of ruin'.

In discussing the self-confessed failure of descriptive method, it is interesting to look at the way Dickens deals with similar difficulties. In *Bleak House*, the problem of getting clear the full horror of Tom-All-Alone's is met both with humour:

> It is a moot point whether Tom-All-Alone's is uglier by day or by night; but on the argument that the more that is seen of it the more shocking it must be, and that no part of it left to the imagination is at all likely to be made so bad as the reality, day carries it.[8]

and secondly by appeal, not to verifiable fact, not to the number of people crowded into rooms 14 feet long by 8 feet wide, but to the vivid image, to the emotive and expressive quality of extended simile and metaphor:

> Jo lives – that is to say, Jo has not yet died – in a ruinous place, known to the like of him by the name of Tom-All-Alone's. It is a black dilapidated street, avoided by all decent people . . . Now, these tumbling tenements contain by night, a swarm of misery. As, on the ruined human wretch, vermin parasites appear, so, these ruined shelters have bred a crowd of foul existence that crawls in and out of gaps in walls and boards; and coils itself to sleep, in maggot numbers, where the rain drips in; and comes and goes, fetching and carrying fever.[9]

The results of such oblique and suggestive descriptive devices carry the polemical argument much more clearly than Jenkins's factual evidence. It may seem that all I am saying is that Dickens is a better writer than Edward Jenkins, but this is to miss the real point. In trying to find an effective method of expressing social realities, Jenkins deliberately adopts a mode which his readership demands of him, deliberately acknowledges that 'truth to fact' must be a major polemical function for the Victorian writer. The pressures which force Jenkins to maintain such assumptions are clear, yet ultimately the scrupulous retailing of factual evidence is a limited technique, a concession to public demand in an age of committees and reports. Our best understanding of the Victorian slums comes not from Jenkins's factual evidence but from his grasp of the grotesque paradoxes of bureaucratic irresponsibility. The comic potential of the evident inhumanity of institutions set up to be humane, of religious institutions without charity, of the failure of benevolent intentions because of petty disagreements, is what Jenkins's fiction exploits most successfully. His factual account of urban poverty, well intentioned and accurate as it may be in its indignation, is less significant as a polemical technique than his firm grasp of the horrifying humour of social paradoxes and the madness of an industrial society.

Notes

1 Edward Jenkins, *The Devil's Chain* (10th thousand 1876), p. xii.
2 Edward Jenkins, *Ginx's Baby* (5th edn, 1870), note to 2nd edn. All further references to *Ginx's Baby* will be to the 5th edition, and they will be included in the text of the essay.
3 George Eliot, *Essays* (Cabinet edn, vol. XXI, 1885), pp. 192–3.
4 E.Y. Jones, *Father of Art Photography* (David & Charles, Newton Abbot 1973), pp. 38, 107.
5 L. James, *Fiction for the Working Man* (Penguin, Harmondsworth 1974), p. 59.
6 John Ruskin, 'Fiction fair and foul', in *The Nineteenth Century* (June 1880), p. 941.
7 Nathaniel Hawthorne, *Our Old Home* (Centenary Hawthorne, vol. V, Ohio State University Press, Ohio 1970), p. 281.
8 Charles Dickens, *Bleak House* (1853; Penguin edn, ed. Norman Page, 1971), p. 683.
9 Ibid., p. 272.

Fictional suburbia

KATE FLINT

'The suburbs', asserts a character in Arnold Bennett's first novel, *A Man From the North* (1898), 'even Walham Green and Fulham, are full of interest for those who can see it'. He invites the novel's hero – and, by implication, the reader – to look at the average surburban street. Though the roofs form 'two horrible, converging straight lines . . . beneath there is character, individuality enough to make the greatest book ever written'. One should look at the varying indications supplied by bad furniture seen through curtained windows, observe the fluttering blind,

> examine the enervated figures of women reclining amidst flowerpots on narrow balconies. . . . In all these things there is character and matter of interest, – truth waiting to be expounded. How many houses are there in Carteret Street? Say eighty. Eighty theatres of love, hate, greed, tyranny, endeavour; eighty separate dramas always unfolding, intertwining, ending, beginning – . . . Why . . . there is more character within a hundred yards of this chair than a hundred Balzacs could analyse in a hundred years.[1]

This, so far as I know, is the first sustained plea for a literature of suburbia: a recognition of the suburbs as an environment with a sufficiently separate – and varied – identity to provide subject matter enough to sustain whole novels.

There is nothing new about the presence of the 'suburbs' in English literature. From Chaucer's time to the early eighteenth century, the location was used as an acceptable point of reference designating not merely the fringes of a large city but, in the case of London in particular, the undesirable habitat of its criminal population. But, by the late eighteenth century, the growth of London had led to a decentralization of middle-class housing, with consequent literary appraisals of rural peace in contrast to the city. However, even by 1782, when the dormitory suburb in the modern sense had not yet come into being, such 'suburban villas, highway-side retreats' had been perceived in terms of slowly stifling claustrophobia. Cowper, in his poem 'Retirement', describes the growing streets of

> Tight boxes, neatly sash'd, and in a blaze
> With all a July sun's collected rays,
> Delight the citizen, who, gasping there,
> Breathes clouds of dust, and calls it country air.
>
> There, pinion'd in a parlour snug and small,
> Like bottled wasps upon a southern wall,
> The man of business, and his friends compress'd,
> Forget their labours, and yet find no rest.[2]

For much of the nineteenth century, imaginative writing did not focus so much on the conditions which became established within the suburbs as on the rapid expansion itself, the expansion of what Ruskin terms those

> pitiful concretions of lime and clay which spring up, in mildewed forwardness, out of the kneaded fields about our capital . . . those thin, tottering foundationless shells of splintered wood and imitated stone . . . those gloomy rows of formalised minuteness, alike without difference and without fellowship, as solitary as similar.[3]

Dickens, in *Dombey and Son*, saw the growth of Camden Town in apocalyptic terms. He describes the cataclysmic upheaval to the environment caused by the northern advance of the railway [. . .] and in the middle of the confusion are speculatively built streets stretching out into the agricultural detritus of 'frowzy fields, and cow-houses, and dunghills'. Yet when the same chaotic scene is revisited six years later, order has been imposed:

the new streets that had stopped disheartened in the mud and waggon-ruts, formed towns within themselves, originating wholesome comforts and conveniences belonging to themselves, and never tried nor thought of until they sprung into existence. Bridges that had led to nothing, led to villas, gardens, churches, healthy public walks. The carcasses of houses, and beginnings of new thoroughfares, had started off upon the line at steam's own speed, and shot away into the country in a monster train.[4]

The figures for the spread of outer London are, indeed, dramatic. Between 1801 and 1898 the population of Camberwell, for example, rose from 7059 to 253,076; that of Lewisham from 4007 to 104,521. Dyos, in his invaluable study of the growth of Camberwell, *Victorian Suburb*, states that the suburban trend is most marked from the 1860s onwards, and estimates that 'the outer ring of suburbs of Greater London . . . grew by about 50 per cent in each of the three intercensal periods between 1861 and 1891 and by 45 per cent in the decade 1891–1901'.[5] As press reports indicated, the supply of housing, especially in the earlier years of this expansion, before the suburban train services were fully developed, even exceeded the number of people willing to move into them.[6] So rapid was the growth of London's suburbia that its precise location had to be continually redefined. Yesterday's terrace houses, each with the luxury of a separate garden, became today's 'huge and smoky area of tumbled tenements' over which the commuter's train thunders on its way to work. Masterman, in *The Heart of the Empire* (1901), searching for a solution to the housing problems of inner London, finds that: 'From day to day the venue for the solution of the problem is changed. Yesterday it lay in West Ham, in Streatham, Hackney, and Tottenham; today it lies in East Ham, in Croydon, and Harrow; tomorrow it will be in the belt of country lying beyond.'[7] Yet he envisages this pushing out of the boundaries in the melodramatic terms of terminal disease. Rather than the suburbs offering the pseudo-countryside promised in building speculators' advertisements, the overcrowding, 'vacuity of labour, and lust for artificial excitement' which he associates with central London is spreading: 'North, East, South, and West the aggregation is silently pushing outwards like some gigantic plasmodium: spreading slimy arms over the surrounding fields, heavily dragging after them the ruin of its desolation.[8]

But the word 'suburbia' continued to bear the connotations of fresh air, space, and, above all, separation from its inhabitants' places of work. It was envisaged primarily as a retreat and, perhaps even more importantly, residence in the suburbs was regarded as an indication of one's ability to purchase leisure. In 1838, Loudon, in *The Suburban Gardener and Villa Companion*, laid expansive claims that the small portion of land attached to such a home can contain 'all that is essential to happiness, in the garden, park, and demesne of the most extensive country residence'.[9] That one is buying oneself, at least in the imagination, into the tradition and culture of the aristocracy is not lost on the narrator of *Cecil: or the Adventures of a Coxcomb:*

> In all direction, for ten miles round the capital – villas – villas – villas! A villa is one of the first indications of prosperity on the part of the professional man. Thriving merchants – popular actors – popular dentists – popular lawyers – popular all sorts of things, are sure to have their Tusculum, their *rus in urbe*, their Eden, their 'appiness 'ouse.[10]

It is towards the end of this period of rapid expansion – from the early 1890s onwards – that a distinctive fiction of suburbia appears. A certain amount of critical attention has been paid to the writers of the late nineteenth and early twentieth century – writers like Gissing, Wells and E.M. Forster – who, while not approaching the Nordau-esque gloom of Masterman's prophesying, attacked the triviality, the conventionality, the blinkered morality, and above all the boredom which they found in London's outskirts. But what has remained almost entirely submerged is the popular fiction, found both in novel form and serialized in magazines, which supports, even actively promotes, the way of life in the suburbs. No longer does the observer of the suburban scene choose a vantage point of implicit superiority – as Dickens did – a vantage point which reinforces the identification of the focal point of culture with the centre of London. It is these new novelists – people like Keble Howard, Shan Bullock and, in his later novels, William Pett Ridge (to name but a few) – on whom I wish to concentrate in this essay.

What characterizes this fiction of suburbia – apart from, of course, a certain homogeneity of setting? In the first place, its protagonists are almost always middle-class, dependent for their incomes on the man's employment in some type of administrative or clerical office work. Invariably, he commutes to this occupation: Pett Ridge, in several of his works, repeats the motif of the husband hurrying from his front gate to catch the 8.35, wearing a silk hat, and carrying a small brown leather bag. Travelling plays an important part in these novels – in Pett Ridge's *69 Birnam Road*, the chapter headings place the central characters' married life into the metaphoric terms of a railway journey – 'The Train Starts', 'Special Announcements', 'Sunday Services', 'Arrival Platform', and so on. The commuting train can, on occasion, be used as a location for chance meetings, but, more importantly, it serves to establish a space between the sites of work and leisure: it separates the frequent tedium of employment from the desirable, material rewards. And rewards certainly fall to the virtuous. For all the good-humoured lampooning of suburban life styles in the Grossmiths' *Diary of a Nobody*, Mr Pooter manages to introduce a wealthy American into the City firm for which he works, and is amply acknowledged:

> I find my eyes filling with tears as I pen the note of my interview this morning with Mr. Perkupp. Addressing me, he said: 'My faithful servant, I will not dwell on the important service you have done our firm. You can never be sufficiently thanked. Let us change the subject. Do you like your house, and are you happy where you are? "The Laurels", Birchfield Terrace, Holloway – a nice six-roomed residence, not counting basement, with a front breakfast parlour'.
>
> I replied: Yes sir, I love my house and I love the neighbourhood, and could not bear to leave it.
>
> Mr. Perkupp, to my surprise, said: Mr. Pooter, I will purchase the freehold of your house, and present it to the most honest and most worthy man it has ever been my lot to meet.[11]

[. . .]But work, except as the means to an end, very rarely occupies much narrative space. An exception is in Shan Bullock's *Robert Thorne*, mistakenly cited by Dyos as a novel favouring suburbia. Here Thorne, working as a city clerk, voices an increasingly bitter attack on his occupation as part of what he – and, he says, all other workers in his position – see as a Mill, a Machine. He attacks, too, the obligations which living in the suburbs place on the individual to keep a brave face, to hide much and make a show of it: 'For the sake of safety, a small chance, a sure fortune, they were content to sell their birthright and plod on in a rut. Clerks. Servants. Tame cats. Machines. . . . We were all the same. The black-coated brigade. Miserable little pen drivers.'[12] The only way out into 'freedom – life – the open air – the big world' – the course he indeed adopts, so that his children shall grow up 'strong and well', with a 'chance of being something better than typists and clerks' – is to emigrate, in his case to New Zealand. Incidentally, this is the only novel I have discovered which convincingly presents the clerk's life as that of the perpetual financial anxiety suggested by Masterman. The middle-class suburbanite 'is almost always living beyond his income. He has been harassed with debts and monetary complications; and the demands of rent and the rate-collection excite in him a kind of impotent fury.'[13] To support suburban house, wife and children, Thorne is forced into correcting students' papers for a Coach, addressing circulars for a draper's firm, and – under an assumed name, to save his pride – working at night on the books of another local draper. Bullock's phraseology is echoed in a lament found in *The Clerk* of 1909: 'We aren't real men. We don't do men's work. Pen drivers, miserable little pen drivers – fellows in black coats with inky fingers and shiny seats on their trousers.'[14] The bitterness on the lack of manliness which seems here to be associated with a clerical career is doubtless partly a reflection of the significant increase in the number of women clerks (in the commercial sector, from 19 in 1851, to 17,859 (1891), 55,784 (1901), 177,057 (1911)).[15] But in the suburban novel, the economic burdens are invariably born by the male head of the family, working women appearing with extreme rarity. Notwithstanding the promising title, Olive Pratt Rayner's (a pseudonym for Grant Allen) *The Type-Writer Girl* (1897) is no ordinary office employee but a Girton graduate whom circumstances have rendered both penniless and fashionably independent. Lasting only three days in the Outer Office of a solicitor before escaping on her bicycle to the temporary refuge of an anarchist commune near Horsham, she is a spirited model of the fictional New Woman.

For the woman to be seen as working would be to contravene the image of leisure bought by achievement. Central to the suburban dream was the notion of the nuclear family, with a wife who is seen to obtain her fulfilment through passive acceptance of her material good fortune – creating the comfortable and relaxing home atmosphere which sustains the physical and emotional well-being of the all-essential breadwinner, and breeding and rearing the dynasty which is to carry on these ideals. Unlike the aristocracy, it is not a dynasty which is later perceived as being under threat as a result of the social effects of war: *The Smiths in War Time* (the second sequel to *The Smiths of Surbiton*) closes with Enid Smith's thanks to Heaven (after her grandson's miraculous escape and return home from a German prisoner of war camp): 'it had been granted to her and to Ralph to found a family that would help to carry the British traditions with honour down the Ages'.[16]

Very seldom do we read of the members of the working class whom Masterman – among many social observers – hoped would benefit from the virtues of suburban rehousing. Indeed, perhaps the only example are the Hewetts in Gissing's *The Nether World*, uncomfortably transported to a one-storey, jerry-built, leaky cottage in Crouch End – 'villas, the advertiser calls them' – an area which exemplifies the rapid tendency towards decay in the inner suburbs:

> The streets have a smell of newness, of dampness; the bricks retain their complexion, the stucco has not yet rotted more than one expects in a year or two; poverty tries to hide itself with venetian blinds, until the time when an advance guard of houses shall justify the existence of the slum.[17]

But the presence of the casual labourer in novels written about suburbia would be surprising. As Stedman Jones points out in *Outcast London*, few could afford to take advantage of the cheaper rents and the workmen's trains – trains which, in any case, did not help the frequent necessity for the workman to turn up in the very early hours of the morning to be on hand for hiring. But nor do we hear about those working in the enterprises which sustained suburban economic growth, apart from the occasional schoolteacher or trusted shop assistant. Nothing is heard of those building or servicing the area, of those who run the pubs and music halls, of the workers on bus, tramway or railway. Once again, perhaps, Gissing provides an exception in *In the Year of Jubilee*, a novel about Camberwell, though certainly not singing its praises, which gives an indication of the complexities of the market relations within suburbia which finance all the major protagonists – the French money comes from building; the Lord money from piano making; Peachey sells disinfectants; while other characters serve the market through fashion and the provision of holidays. The cast list of suburban fiction reinforces the suburban dream: it is largely composed of those with secure employment and with the leisure and money to spend on travel. In addition they occupy an arena, as Dyos and Reeder put it, for 'the manipulation of social distinctions to those most conscious of their possibilities and most adept at turning them into shapes on the ground.'[18] Hence Fred Hartley, in *69 Birnam Road*, rapidly promoted to the post of superintendent of a railway line, feels anxious when a clerk from his office moves into the same Clapham street: 'He earns £180 a year, and the road is suitable for him and for his wife: by letting a room or two, they will manage very well.'[19] Yet if the road is suitable for a clerk and his wife, the time has clearly come for the Hartleys to move on somewhere else. Fred must entertain sometimes, and it is important that those who come to his house realize that he is keeping up his position.

Occupation and income could easily be correlated with district. Thus G.S. Layard advised a solicitor's cashier earning £200 a year to do what Hartley's younger colleague had done: move to the clerk's districts of Clapham, Forest Gate, Walthamstow, Kilburn or Peckham.[20] When Keble Howard was initially commissioned to write a serial about 'the lives of a quite ordinary married couple' for *The World and His Wife*, Leicester Harmsworth initially specified that the couple should be 'quite humble folk. The sort of people who would live in a twenty-six pound a year house.'[21] This, according to *The Suburban Homes of London*, would place them in perhaps Peckham, or that part of South London along the Wandsworth Road where 'the houses are no longer neat villas, but have that grimy neglected appearance always to be found associated with the dwellings of what may be termed the struggling classes'.[22] Perhaps Harmsworth decided that such a family would be too far removed for his intended readership, since a day before the serial was advertised, he let Howard know that he wished the first instalment to be rewritten, with the central couple having an income of £600 p.a. Howard's response, in terms of economic (and alliterative) association, was instantaneous: 'Six hundred a year? That means the suburbs. And they're to be quite ordinary typical everyday people. How would "The Smiths of Surbiton" do?'[23]

If the geography of suburbia offered a tangible means by which one's social means could be seen to be 'improving' – the move to a bigger house, to a better area – so the fictional space manipulated by Ridge, Howard and others was so structured that its linear, cumulative method of story-telling parallels that longed-for social advancement. The repetitive form of suburban fiction is its second major distinguishing element. At a time when Gissing, Henry James and others were experimenting with inconclusive endings, with themes of unfulfilment, of wrong choices made, of the sadness of middle-aged protagonists facing a future certain of nothing but its tedium, this popular fiction maintained the convention of events leading to a happy ending: an ending which is sometimes the old traditional one of a happy marriage; sometimes, since many of these novels are, after all, about married life, the removal to a new and larger establishment. Bennett's protagonist's view of suburban life – 'eighty separate dramas – and every drama a tragedy' – is tamed to the deliberate level of commonplace in suburban fiction: seldom does anything more dramatic happen than the unexpected (yet, nevertheless, of course, highly deserved) promotion – or the alarming illness of the adored baby. Such narration of everyday details, with no stretching of the reader's credulity, acts as bait, luring him or her into an acceptance of the actuality of what is described, into a belief that life does, indeed, have the tidiness of carefully manipulated fictional structures. Only occasionally – as in Howard's *The Bachelor Girls in Search of Independence* – does the author show such an awareness of current fictional trends that he feels obliged to apologize for, and assert the authenticity of, a happy ending.

A number of necessarily interrelating modes of analysis can be applied to make this suburban fiction release its meanings. First, its clearly defined, decidedly limited range of social reference suggests a specific readership, a readership which finds security in seeing itself faithfully depicted, its ideas realized in fictional form. A closer examination of the publishing and distribution of these novels than I have the space to outline here reveals much information about the reading and leisure habits of suburbia from late Victorian times onwards. Unsurprisingly, the growth of this type of fiction occurs in conjunction with the founding of publishing houses specializing in popular novels – for example, Hodder & Stoughton, Chapman & Hall, even Mills & Boon – and with the expansion of a distribution network which served the increasing number of suburban bookshops. Clearly, publishers competed among themselves for the copyright of fast-selling fiction. The rights to *The Smiths of Surbiton*, for example, which first appeared in serial form in *The World and His Wife*, published by Harmsworth in 1905, passed in the next twenty years through Cassells, Skeffington, and finally Fisher Unwin. Second, the importance which material objects play in this type of fiction encourages a reading based on reflection theory, using the descriptions of houses and interiors, of gardens, station platforms and local commons as repositories of factual information, verbal photographs by which we imagine we can re-create a visual impression of living conditions. Thus, for example, Pett Ridge, describing 'The Crescent' in *Outside the Radius*, presents, with admittedly a certain amount of good-tempered amusement, the front windows of the street, where

> occur here and there attempts in the direction of individuality, and of these I give you complete inventory:
> Bamboo stands with ferns in giant egg shells
> Webster's Dictionary
> A stuffed cockatoo
> St Paul's Cathedral in white wax
> Bust of the late Mr Spurgeon
> Photograph of Her Majesty
> The Three Graces under glass shades.[24]

Each of these households appears to be engaged, like Robert Thorne, 'in making the best show we could. The brass knocker, the bay window, the dining and drawing rooms, establish the fact we had in view, the great suburban ideal of being superior to the people next door' (p. 249).

Most of the citations from suburban fiction that I have made so far depend on the implicit assumption that this fiction faithfully reproduces material circumstances. The detail partly served the function of allowing the contemporary reader to 'place' the precise social situation of a novel's protagonists, and consequently to define his/her own position within the structures of suburbia. But for the reader today, this solid specificity of detail combines with the conventions of fictional form to produce a third type of analysis, based on the dialectical relationship between the given, the text of the novel, and the possibilities which its closed structure represses and denies. Such a reading must necessarily expose the ideological assumptions on which this suburban fiction was consciously or unconsciously grounded, and which it attempts to serve and perpetuate.

I wish to isolate one novel, Pett Ridge's *A Clever Wife*, in order to show in more detail the repressive structures at work within it. I have selected *A Clever Wife* for three reasons. First, the acceptance of the values of suburbia runs through it as a motif against which to judge the central characters' common sense, and exists as a goal towards which the reader can see them moving. Second, it follows a traditional pattern: courtship, marriage, estrangement, misunderstanding and rapturous reconciliation. Third, appearing as it did in 1895 – the same year as *Jude the Obscure*, Meredith's *The Amazing Marriage*, and Grant Allen's *The Woman Who Did* – it can be seen taking its place alongside these as a contribution to the marriage debate and to the theme of the 'New Woman'.

Cicely Westerham, with whom Henry Halliwell, the novel's hero, falls in love, is a writer working for the emancipation of women, arguing in public meetings against the tendency of women who shed their maiden name to lose their identity and swell the army of helpless wives. She makes her acceptance of Henry's proposal conditional:

'It is quite understood that you have no objection to seeing me preserve my perfect independence?'
    'Why, certainly'.

'And you won't expect me to become domesticated and
suburban, and interested in back gardens . . . ?'[25]

On honeymoon, she confuses Henry by appearing more interested in checking the proofs of her first novel than in listening
to his protestations of affection. She maintains marriages are
most likely to succeed when the partners allow each other a
measure of independence, are less 'persistent in their internal
companionship'. Discussing Henry's proposal that, on their
return to London, they should spend a few days in a hotel while
looking for a flat, Cicely interrupts:

> 'I don't think we want a flat, dear.' 'My love, we can't afford a
> whole house unless we want to go to the suburbs. And neither
> of us wants to do that.' 'What I propose is – that *you* should
> continue in your rooms at Chancery Lane, and that *I* should
> stay on in –' 'That you should keep your rooms in Victoria
> Street?'
>
> (p. 147)

Henry is not pleased to find that this isn't a joke: still less pleased
when his wife firmly supports his newspaper's plan to send him
as a war-artist to South Africa; and, angered on his return to
find Cicely's novel (published, to add insult to injury, under her
maiden name) has brought her a huge amount of social success,
and that her husband – if remembered in conversation – is
perceived as an unimportant nobody, he leaves to study art in
Paris.

There is an atypical Bohemian aura around the occupations
of the central characters, but they create no disturbance to the
general pattern of this type of fiction since they are not represented as being ultimately successful or fulfilling. For Cicely's
second novel is an appalling flop. She longs for her husband's
supportive company after all. He calls at her flat and, due to a
maidservant's imperfect grasp of the situation, believes her to
have run off with another man. Somewhat disconsolate, he goes
to visit his sister Bertha near Clapham Common – that paradise
described in *The Suburban Homes of London*. In contrast to the
newness of Brixton, it is 'one of the most picturesque spots to be
found within an equal distance of the heart of the metropolis'
(p. 60).

To Henry, the southern suburbs were a 'pays inconnu', and he was astonished, as he neared the Common, to find how agreeable it was. Houses of a moderate size, houses of an immoderate size, with none of the monotonous rows of villas that appal the senses.

(pp. 371–2)

His happiness in these surroundings is instantly consolidated when it is revealed that his wife is safely installed at his sister's. Henry and Cicely take a reconciliatory stroll:

The stars looking down on the north side of Clapham Common, where the houses have before them moats, and look at a distance quite baronial, saw two people walking together. . . .

'Dear heart', said the silk scarf, 'I wish I could tell you how happy I am.'

'I think,' said the opera cloak, in a voice that was agreeably low, 'I think I can guess.'

'I had no idea,' said the silk scarf, 'I had no idea that the suburbs could contain joy.'

'I am sure, dear,' remarked the opera cloak, 'that if you offer an apology to Clapham Common it will be accepted.' . . .

'I wonder how it would be,' said the silk scarf, 'for Mr. and Mrs. Halliwell to live away from town. Would Mrs. Halliwell mind?'

His hand held gently to her arm, and she pressed the hand to her side with a charming little movement of affection.

'So long as she is with her dear husband,' said the scarlet opera cloak decidedly, 'she does *not* mind where she lives.'

(p. 392)

The link connecting the 'correct' at the level of marriage with the ideals of suburbia is inescapable. Yet this connection, this conclusion, has been largely determined by the demands of the text: firstly, that it work out its thematic thesis (blindness to the virtues of suburbia is equated with blindness to the true responsibilities of marriage); secondly, that a point of equilibrium is reached: a point at which Pett Ridge can halt his story to supply the conventional demand for a happy ending.

Since the emotional conflict between the couple is seen to be resolved through acts of submission – Cicely to Henry, Henry to

Clapham – these cancel out the other opportunities which have been offered during the novel – women's independence/exile in Paris. Such choices, through being eliminated by the moral and logical structure of the work, help give the text its significance but are repressed: repressed in a way which ultimately underlines the repression of the central characters. For, in many ways, acceptance of the suburban ideology – of the optimism of social planners, of the promises of house agents' advertisements, of the life style depicted in these novels – is to be equated with submission: the submission, with greater or less unwillingness, of both the worker and his wife to forms of social and economic repression. This capitulation is something which Gissing, Wells, Bennett and Forster, in contradistinction to the novelists I have been discussing, are at pains to point out.

The hero of Bennett's *A Man From the North* – Richard Larch, the person to whom the opening remarks about the variety of suburbia were addressed – comes to London in search of a literary career and exciting social life. But, having difficulty applying himself to his own writing, it is his methodical work in the accounts department of a solicitor's office which meets with recognition. Similarly, the woman he proposes to is far from the combination of aesthete and siren he dreamt of – in fact she is the cashier in a vegetarian restaurant. He knows he has sold himself short and looks, at the end of the novel, without much real optimism into his potential married future: 'He knew well that he would make no further attempt to write. Laura . . . worshipped him, he felt sure, and at times he had a great tenderness for her; but it would be impossible to write in the suburban doll's house which was to be theirs' (p. 264). No late nineteenth-century reader who knew their Ibsen would be likely to remain unmoved by this particular hint at the stifling life in store – for both partners, even though, in this novel, Bennett remains blind, except through implication, to the woman's point of view.

> No! In future he would be simply the suburban husband –
> dutiful towards his employers, upon whose grace he would be
> doubly dependent; keeping his house in repair; pottering in
> the garden; taking his wife out for a walk, or occasionally to
> the theatre; and saving as much as he could.
>
> (p. 264)

He is consigning himself to the cultural desert which South London represented for Walter Besant: far be it from him, he disclaims, with little energy, 'to deny the culture of Sydenham and the artistic elevation of Tooting. Yet one feels there must surely be some disadvantage in being separated from the literary and artistic circles whose members . . . live for the most part in North London.'[26] Richard's vision, in all its typicality, is brought near to the level of tragedy on the last page of the novel as he muses: 'perhaps he had no genuine talent for writing. And yet at that moment he was conscious that he possessed the incommunicable imaginative insights of the author. . . . But it was done with now' (p. 265).

The 'incommunicable imaginative insight' would seem to be, for the instant, that there is no tidy, fictional insight into the combination of personal and social factors which lead characters to seek safety in suburbia. Yet, nevertheless, the novel ends here. Suburbia having been reached – one can hardly say, in this example, achieved – there is, for Larch and Bennett, nothing left to write about. The novel, by ending at this point, with the cessation of writing as its theme, indicates that suburbia, rather than being perceived as the initially-promised complex of choices, now appears no more than a limited set of known systems. The ending of this novel serves to emphasize the close link between the fictional closure in the suburban novel – meaning not just the finishing of the novel but the resolution of the possibilities inherent within the text – and absorption into the closed social structures of suburbia.

Notes

1 Arnold Bennett, *A Man From the North* (London 1898), pp. 102–3. All further references are to this edition.
2 William Cowper, 'Retirement', *The Poems of William Cowper*, ed. John D. Baird and Charles Ryskamp, vol. I (Oxford University Press, Oxford 1980), p. 390.
3 John Ruskin, 'Seven lamps of architecture', *Collected Works*, ed. E.T. Cook and A. Wedderburn (London 1903–13), vol. VIII, p. 226.
4 Charles Dickens, *Dombey and Son* (Clarendon edition, Oxford University Press, Oxford 1974), p. 218.
5 H.J. Dyos, *Victorian Suburb* (Leicester University Press, Leicester 1961), pp. 19–20.

126   Popular Fictions

6 Donald J. Olsen, *The Growth of Victorian London* (Batsford, London 1976), p. 191. The chapter 'The villa and the new suburb' is invaluable to the historian of suburbia.
7 C.F.G. Masterman, *The Heart of the Empire* (London 1901), p. 81.
8 C.F.G. Masterman, 'The burden of London', *In Peril of Change* (London 1905), p. 165.
9 J.C. Loudon, *The Suburban Gardener and Villa Companion* (London 1838), p. 8.
10 Catherine Gore, *Cecil: or the Adventures of a Coxcomb* (London 1867), p. 129.
11 G. and W. Grossmith, *The Diary of a Nobody* (1892; Penguin, Harmondsworth 1975), p. 233.
12 Shan Bullock, *Robert Thorne* (London 1907), p. 282. All further references are to this edition.
13 C.F.G. Masterman, *The Condition of England* (1909; Methuen,London 1960), ed. J.T. Boulton, p. 60.
14 Gillian Squirrell, *H. G. Wells: Novelist of, and for, the Lower Middle Classes?* Unpublished BA dissertation, University of Bristol, 1981, p. 21.
15 Gregory Anderson, *Victorian Clerks* (Manchester University Press, Manchester 1976), p. 56.
16 Keble Howard, *The Smiths in War Time* (London 1917), p. 307.
17 George Gissing, *The Nether World* (1889; Harvester, Brighton 1974), ed. John Goode, p. 364.
18 H.J. Dyos and D. Reeder, 'Slums and suburbs', in *The Victorian City*, ed. H.J. Dyos and M. Wolff (Routledge & Kegan Paul, London 1973), vol. II, p. 369.
19 William Pett Ridge, *69 Birnam Road* (London 1908), p. 294.
20 G.S. Layard, 'A lower middle class budget', *Cornhill Magazine*, vol. 10 (1901), p. 301.
21 Keble Howard, *My Motley Life* (London 1927), p. 218.
22 W.S. Clarke, *The Suburban Homes of London: A Residential Guide to Favourite London Localities* (London 1881), p. 318. Clarke provides a careful breakdown of the cost of housing, area by area. All further references are to this edition.
23 *My Motley Life*, p. 219.
24 William Pett Ridge, *Outside the Radius* (London 1899), p. 5.
25 William Pett Ridge, *A Clever Wife* (London 1895), p. 131. All further references are to this edition.
26 Walter Besant, *South London* (London 1899), p. 320.

8
Philip Gibbs
and the newsreel novel
STUART LAING

In an article on 'Writers and the General Strike' it has been
recognized that:

> there is often a considerable time-lag between the occurrence
> of a particular event and its incorporation into literary and
> artistic products. In this instance the phenomenon of lag is
> particularly vexing because it often means that apparently
> straightforward reactions to the General Strike are in fact
> mediated by the economic and political experience of the
> thirties.[1]

The earliest examples of novels dealing with the General Strike
discussed in the article are Wells's *Meanwhile* (1927) and Galsworthy's *Swan Song* (1928). Both however had been preceded by
a novel published in 1926, the year of the strike itself – Philip
Gibbs's *Young Anarchy*. Gibbs's novel certainly, then, avoids the
mediating element of any considered hindsight; it does, however, clearly fall within the general terms of the analysis offered
by the article. The authors note that 'each literary position may
quite clearly be seen as the expression of a distinct social class,
or – more often – of a distinct stratum within a class'.[2] What is
then in question is the development of a field of sharply conflicting and competing interpretations of the General Strike, in
Wells and Galsworthy and in such 1930s novels as Grassic

Gibbon's *Cloud Howe* (1933) and Storm Jameson's *None Turn Back* (1936). *Young Anarchy*, in retrospect, stands as one of the earliest statements in this field – its timing being, in one sense, as of much significance as the particular interpretation of the strike which it gives.

The phrase 'the expression of a distinct social class' should not, however, as far as this essay is concerned, be taken to denote the acceptance of any idea of literature as reflection (even if mediated by a Goldmannesque 'world-vision') as an adequate explanatory model. The aim of this essay is to discuss the development of a particular novel-form by Philip Gibbs, emphasizing the ways in which political events and contemporary 'social problems' are handled and made sense of by being 'passed through' a specific fictional structure. The texts may then more usefully be termed works of ideological production than seen as expressions of a pre-given position inscribed in the culture or consciousness (actual or potential) of a social group. Such production is of course not to be regarded as the sole prerogative of literature but rather as the very condition of existence of ideology – literature being one form of ideological production among many others. It is for this reason (not because literature is merely an expression of something which originates elsewhere) that Gibbs's novels may be understood in terms of their relation to more general fields of such production – particularly both formal political philosophies and rhetoric and the production of news in both the press and the cinema newsreel.

Before discussing the novels themselves and situating their particular narrative form, it may be useful, given the lack of critical or historical accounts of Gibbs's writings, to provide a few general comments on Gibbs's career and cultural position. Between 1905 and 1961 Sir Philip Gibbs published over fifty novels. Their popularity at its peak (in the inter-war period) was such that in 1939 an advertisement for his latest novel could claim 'over 20,000 sold before publication'.[3] However in terms of standard literary history his work has vanished without trace – indeed it has never been acknowledged. On the other hand his novels do not fall easily into the category of 'popular literature' either in terms of its accepted genres (western, thriller,

romance) or of the general definitions offered, for example, by
V.E. Neuburg.[4] Gibbs's novels have been effectively relegated
to the status of marginal documentary evidence for the
historian.[5] One clue immediately available as to the cultural
space they occupy is contained in the sole reference made to
Gibbs in the whole of Orwell's *Collected Essays, Letters and
Journalism*. In the essay 'Inside the Whale', Orwell refers to the
time when, in the 1920s: 'Squire ruled the London Mercury,
Gibbs and Walpole were the gods of the lending libraries, there
was a cult of cheeriness and manliness, beer and cricket, briar
pipes and monogamy.'[6] The description provides a neat pigeon-
holing of Gibbs within Orwell's polemical and over-simplified,
but indispensable, literary history of the period. A more detailed account of Gibbs's position may begin with a brief review
of his life and literary career.

Philip Gibbs was born in Kensington in 1877. His father was
a civil servant in the Education Department in Whitehall and
other members of his family (including an aunt and a grand-
father) had been directly employed in the service of the Royal
Family. In an autobiographical volume *The Pageant of the Years*
Philip Gibbs characterized his family's status: 'We belonged
definitely to that shabby genteel middle class which, however,
produced in the Victorian era so much quality and character.'[7]
He was, with his brothers, educated at home by his father. His
father had himself published novels and numbered among his
literary friends Hope Moncrieff (editor of the *Boy's Own Paper*)
and G.A. Henty, writer of historical novels for boys. He first
succeeded in publishing articles and short stories at the age of
sixteen. At eighteen he took a job at Cassell, the publishers who
subsequently published his first book, *Founders of the Empire*.
After working as head of a literary syndicate in Bolton he
moved, in 1901, to work on the literary page of the *Daily Mail* (at
that point, under Harmsworth, later Lord Northcliffe, leading
the development of new styles and commercial success in
popular journalism). During the period up to the Great War he
worked for a number of the leading Fleet Street papers including the *Daily Express* and the *Daily Chronicle* as well as for the
short-lived *Tribune* (a paper intended to be the new Liberal
daily). Among the novels he wrote in this period were *The
Street of Adventure* (based on his Fleet Street experiences) and

Intellectual Mansions S.W. (which included episodes dealing with the suffragette agitation).

In the Great War he became, from 1915, one of the few official war correspondents on the Western Front, for which work he was knighted in 1920. He left newspaper journalism after resigning from the *Daily Chronicle* over the paper's attitude to the 'Black-and-Tans' in Ireland. He became then a full-time free-lance writer, as well as undertaking lecture tours in America and becoming involved in a variety of public causes and issues – for example, supporting the 'Big Brother Movement', designed to help the emigration of the young unemployed to the Do-minions, and serving as a member of the Royal Commission on the manufacture and sale of armaments in the mid-1930s. Throughout the whole pre-war and inter-war period he spent a considerable time abroad – before 1914 in France, the Balkans, Portugal and Germany, in the 1920s in Turkey, Greece, Egypt and Soviet Russia and in the 1930s in many parts of Europe. In 1934 he was commissioned to write *European Journey*, a book based on the idea of J.B. Priestley's successful *English Journey*. Again after the Second World War he visited much of Central Europe, particularly occupied Germany, and published novels based on his experiences there. He continued to publish novels and books of social and political commentary until his death in 1962.

Although the majority of his published works were novels, the very limited space he gives in *The Pageant of the Years* to dis-cussion of himself as a novelist suggests that he saw himself more as a writer than as an artist (there is no evidence of any sustained interest in formal aesthetic issues). The idea of being a writer here comprises, as well as novels, journalism, political and travel reportage, history and social commentary of many kinds. For example, in the mid-1930s, as well as regularly publishing novels, he edited the Hutchinson compendium *The Books of the King's Jubilee* (The Life and Times of our King and Queen and their People 1865–1935) and wrote *Ordeal in England*, published in 1938 by the Right Book Club, dealing with the deepening crisis of the late 1930s (in part symbolized by the Abdication, although the book consists mainly of reflections on Anglo-German relations).

There is a sense then in which his novels must necessarily be seen as part of a total corpus of writings, rather than as a separate 'literary' career. However, with this reservation in mind, it is nevertheless possible to view the novels in relative isolation in order to note their development of a particular fictional structure for the interpretation of contemporary history. Of the fifty novels he wrote no one is completely typical; however, the analysis of *Young Anarchy* which follows is intended to suggest the general characteristics of Gibbs's mode of operation as well as the particular problems of interpreting the General Strike. [. . .]

Young Anarchy's particular perspective is determined and communicated by its mode of narration. The novel is set in the first person, narrated by an unnamed character who is 'a bachelor of good habits with novel-writing as an incurable disease'.[8] He is the uncle of two of the main characters ('Glad Young Things' Mervyn and Lettice Wingfield) and acts as a kind of substitute uncle to their friends. He describes himself as 'middle-aged' (age being an important element in the novel) and functions as something of an intermediary between the younger and older generations – he is simultaneously observer and conciliator. In response to an attempt to persuade him to identify himself with socialism he records: 'I refused to identify myself with any side. . . . I've no political convictions. I'm just a looker-on, trying to get at the truth of things with an open mind' (p. 77). His intermediate political and cultural position leads to his being asked for advice by representatives of both the younger and older generations and his characteristic response is that which he makes to one of his nephew's friends: '"If I were you" I suggested, "I'd cultivate a sense of humour and meet your father half way, without exasperating him. There's a lot to be said on his side, you know"' (p. 100).

A Gibbs novel written only four years before *Young Anarchy* was called *The Middle of the Road* and this title, together with the key phrases in the preceding quotations ('no political convictions', 'an open mind', 'meet your father half way'), reflects both Gibbs's sense of his own position as a writer formed in the traditions of journalism and the stance of the narrator in *Young Anarchy*. This stance of centrality and apoliticism (the narrator is mid-way between youth and age and right and left) both

'guarantees' the unbiased nature of his observations and interpretations and prefigures the kind of solutions to political and
social problems which are put forward at the end of the novel.

From this position of apparently neutral observation the
narrator, at the opening of the novel, identifies two general
questions which serve as the basis of his analysis of the problems
of English society in the mid-1920s. The first of these is the issue
of how to cope with a pervasive social and economic decline
which is perceived as being a direct consequence of the aftermath of the Great War. This decline is seen as manifesting itself
most clearly in the unemployment of so many ex-servicemen:

> England was going through troubled times. It hadn't been
> easy to get back to normal conditions, and something like a
> million men had never found work. Should we ever get back, I
> wondered, with melancholy pessimism, or had we lost our old
> chances, our old means of wealth, our spirit and tradition,
> with all that young manhood which had gone down in the
> war?
>
> (p. 27)

At other points of the novel this sense that 'something had gone
wrong' is linked to a more global analysis in terms of the collapse
of world markets. However, the key phrases in the narrator's
diagnosis tend to refer to the apparent loss of English 'spirit and
tradition'.

The second question concerns the fate of contemporary
youth. The novel opens with a discussion between the arch-
conservative Bishop of Burpham and his philanthropic liberal
sister Elizabeth Pomeroy. To the Bishop post-war youth are
'lawless, anarchical and utterly lacking in any sense of duty and
discipline' (p. 9); he speaks later in the novel of 'the open
immorality of post-war youth who are dancing their way to the
devil' (p. 57). The narrator is more tolerant, but at times he
offers a similar analysis, although characteristically phrasing it
as a question: 'These young people were rather distressing
sometimes. Young anarchy to the tune of jazz bands – was that
the way to happiness and the higher life?' (p. 57). The novel's
narrative is predominantly concerned with tracing the exploits
of a few representatives of this 'post-war youth'. Most promi-
nent is a group of characters who describe themselves as the

'Glad Young Things', particularly represented by Mervyn and Lettice Wingfield. Their life style is marked by a taste for jazz, a passion for dancing and generally irresponsible behaviour; they are seen, at worst, as cynical aesthetes with questionable morals. In particular the freedom with which Lettice can engage in all-night escapades is, to the narrator, symptomatic of a decline in the standards of female manners and morals:

> I was overcome by a kind of panic at the thought of what might happen to this niece of mine, so lovely, so exquisite, so gay, in her adventurous mood. These young people of the post-war world could go about together in a way that would have horrified their grandparents, that alarmed and sometimes terrified their parents.
>
> 'Coming Ivo?' Lettice had said. Coming where? To his rooms above the garage? . . . 'I hear the pipes of Pan', she said. . . . Dangerous music for young ears with jade earrings below shingled hair. It was the music of paganism. In the rhythm of that jazz which had bewitched the world, the old god with the goat's feet had come back, leering at authority, religion, discipline, morality – and youth was dancing to its tune.
>
> (p. 170)

The 'Glad Young Things' are in fact accused of two related sins – a frivolous and potentially immoral life style and the consequent avoidance of any serious involvement in the problems of English society and politics. The close relationship between the two is neatly exemplified by Mervyn's proposal of a career for himself as a dancing-teacher. Mervyn's lack of serious purpose leads him to be contrasted, by his father, to his elder brother who died in the Great War and the failure of this new generation to live up to the memory of those who were killed in battle. [. . .] Among this 'post-war crowd' is Jocelyn Pomeroy (son of the Bishop of Burpham), the character who serves as the novel's hero. Initially he is a typical member of the 'Glad Young Things' who, early in the novel, is sent down from Oxford for 'breaking college rules persistently and flagrantly' (particularly by taking Lettice to an unsuitable 'dancing-hall'). He also runs up debts, has a fast car and goes to late-night clubs in London. He, while still at Oxford, refutes a suggestion from his aunt that young men like himself should 'give a lead to our muddled old age': 'They have no convictions. They are lookers-on at this rather ridiculous game called life, trying to find some clue to its tangle of absurdities, but very doubtful whether such a clue is there. They are amused and interested at times, but generally a little bored' (p. 40). This state of mind is attributed by Jocelyn to the effect of the Great War which led to the post-war generation having 'no faith in human nature or human progress' (p. 41).[9] Jocelyn is, however, involved also with a second and rather different element of 'young anarchy'. While at Oxford he meets David Swayne, a former miner who has become a student at Ruskin College. Partly through David Swayne's influence he becomes a supporter of the Labour Party, at times even showing an interest in communism. This leads to a major rift with his father, an ambivalence towards his 'Glad Young Things' life style and finally to an almost successful Labour candidacy for Parliament in a London by-election. Jocelyn does retain some of his scepticism, particularly towards elements of the Labour leadership ('They'll play their own hands and feather their own nests if ever they get the chance. They're out for power, like all the rest' (p. 133)); however, his acceptance of the Labour philosophy is seen as an element of youth's general revolt against traditional values exemplified, in Jocelyn's case, by the particularly inflexible attitudes of his father, the Bishop.

David Swayne is the chief advocate of Labour philosophy within the novel. His sincerity and honesty are emphasized, but above all the narrator notes and transmits his lack of manners and style. From the beginning descriptions of him emphasize his ugliness and shabbiness:

> He was a tall, sturdy young man of about twenty-three or four with a shock of untidy hair, brick red, and a square ugly pale face. It seemed to me that he wore the last things in clothes. That is to say he had a pair of flannel bags ludicrously too short for his long legs, so that they showed his woollen socks above a clumping pair of boots badly down at heel, and a ragged old jacket positively out at elbows.

> (p. 44)

Two scenes early in the novel particularly emphasize this lack of grace by contrasting David Swayne with the Wingfields, particularly Lettice. They first meet in Jocelyn's rooms where the narrator contrasts David Swayne's 'bony paw' with Lettice's elegant 'little gloved hand'; his clumsiness is such that he upsets his cup of tea over her dress and offers her a 'grubby rag' of a 'well-used handkerchief' to mop it up with. Lettice is initially 'aghast' at this, but wins the narrator's approval by the way she pulls herself together and 'gallantly' refuses his offer (p. 53). Subsequently, at Jocelyn's instigation, he is invited to dinner at Southlands (the family seat of the Wingfields) where he becomes involved in a heated political debate and walks out in the middle of dinner, accidentally breaking two wine glasses in the process.

There is some modification in his character and behaviour after he completes his chapter of accidents by being involved in a car crash while being driven home from Southlands. He is forced to stay at the house to recover and the kindness shown to him (and to his mother who visits him there) leads him to reject 'class hatred and civil war' as a political strategy. He makes Lettice a promise: 'A resolution for the future when I may have a bit of power. It's just this – politics are a dirty game, they say, but it's going to be a fair game, as far as I'm concerned, and I'm going to play for England as well as my own class' (p. 74). The important element here is his substitution of 'game' for 'war' as a metaphor for political conflict. It is his adoption of this kind of moderation which allows him to be differentiated from a group of London Communists who make a few brief appearances in the novel as representatives of the fanatical extreme of dissension from traditional values.

Two other characters complete the cast of those upon whom the narrator bases his analysis of contemporary youth. These two are significant since, from their first appearance, they offer evidence for the narrator's underlying faith that youth will ultimately vindicate itself. Frank Hardy, the first of these, is neither a 'Glad Young Thing' nor a committed socialist, but rather an unemployed ex-officer, who, like the narrator, acts as something of a mediator between traditional values and post-war youth. The novel takes, as a premise, the existence of an extensive cultural gap between the pre-war and post-war worlds; Frank Hardy, as a survivor of the 'Lost Generation', is able to bridge at least part of it. The narrator emphasizes his allegiance to traditional values, but he is also on the side of youth, as is demonstrated when he loses his job (procured for him by the narrator) as librarian to the Bishop of Burpham for drinking whisky and dancing to gramophone music with the Bishop's daughter, Nancy, in his room at the Bishop's palace (even though chaperoned by the narrator and by Nancy's brother). He subsequently becomes secretary to the Bishop's sister, and ultimately becomes engaged to Nancy who, throughout the novel, together with Frank, represents the unambiguously positive qualities of youth.

[. . .] In the middle of the novel is a summarizing chapter (Chapter XXI) in which the narrator attempts to make an explicit analysis of young anarchy in the post-war world:

> those young friends of mine, whom I have not selected with any novelist's art, . . . are certainly typical of their age and class in recent history, not only in England, perhaps, but in many countries. In thousands of English homes . . . there has been this clash of ideas between parents and children, this tug of war between two different codes of character and conduct, this claim to absolute liberty by youth resisting and ridiculing all restraint or authority on the part of those to whom, in an older code, they owed obedience and duty.
>
> (p. 122)

This passage performs two related functions. There is, first, a generalization of the concept of 'young anarchy' if not quite to the whole society then certainly to the particular class (a generalization which may apply to 'many countries'). Crucially also there is the suggestion of the representative nature of the particular young people with whom the narrator is involved (they are 'certainly typical of their age and class'). The idea of typicality is re-emphasized throughout the chapter, as in the narrator's comments on Jocelyn's quarrel with his father: 'It was as though he stood for the spirit of his own generation, outraged by an attempt to thrust him back into the servitude of a past epoch' (p. 123). As the language here implies ('servitude', 'past epoch'), the Bishop's degree of strictness is seen by the narrator as archaic. This allows Jocelyn's revolt to be viewed with some sympathy and, through the idea of typicality, explains the narrator's partial endorsement of some aspects of the 'spirit' of the younger generation.

The narrator then moves on to extend the terms of his analysis:

> It was not the spirit of one class, but of all classes. I saw exactly the same spirit in Elizabeth's club for working men. Those youths of Walworth . . . too repudiated such words as obedience and discipline. They had no reverence for age in their own homes or in the abstract.
>
> (p. 124)

Post-war youth of all classes is seen as a single entity in its rejection of the old values, presented most strikingly in its lack of 'obedience' to parents and elders. The narrator, while recognizing the reasons for such rejection, sees great dangers in it, particularly in terms of two possible extreme developments – sexual immorality (Mervyn is seen as having 'no respect for womankind in the old-fashioned sense' (p. 123)) and Bolshevik revolution (Frank Hardy warns the narrator that 'There's a lot of this Red stuff about. . . . Of course all this unemployment is a pretty good breeding-ground for young anarchy' (p. 209)). The breadth of the analysis is striking – linking the behaviour of the 'Glad Young Things' and the young Communists as symptoms of a single social malaise. The message of the chapter is clear: 'Young anarchy was not confined to one social sphere. It was in all strata of English life in these post-war years' (p. 124).

As already suggested, the narrator's analysis of English society is conducted largely in terms of the categories of youth and age. Age, like youth, is represented by a spectrum of characters. At one extreme is the Bishop of Burpham, whose social and political philosophy is, in his own words, reactionary. In his view 'the curse of the dole has led to the demoralization of the younger men' (p. 108), and the Labour Party is 'in receipt of Bolshevik money which is paid to them to corrupt and undermine the Constitution and liberties of this country' (p. 93). He has also 'a profound admiration for Mussolini and believed that England needed a leader of that kind' (p. 96). These views and his attempts to exercise an authoritarian parental control lead to estrangement from both his children and to a judgement of intolerance by the narrator who does, however, endorse some of the Bishop's social analysis. Lord Southlands, father of Mervyn and Lettice Wingfield, is also unable to understand his children. Initially, however, his behaviour to them is (in contrast to that of the Bishop) tolerant and forgiving, although eventually he too explicitly condemns his son's lack of responsibility. Lord Southlands (elevated to the peerage for his success in the engineering business) is presented as a rather straightforward, simple man unable to comprehend the social change occurring in the aftermath of the Great War.

The two characters representing age who are allowed some comprehension are the narrator, whose position has already been discussed, and Elizabeth Pomeroy, the Bishop's sister. She is a philanthropist whose ideas are sometimes seen as valuable, as when running a canteen for soldiers in the war or in the formation of her club for working men in post-war London, but are also at times seen as unrealistic and wrong-headed, as in the case of the butler, a 'reformed burglar' who has a moral relapse and steals 'most of her silver and a diamond brooch' (p. 29). Her most spectacularly unsuccessful idea is to found a League of Youth which will bring about a 'spiritual revival' in the younger generation. She finally goes 'clean over' to the Labour Party, an allegiance which causes her problems of loyalty during the General Strike.

The General Strike provides the occasion and setting for the answering of the narrator's two initial questions, and the resolution of the novel's conflicts and problems. The narrator introduces it into the narrative in a way which indicates the role it is to play: 'I need not chronicle its story here, except as it touched the lives of those people in whom I am so deeply interested. Its drama did indeed touch all their lives, not because they played great parts in it but because they, like all the rest of our people, were put to a test of character by this sudden menace of social upheaval' (p. 243). The idea of a 'test of character' is central to the meaning given by the narrator to the General Strike. This is, first, a matter of individual testing. On the evening before the first day of the strike Mervyn, the leading dissolute of the 'Glad Young Things', orders his breakfast for half-past seven, instead of his usual half-past ten, so that he can report for Government duty to do 'anything that's wanted . . . scavenging, engine-driving, despatch carrying, stoking' (p. 250). He later appears 'stoking a train from Paddington to Plymouth' (p. 281). Lettice also plays her part in defeating the strike 'serving sausages and mashed in a canteen for motor drivers' (p. 280).

The involvement of Mervyn, Lettice, Ivo and their friends in maintaining services and defeating the strike is one kind of vindication of the spirit of youth. The reversal in Jocelyn's attitude and behaviour is more complex. He overcomes not only the cynicism and apathy of the 'Glad Young Things', but also his political allegiance to the Labour Party. He volunteers to drive milk-supply lorries with the comment: 'It won't do Labour any harm to know that our crowd aren't afraid of dirty work' (p. 281).

[. . .] The General Strike, then, provides the opportunity for post-war youth to vindicate itself and to give a positive answer to the narrator's question about the implications of 'young anarchy'. The General Strike also provides the answer to the narrator's more general question concerning the 'spirit and tradition' of England as a whole:

> We stood revealed to the whole world and to ourselves as a people whose spirit is still high and splendid. In no other nation in the world, I think, could such a thing have happened without bloodshed and anarchy. No shot was fired from first to last. The strikers were as well-behaved as those who took their place for a time or rallied up in defence of ancient liberties. The good-nature of our people staggered the imagination of our friends and enemies.

> (p. 288)

The importance of the General Strike is seen then in terms not of the economic conflicts or political differences which caused a situation of extreme crisis, but rather of the style and spirit of the participants' behaviour – in avoiding bloodshed and physical violence. This resurgence of 'the spirit of the old tradition' is an indication that the apparent decline in standards (moral and economic) since the Great War is temporary or even illusory.

The narrator in fact specifically links the crisis of the General Strike to the crisis of the Great War in a way which foreshadows the more recent use of appeals to the 'Dunkirk spirit' in post-1945 political rhetoric [. . .] and the novel's account of the General Strike maintains this parallel with the Great War in

terms of the nature of the experience and of the general response
to it on both sides. One striker compares the situation to
'fighting in the bloody dark in No Man's Land' (p. 262), while
another defends the solidarity of the strikers as a re-creation of
the 'spirit of the trenches' (p. 268). On the other side Frank
Hardy, strike-breaking in the docks, comments: 'It's like being
back in the Army again. . . . Twelve years wiped out, and the
same spirit' (p. 272). The idea of a recaptured national 'spirit'
runs through all these comparisons and the word is invoked
repeatedly to allow the narrator to present the General Strike as
a national triumph which points the way to a better future based
on co-operation between the classes:

> Ivo Tremayne, fighting the General Strike, took off his hat to
> the strikers. Lettice, my intolerant Lettice, so haughty, so
> steeped in class tradition, could not help being sorry for the
> 'poor dears'. It would be fine if somehow we could make use of
> this good-nature, this chivalry to our opponents in the game,
> this national spirit of fair play. How great would England be
> again if all classes would get together in that spirit for
> common service!
>
> (p. 286)

The idea of 'fair play' here echoes David Swayne's promise to
Lettice to 'play' a 'fair game'. It is here worth recalling Orwell's
description of 'a cult of cheeriness and manliness, beer and
cricket' as the pervasive atmosphere of Gibbs's world. In fact
the rhetoric and the programme of action offered as the solution
to social conflict by the narrator of *Young Anarchy* is very similar
to that offered directly by Gibbs himself shortly after the end of
the General Strike. In a letter to *The Times* on 18 June 1926
(while the miners were, of course, still in bitter dispute), he
made a suggestion which he felt would 'give to both sides
everything for which they are fighting without surrender of
pride or principles'. The precise solution proposed concerned
concentrating on output rather than wages or hours as the key
issue. The letter continued:

> I believe that our miners have as much love for their country
> as any class in the nation and that they have a pride and spirit
> and energy not surpassed by any other body of workers . . . if

the truth about their industry and an appeal to their manhood for the nation's sake can reach them through the barrage of political strife between owners and leaders, then I believe that the response would be as splendid as when ten years ago our national life was threatened by that other peril.[10]

As in the novel, the aim here is to identify a central position (apart from the 'strife between owners and leaders') which the terms 'nation' and 'spirit' can be used to identify; the comparison with the Great War is important here in implying the need for a patriotism which transcends sectional interest.

Within the novel itself the claim is made that the response to the General Strike did indicate the existence of such a national spirit and in doing so provided positive answers to the narrator's two initial questions concerning the fate of post-war youth in particular and post-war England in general. There is, however, clearly a third major question which the novel answers, a question of pressing importance in the latter months of 1926 – how to interpret the General Strike. A number of interpretations were possible, but the particular one offered in *Young Anarchy* is to suggest that the General Strike's importance lay not so much in the political or economic issues involved, but in its demonstration of the style of English behaviour in a crisis. The manner of the strike's defeat, seen as caused by the good sense of the strikers (their 'fair play'), by the rallying of youth to the service of the nation and by the ultimate moral courage of moderate Labour leaders, is seen as a triumph for the middle way of the narrator, of Jocelyn, of Frank Hardy and even of David Swayne (who supports the strike reluctantly, seeing it as a 'hideous outrage' against 'moderate Labour' (p. 266)). The novel's conclusion offers simultaneously the final coming together of Jocelyn and Lettice (earlier estranged by Jocelyn's allegiance to Labour and Lettice's flighty 'Glad Young Things' attitude to their relationship) and the perspective of a nation unified in style and spirit.

A considerable number of Gibbs's novels conform to a narrative pattern similar to that of *Young Anarchy*. This pattern is composed of a combination of two elements – a focus first on a small group of characters, centred on some form of 'romantic interest' of a traditional kind, and second an explicit presentation of a specific contemporary social problem or political train of events as the occasion and setting. These two elements are, however, not in a simple foreground/background relation since the social or political problems presented are of direct consequence to the problems of the individual characters and the solution to one set of problems tends to constitute a simultaneous solution to the other. These points, together with the speed of production of the novels, constituted the main concerns of a 1939 *Times Literary Supplement* leader on Gibbs's novels under the heading of 'The newsreel novel':

> It is nothing new for the novel to be contemporaneous. But Sir Philip Gibbs's device of publishing under the forms of fiction a continuous commentary on the world as it passes – a commentary of which the latest instalment is reviewed on another page – is surely original? It introduces the newsreel novel. . . . In attempting the interpretation of historical events (almost before they have happened) through the mouths of imagined characters Sir Philip Gibbs, a close and untiring student of world affairs, exercises an undoubted right, and exercises it with skill and power.
>   . . . There is however one awkward point confronting the newsreel novelist. He cannot ever bring his story to more than a material conclusion. He can write a last page but never a 'Finis'. Old-fashioned opinion holds that a novel should come to a conclusion, that every work of art should have some mould. Some revolutionaries of fiction seem to hold that their art should simply mirror the 'manifold of sensation' from without, just as it should let itself drift down the stream of imagery that rises perpetually within. The inventor of the newsreel novel has too nice a sense of form to accept a theory that would abolish the distinction between art and life. But he will have to find some solution to his own problem; he must find some port where his people can come to harbour.[11]

The summary contains a number of important observations on the form and method of Philip Gibbs's novels, including the comparison with the presentation of news (based partly on the speed with which his novels appeared – often, as the article notes, only a few months after the political events with which they deal) and the partial convergence in his novels between historical and fictional writing. Perhaps most significant, however, is the recognition of the problem of narrative conclusion. The article makes it clear that Gibbs is not to be aligned with the 'revolutionaries of fiction' (presumably led by Joyce and Virginia Woolf) who rely on the 'manifold of sensation' and a 'stream of imagery'. The implication here is that there is a loss of responsibility in this alleged privileging of consciousness and the subjective. Gibbs's attention, by contrast, to the public, objective, world is implicitly preferred. However, a conflict is suggested between the attempt of a 'newsreel' to follow history as a continuous development and the need for a novel to have a beginning, a middle and an end.

In fact, this problem was particularly acute in Philip Gibbs's fiction in the late 1930s, as can be exemplified by reference to his novel *This Nettle, Danger*, published in 1939. The novel's title is taken from Hotspur's speech in *Henry IV Part One* – 'Out of this nettle, danger, we pluck this flower, safety' – a speech quoted by Neville Chamberlain on his way to Munich. The novel deals with the events leading up to the Munich crisis (seen mainly through the eyes of John Barton, a young American journalist). Its conclusion however shows a radical uncertainty as to how to interpret the Munich agreement. The dominant suggestion is that 'Neville Chamberlain had broken the threat of the mailed fist by the substitute of reason',[12] although the last three pages of the novel indicate the reservations caused by Nazi anti-Jewish activity in the weeks immediately after Munich. The composition of the novel appears to have been overtaken by events in a way that illustrates the criticisms of the *Times Literary Supplement* article. The outbreak of the Second World War was of course to provide a clear frame of reference for Munich and indeed for all political and military events until 1945 and Gibbs's novels of the war years show a much greater certainty in 'the interpretation of historical events'.

[. . .] The use of the phrase 'newsreel novel' opens, additionally, a number of question which the *Times Literary Supplement* article does not address explicitly – questions about both the form and the implicit purpose of Gibbs's novels. In particular three possible contexts for situating the novels are suggested by the phrase – those of the cinema newsreel itself and of its two components, the medium of film and the idea of news, as embodied particularly in the national press. To consider the second of these first, it is perhaps tempting to take the phrase 'newsreel novel' as suggesting that Gibbs's work may profitably be viewed as having analogies with new techniques of presenting reality, developed within film. Certainly within the field of 'documentary', in particular, there is, in the inter-war period, considerable evidence of attempted convergences between forms of verbal and visual presentation, ranging from Dos Passos and John Sommerfield's *May Day* in the novel, through the much maligned 'camera eye' of Isherwood's *Goodbye to Berlin*, to the whole project of Mass Observation (see particularly Humphrey Jennings's work and *May 12: Coronation Day Survey*). However, precisely the most important developments in this area involved questions of 'montage', of narrative sequence, of narrative voice – all areas in which Gibbs's novels are rigorously traditional and conventional. This does not, though, exclude the question of formal similarities between the novels and cinema newsreel. In the general area of film production (as in literary production) the documentary theoreticians and practitioners in no way constituted a dominant influence – in particular the newsreel has a very different history and formal structure from that of the Grierson school of documentary. To consider this point in more detail it is necessary to deal briefly with something of the development and the determining influences of the cinema newsreel in the inter-war period.

A particularly significant development, as in all forms of film, was the moment when (and the way in which) synchronized sound became incorporated into newsreel. After the major role of newsreels in war propaganda and recruitment in the Great War, the early 1920s saw something of a decline in popularity and also in British control of the national and international newsreel combines – as the pre-war central European and Russian markets had been lost and as American control of the multi-nationals (particularly Gaumont and Pathe) strengthened. Nicholas Pronay suggests additionally that the lack of sound prevented any significant amount of political reporting: 'So, silent films came to be driven after the war away from real news, and towards intrinsically spectacular rather than political events, coronations, state openings, civic ceremonies, military tattoos and the like'.[13] In accepting this point, however, it is important to recognize that what is in question is not an issue of technical determinism, but of the uses of a determinate medium. The films of Flaherty, Ruttmann, Pudovkin and Grierson indicate that other uses of silent film as reportage were possible; the problem was that by definition the newsreels covered 'news', i.e. predominantly specific individual events and the story of them. Pronay notes that from the earliest newsfilm the emphasis was placed on the construction of a story (i.e. a sequential linear narrative).

The development of synchronized sound newsreel (begun in 1927 and completed by 1931) transformed the technical possibilities but did not alter the underlying operative definitions of form and function. Precisely because the sound – in particular as embodied in the directive voice of the commentator/ journalist – now 'anchored' the visual element, that element could now be composed of a much wider range of material, whether newly-shot or simply extracted from the continually expanding film libraries of the five major newsreel companies (all American dominated). However, the central emphasis on event-as-story did not change, nor did the conditions of reception about which Pronay comments:

> In the case of newsreels (and equally so in television news and radio news) it is the editor who determines *all* these factors of reception. He and not the reader imparts a sequence – hence a sequential/causal connection if he chooses to do so – to the items, and determines the speed with which the reader is given the story without the chance of the reader omitting anything and without any opportunity whatever for 'reading it again' or comparing it with another version side by side.[14]

One final point about the history of cinema newsreel is needed in order to contextualize fully the *Times Literary Supplement* use of the word. By 1939 newsreels had a weekly audience of 20 million, including 'that very substantial lower section of the population which was by education or background not in the position to be an effective reader of the press'.[15] Undoubtedly part of the implied opposition between 'newsreel' and 'novel' in the *Times Literary Supplement* phrase is due not merely to differences of form but to assumed differences of level, of audience, of social status. A more speculative view of this point might suggest that Gibbs's novels, in their way, performed the same function as the newsreels, but for a different audience. Such a view would however need to be seen in relation to the role of the dominant (although as such increasingly under challenge) news medium of the period – the national daily newspaper. Gibbs, as has been noted, was a working journalist for much of his life, and in *The Pageant of the Years* he offers a revealing comment on the ideas of Harmsworth, one of his earliest employers:

> he wanted his young writers to dramatise their news stories. In fact everything had to be a 'story' rather than a report. He sent them out to search for oddities of character, strange ways of life, out-of-the-way adventure. In the description of an historic scene, or an affair of public ceremony, he gave his praise to the descriptive writer who had . . . avoided the obvious by seeing the human stuff on the side walk while some pompous pageant passed.[16]

Here again is the binary structure of a Gibbs novel, on the one hand the 'pageant' of historical events[17] and on the other the 'human stuff' behind the scenes. The emphasis on 'story' also recalls the characteristic newsreel structure already discussed. It is, however, important here to indicate some general differences and similarities between the three forms. Although a Gibbs novel and cinema newsreel are radically dissimilar in the composition of their audience, their mode of presentation is, in some ways, similar – they are both simple linear forms offering a single sequential narrative. This may also be true of the individual newspaper story, but not of the newspaper as a whole – to put it simply, a newspaper does not have a beginning, a middle and an end. Undoubtedly certain areas (the front and back pages – perhaps the editorial) are privileged as of greatest importance and equally the whole paper will tend to present a consistent (or at least coherent) way of seeing the world. However, it is for the individual reader to combine any number of different items to complete his or her particular total reading. It is then not surprising that in the inter-war period the newspaper, as well as the documentary film, offered models for novelists who (unlike Gibbs) were interested in breaking conventional sequential narrative – as in the cases of Evelyn Waugh's use of the gossip-column format in *Vile Bodies* or Graham Greene's use of newspaper headlines in *It's a Battlefield*. It is in this sense that, paradoxically, Gibbs's highly conventional narrative form constructs 'news' in a way closer to that of the newsreel than of the much older form of the newspaper.

Nevertheless it is worth noting the degree to which Gibbs's career as a novelist runs parallel to the rise of the daily press and its achievement of almost saturation mass circulation. When Philip Gibbs entered Fleet Street at the turn of the century daily papers were read by one adult in five or six. By 1920 the figure was one in two and by 1947 every ten adults read twelve daily papers (in all cases Sunday papers were read at least twice as intensively).[18] The significance of the press within Gibbs's world is brought out by a comment of the narrator in *Young Anarchy* just after the outbreak of the General Strike:

> One sign scrawled in chalk on wooden boards outside the newsagents' shops, struck me as a sinister announcement which would have an astonishing effect upon national life. *No papers printed.* For the first time in our experience of life we should be cut off from all news of what was happening in the world and in our own country . . . unless one had one's ear to a 'loud speaker'!
>
> (p. 255)

The existence of a mass circulation daily press here stands as the key example of normal daily life. When this is put alongside the development of radio (2 million licence holders in 1927 – 9 million by 1939)[19] and of the cinema newsreel, then the distinctive structure of Gibbs's novels makes sense in terms of a period in which the production and dissemination of 'news' through the whole society were unprecedented in terms both of scale and speed.[20] This structure has been examined in *Young Anarchy*, where the difficult task of encoding the General Strike as a triumph of national spirit was attempted. [. . .]

With this particular framework for interpretation the novel 'processes' the political events and social issues of the period so that they deliver a specific set of messages. The preceding analysis has shown how the pressure of political crises, social disturbance and new moral codes made the idea of continuity of values problematic. The work of the novel is to absorb this pressure and then to interpret the events and problems themselves (including the response to them) in such a way as to testify to the resilience of the traditional English national character – particularly the virtues of national unity, reconciliation and fair play. As has been argued, it is important also to regard the novel, in undertaking this task, as responding to a particular transitional moment in the development of forms of communication, particularly news-production – in the national press, cinema newsreel and radio. *Young Anarchy* may not be among the most carefully constructed literary works of the twentieth century but it does offer some remarkable instances of the process of constructing the 'story' and meanings of a common-sense history.

Notes

1 A. Mellor, C. Pawling and C. Sparks, 'Writers and the General Strike', in M. Morris (ed.), *The General Strike* (Penguin, Harmondsworth 1976), p. 339.
2 Ibid., p. 338.
3 *The Times Literary Supplement*, 4 February 1939, p. 69.
4 V.E. Neuburg, *Popular Literature* (Penguin, Harmondsworth 1977). He states that: 'At its simplest, popular literature can be defined as what the unsophisticated reader has chosen for pleasure. Such a reader may, of course, come from any class of society, although the primary appeal of popular literature has been to the poor' (p. 12). My guess is that although Philip Gibbs's novels may have appealed to the 'unsophisticated', their primary appeal was not to the poor. Neuburg however suggests also that the study of such literature has a role to play in uncovering the 'assumptions, beliefs, feelings and modes of thought of men and women in the past' (p. 11); this is, I believe, true of Philip Gibbs's work although it need not be a case only of the 'relatively unlettered members of society'. In his reply to a questionnaire, contained in Q.D. Leavis, *Fiction and the Reading Public* (Chatto & Windus, London 1932, reprinted 1968), Gibbs reported that his readers included 'all classes and types, both men and women – ex-servicemen, miners, settlers in the Dominions, city clerks, professors, scientists, students, the mothers of the younger generation, the fathers of grown-up daughters, the daughters themselves, American university girls, German officers, British officers'

(p. 73). Q.D. Leavis herself classifies Gibbs among those writers who were '"middlebrow" not read as literature, but not writing for the lowbrow market' (p. 45).

5 See C.L. Mowat, *Britain Between the Wars* (Methuen, London 1955). Mowat cites Philip Gibbs's novel *The Middle of the Road* (first published 1922) for its account of the formation of a 'Defence Force' to act against industrial troubles in 1921.

6 G. Orwell, *Collected Essays, Letters and Journalism*, vol. I (Penguin, Harmondsworth 1971), p. 555.

7 P. Gibbs, *The Pageant of the Years* (Hutchinson, London 1947), p. 6.

8 P. Gibbs, *Young Anarchy* (Hutchinson, London 1926), p. 13. All further page references to the novel are incorporated in brackets within the main text.

9 The self-analysis made by Jocelyn here, particularly in the emphasis on loss of faith, recalls the analysis of the 'Bright Young People' made by Father Rothschild in Evelyn Waugh's *Vile Bodies* (1930). It is significant that this novel, regarded now as a definitive evocation of upper-class youth in the 1920s, was published four years later than *Young Anarchy*. Father Rothschild's analysis implies that at root there is a valuable element in the younger generation, echoing the vindication of youth in Gibbs's novel. This is often taken to shown an underlying seriousness in Waugh's analysis; however Christopher Sykes, Waugh's biographer, states that Waugh's later view was that the passage containing Father Rothschild's apologia was 'very silly'. (See C. Sykes, *Evelyn Waugh* (Penguin, Harmondsworth 1977), p. 146.)

10 *The Times*, 18 June 1926.

11 *The Times Literary Supplement*, 19 November 1939, p. 655.

12 P. Gibbs, *This Nettle, Danger* (Hutchinson, London 1939), p. 460.

13 Nicholas Pronay, 'The newsreels: the illusion of actuality', in *The Historian and Film*, ed. P. Smith (Cambridge University Press, Cambridge 1976), p. 108.

14 Ibid., p. 111.

15 Ibid., p. 111.

16 *The Pageant of the Years*, p. 40.

17 The term 'pageant', as a description of history, has a number of connotations. The medieval reference suggests both the idea of the long continuity of English history and, in some instances, the idea of history as, ideally, a chivalric game. There is a more immediate reference in the apparent popularity, during both pre- and post-Great War periods, of the village pageant re-enacting the glories of the past through a particular village (see accounts of pageants in Gibbs's own *The Pageant of the Years* and of E.M. Forster's part in the Abinger Church Pageant of 1934, discussed in P.N. Furbank, *E.M.*

Forster: A Life, vol. II (Secker & Warburg, London 1978), pp. 197–8). Also see Noel Coward's *Cavalcade*, a successful play of the early 1930s (and subsequent mid-1930s film) in which contemporary historical events (the Boer War, the sinking of the *Titanic*, the Great War, the Jazz Age) are seen against a backcloth of the depth and continuity of English tradition.

18 R. Williams, *Communications* (Penguin, Harmondsworth 1968), chap. 2.

19 See J. Walvin, *Leisure and Society 1830–1950* (Longman, London 1978), chap. 10.

20 This is not wholly to endorse the *Times Literary Supplement* view that the use of fiction to interpret specific contemporary political events was, in Philip Gibbs's case, 'surely original'. The idea can be traced back at least as far as Disraeli's *Sybil* (1845) and its treatment of Chartism. Disraeli's aim was perhaps more overtly party political – evidenced by a letter from a fellow Tory MP which read: 'Unless I greatly err *Sybil* will be pronounced full worthy to succeed Coningsby, and will sow still more widely and deeply the seeds of old Toryism in the English mind. It's not a bit too democratic.' Disraeli replied: 'You have clearly apprehended and expressed what I wished to convey.' (Sheila M. Smith, *Disraeli's Readers*, Nottingham University Miscellany No. 2 (1966); p. 22.) Although there are some senses in which the fictional strategies are similar, however, the sheer volume and speed of output of Philip Gibbs indicates the degree to which he, unlike Disraeli, saw his task as a kind of fictional journalism.

9

The gentry, bourgeois hegemony and popular fiction: *Rebecca* and *Rogue Male*

ROGER BROMLEY

First published in 1938, at a time, that is, when capitalist society was experiencing one of the deepest crises in its history, Daphne du Maurier's *Rebecca*[1] at first sight seems remarkable for its total lack of reference to anything that might even hint of that crisis. The simplest way of accounting for this would be to consign the text to the category of 'escapist fiction', a means of relief for people whose everyday experience was dominated by the reality of the depression. Another response would be to describe the text as likely to be read by those upon whom the realities of unemployment and deprivation would have had little impact. It is very difficult, now, to reconstruct a map of the possible readership of the novel, but that it was an immediate bestseller indicates that it is improbable that a simple pattern of readership along class lines could be produced. This would certainly be even more improbable for an analysis of the cinema audiences that saw the film version in 1941. Again, Daphne du Maurier was involved in 'political' activity in the 1930s and it could be argued that what she left out of *Rebecca* was contained in *Come Wind, Come Rain*, a collection of short stories and essays which articulated a solution to the current crisis in the terms of moral rearmament. When the film version of *Rebecca* was produced this publication was sold, fairly cheaply, in the foyers of various cinemas throughout Britain.

As surface explanations these accounts might seem adequate,

but a cultural analysis of *Rebecca*, using Gramsci's concept of hegemony and his idea of 'Caesarism', argues for a reading of the text that sees its apparent absences as determining presences at the level of its deep structures. In other words, *Rebecca* can be read as a response to the crisis of the 1930s, if it is seen in the broader context of the various means sought to resolve what was not only an economic crisis but also a crisis in hegemony. This kind of reading indicates the need for a serious reconsideration of the social functions of mass-produced cultural productions. Geoffrey Household's *Rogue Male*,[2] published a year later than *Rebecca*, is similarly marked by an explicit absence of reference to the depression, although it does contain material which bears directly on the imminence of the Second World War. Its interest lies in the fact that it characterizes the enemy as communism and as fascism, which is itself an important ideological variation on the dominant preoccupations of the period in the minds of most people. In fact, the text presents a deliberately ambiguous fusing of the two systems at several points: 'In fact it was a speech that would have gone equally well in the mouth of his boss's opposite number on the other side of Poland.'[3]

These two texts have not been selected for typicality, but because both seem to raise and explore, at their deep structural level, the nature of crisis in the period, and offer evidence in relation to the shifting nature of class composition and hegemony. In both cases, as is the nature of popular fiction, the crisis is articulated exclusively in personalized terms: the central male figure is a member of the landed gentry; the basic determinant of each figure's social class being signalled not only by relationship to property (capital in the form of land) but also by a set of signs which denote a whole style of life, and a set of cultural practices and attitudes by means of which, in terms of deference and recognition, wealth is very much secondary to birth and breeding.

The questions which each text asks are based on a single problem: how does a residual fraction of the ruling bloc *re-present* itself in the cultural/ideological formation; how does a class fraction survive when its original power and function is displaced? On the other hand, if it is true that each succeeding ruling class has incorporated and transformed the ideology of its predecessors, then a subsidiary question raises itself: how does the dominant class in the ruling bloc negotiate its basis of alliances with other fractions, whose existence and survival may be vital in the complex process of hegemony whereby relations of domination and subordination are sustained in class society? One possible answer is offered by Gramsci in his 'Notes on Italian history':

> The class relations created by industrial development with the limits of bourgeois hegemony reached and the position of the progressive classes reversed, have induced the bourgeoisie not to struggle with all its strength against the old regime, but to allow a part of the latter's facade to subsist, behind which it can disguise its own real domination.[4]

It is, arguably, the *style* of that mode of hegemony which is being rehearsed and reproduced in the two texts under discussion here. Time and time again in both masculine and feminine romance an aristocratic façade subsists, and acts as both an alibi and a disguise for the bourgeois forms, values and perceptions which the texts consecrate and naturalize. More accurately, these cultural forms constitute evidence of the distinctive route which the British ruling class has taken to develop its own 'peculiar' mode of hegemony. The fusion of old and new in the ruling bloc in the early Victorian period produced the conditions for certain features and attitudes, the ideological components of which still persist long after the real conditions which have produced them have passed. Obviously these components have undergone considerable modification and transformation (the notion of *continuity* is, in fact, one of the features of the ideology) and I would claim that one of the sites where these can be examined is in the complex negotiations established in the mediations of popular fictions.

If we accept that the period from 1936 to 1957 was one of transition characterized by challenges to 'order' and by manifest contradictions, what cultural resources were available to mediate class relations to an extent that relative stability, consent and a partial resolution of contradictions could be produced at a level that would witness the aristocratically-styled, yet undoubtedly popular, government of Macmillan in 1957?

The role of the *adaptive* landed gentry was an important factor in the complex relationship of ruling class fractions which combined to produce the dominant bloc in the Victorian period, and it is of interest that both of the texts considered here contain extended moments where the gentry figure is intransigent and reactionary, preoccupied by 'maddening' moods or anarchic, cynical attitudes which act as a block to his adaptability and emergence into a new assimilation of alliances and ways of seeing. The *block* is the cultural/fictional metaphor of crisis, a suspended time of contradictions, disharmony and threatening instability. It is the resolution of these crises that the fictions turn upon and are thus able to present endings which suggest continuity, harmony and order. The basic motif in both is *renewal*. In each case the procedural agencies are different (though both women) but the resolutions similar. In *Rebecca*, Maxim has to deconstruct a dead woman from his memory and existence [. . .] in order to face and ally with a living woman [. . .] whom he can possess freely. In *Rogue Male*, the hero has to re-create a dead woman in order to be re-born, to find an object for living. The overcoming of recalcitrance in both figures signs their adaptability, their being able to survive purposefully in the contemporary world, albeit only at a personal level.

For a long time, the British bourgeoisie, according to Marx, ruled through a surrogate aristocracy, but the real situation of the landed gentry from the 1920s to the 1950s argues that it is no longer possible to sustain this notion, even at the level of ideology. There is considerable sociological and historical evidence for the erosion of the landed fraction in this period, but these fictions, as 'narratives of exile' written retrospectively, both help to confirm this evidence in literary terms, *and yet* by their ideological affirmations also assert a certain cultural and social continuity of the fraction as the *idea/ideal of a ruling class* through ritual, symbol and style. In Laclau's phrase they sustain 'a subordinate and decorative role'.[5] The aristocratic fraction of the ruling class no longer remains in the ascendant in the real social relations, and, arguably, since the 1920s it has been characterized by an increasing powerlessness. How, therefore, has this subsidiary fraction, in the ruling alliances that compose the dominant bloc in society, *signed* itself in society (Rebecca's first 'appearance' in the text is through signature, which inscribes itself in the consciousness of her successor)? In this case, it is predominantly at the level of style and of codes, and an ideology of personal value, indicated through breeding, gestures of face, hand, eye etc. – 'gestures which reveal quintessences'[6] and form part of what might be called an ethical hegemony, exercising the *idea* of a ruling class but not its practical functions – which have long since been assumed by the bourgeoisie. It is in this way that 'a rising social class acquires a significant part of its ideological equipment from the armoury of the ruling class itself'.[7] It is my argument that this ideological equipment is refurbished and re-presented through the cultural repertoire at the disposal of the dominant class, in this case the mass marketing of masculine and feminine romance, with its formal and contentual anachronisms marked by 'pseudo-feudal' relationships.

At particular times, a ruling bloc may wish, or be forced, to substitute for itself deputies or agents in the social formation who are not of the ruling bloc (e.g. intellectuals, politicians etc.). This not only may occur at the level of personal representatives, but also may be reposed in values, modes of behaviour, ways of seeing, etc., themselves the result of historic alliances represented as a 'lived relation' in the different levels of the social formation [. . .]. In other words, the ruling class may re-present itself socially through a complex network of ideological positions which depend for their effectiveness on the degree to which these positions draw on the values of the subordinated class and its fractions, especially (in the case of *Rebecca*) the petit bourgeoisie. Thus, liberal ideology, dominant for so long in our society, is an odd amalgamation of the landed aristocracy, the leading bourgeoisie and the petit bourgeoisie (with an artisan fraction subscribing to its values) encoded within an anti-aristocratic framework.[8] The keynote is the co-existence of disparate fractions, and it is this resolution which *Rebecca* reproduces. The unnamed heroine, rootless and of obscure origins, without 'beauty, music or conversation' (traditional means of entry into the élite for a woman), is gradually initiated into the world of the landed estate by a process of complex and painful education. Originally a companion to a vulgar *arriviste*, she graduates from servant to mistress of a country house. It is interesting to note that she meets Maxim in Monte Carlo, a capitalist playground and alien milieu to one of his origins, yet at the same time an environment characterized entirely by chance, luck, competition, those factors most appropriate in any ideological account of the lower-class girl's social mobility. At the level of romance, of course, she is seen by Maxim as the one spiritual element in a gross, materialist centre of accumulation. This reflects also on the fact that Rebecca had been 'at home' in this setting, and it is here that Maxim has gone to remember/forget her. [. . .]

The significant point is that the displaced aristocrat can be renewed only through association with the values of the figure from the subordinated class, with her virtues of restraint, modesty, austerity and dedication. Another factor is that for a considerable part of the narrative *their* relationship can only be mediated through his *agent*, Frank Crawley, [. . .] whose self-effacing values are close to those of the heroine. So we have a situation where the middle-aged gentry figure finds himself through a relationship with a lower-class girl half his age (the localized ages have a symbolic historical function), mediated by the agent who handles his estate in his absence, and his personal relationships in his metaphorical absence through distraction.

While the dominant ideology is necessarily systematized and presented as natural and universal (commanding spontaneous consent – hence the deferential presence of the servants and tenantry), it does not spring automatically from the ruling class, but is usually the relation of forces between the fractions of the ruling bloc (symbolically presented here through the surrogate fraction of the landed gentry). Gramsci conceived of the differential appropriation of the dominant ideas within the ruling bloc itself, *and* within the dominated class. It is this differential appropriation which constitutes a definition of hegemony which *Rebecca*, through its narrative of breakdown and crisis, supersession of the past, active mediations of agents from outside the ruling bloc, renewal of personal relationships through the exclusive 'couple formulation', and ultimate exile from the estate, articulates through its arrangements of deep structural significance. The basic motor of the text is *reformation* and the emergence of a new set of reciprocal social alliances. It is a novel about changing differentials in the class composition of the contemporary social structure.

Having said all this, it must be demonstrated how the representative of the landed gentry is transformed and actively incorporated in the new formation. How, in other words, is the crisis negotiated by the articulations of the text? The site chosen might be described as the ethical/personal. In the ethical sphere, bourgeois moral ideals (in which Maxim has to be educated) combine an emphasis on being true to oneself – the unashamed conscience (the opposite of which is Maxim's burden) – with an emphasis on performing one's social obligations. These were accompanied by a belief in male supremacy, family loyalty and romantic love (not originally bourgeois ideas, but transformed into bourgeois modes via the ideology of individualism based on private property and the monogamous couple formulation). Aristocratic family relations were economic transactions – the family/house was the realm of economic life – and love and sexuality were sought outside marriage by *men*.[9] The position of Rebecca in the text is significant here as a mirror-inversion of this model, as she participates in what amounts to an *arranged* marriage with Maxim for the sake of Manderley (i.e. in the family's rather than the individual's interest), and then proceeds to develop a double standard by taking lovers, threatening illegitimacy (so crucial to the line and the blood) and using men as sexual objects. With Mrs Danvers as her 'agent', they carve out a space, literally and metaphorically, in which women can experience a meaningful existence, even if at this stage it is only through a relatively simplified role reversal. The figure of Mrs Danvers broods menacingly over the text as a residual trace of the subversion represented by the liberated Rebecca to the dominant (male) ideology. Rebecca was, in contrast to her homely successor, *too* beautiful and, by all except the immediate family, exalted as a spiritual creature. The immediate family (except, significantly, the blind grandmother) see her as an enchantress, having bewitched Maxim. Being physically beautiful is one of woman's functions as long as she remains an object; the problem with Rebecca is that she demands to be regarded as a *subject*. The second wife has no such physical beauty, and makes no demands to be liberated – she is content to be the domestic half of the monogamous couple.

Aristocratic ideals of romantic love and individuality were developed in explicit opposition to the family, and in its

ideology these had to be spiritualized and related to male concern with personal relations and an ideal of individual self-
improvement and self-realization. All of these were pursued by
Rebecca, which is one of the reasons why she had to be killed
because she usurped male prerogatives and therefore introduced an *unnatural* order. [. . .] The narrative has to kill Rebecca
all over again to facilitate the naturalizing of a new order. Her
sexuality was subversive, a menace to the patriarchal order; she
was man-like in her radical and code-breaking sexuality, treating relationships as game and competition (she also takes part
in sailing races against men) and laughs at men: she has invaded
male territory. Maxim as god, giver and taker of life, has to kill
the 'threat' in an act of justifiable homicide [. . .] – subject to a
higher law, that of natural order. In a text where the emphasis is
on the adaptive, and the assimilation into changing class structures, it is a mark of liberal ideology that Rebecca as the bearer
of aristocratic-feudal residues in an industrial-democratic
world has to be extirpated as the root of all evil; she is the
unrepentant, profligate aristocrat likely to waste the inheritance. This is further signed by the fact that she is unable to bear
children (the women's true and natural legacy to the estate) and
also has terminal cancer, another symbol of inner disease. Of
course, this should all be explored and re-stated in terms of her
sexuality and the subversion of woman's role, but it is the
ideology that is my concern at the moment.

In bourgeois ideology, woman's sexuality and reproduction
have to be incorporated in the sphere of the family which, in
turn, becomes the repository of emotions, of sexuality, physical
well-being, and the space for situating the free choice of a unique
beloved. Both texts are about the 'freeing' of the self to exercise
choice. In *Rebecca*'s extensive crisis of self and family, Maxim's
emotional distress, physical ill-health, absence of affection, and
his 'possession' by Rebecca all thwart the fulfilment of the
bourgeois ideals. The terror and neurosis experienced by the
heroine at Manderley reproduce his experience of crisis, which
can only be resolved in mutuality and exile from Manderley.
Their original return to Manderley could be structurally related
to a desire in the 1930s for a return along the road back to 1913,
the gold standard, free trade and laissez-faire. This was an
economically nostalgic solution to 1931 and the crisis, as was

their attempt to return to a pre-bourgeois Manderley in which the heroine sought to reproduce the image and style of Rebecca. Both actions were doomed, and could only persist at a distance and in retrospect as a cultural memory and image of an *idea* of a golden age: socially marked by grace, beauty and an edenic landscape; economically, by free trade, a non-interventionist state and the gold standard.

The heroine grows as Rebecca recedes, as she expels her shadow self, the image within. The text ritually sheds the 'perverted' woman, Eve incarnate, the spoiler of the paradisal estate, to which there is no going back. It is important that Rebecca's body is recovered from the sea, because until that time her spirit cannot be laid. Her significantly decomposed *body* (vessel of life for woman and, in this instance, the agency of carnality) is buried in the family vault. This burial marks not just her displacement by the heroine (the truly spiritual woman, though materially poor and of 'humble' origin) but it denotes the burying of a model of family also. [. . .]

One of the crucial features of Maxim's crisis was a potential or, on occasions, an actual loss of control. By the end of the novel, this control has been resumed, together with that presence and authority which are the traditional marks of the 'natural' leader. This is how he is seen by his second wife when she first encounters him in Monte Carlo, as a man of grace, ease and authority. Even when close to being exposed as a murderer, when physically threatened, and under great pressure in the coroner's court, he maintains the presence and bearing lost during his period of crisis. The important point is that this recovery has not been self-produced by an effort of will but is the result of the coalition of forces mentioned earlier: the burial of Rebecca, the love of his second wife, and the moral agency of Frank Crawley.

The reference to coalition is not an accidental metaphor, as I should like to conclude this stage by attempting to relate the text to the social and political practices of the 1930s by means of Gramsci's concept of 'Caesarism'.[10] Gramsci uses this term to describe a situation in which the forces in conflict balance each other in a catastrophic manner. In *Rebecca*, although the eponymous figure is dead in terms of the ongoing narrative time, she, Maxim and his second wife represent the forces in conflict in such a way as to produce the text's catastrophe or crisis. The situation is such that a continuation of the conflict can only terminate in their reciprocal destruction. It is this destruction which, as a constant threat, dominates a substantial proportion of the narrative and accounts for the prevailing mood of nightmare, menace and tension. Gramsci talks about the forces in conflict in terms of progressive and reactionary, and these may be applied with equal effect to the text. Basically, Rebecca actualizes the reactionary (in the terms of the narrative's 'ideology') and Maxim (with support) the progressive, but it is limiting simply to discuss the forces in these terms, because at some stage or other every figure in the text, however minor, is brought into the sphere of one or other of the forces. Rebecca is the exception – her literal absence makes this possible as she is immobilized. Every other figure has the potential for change, for mobility and immobility. In his first encounter with the young girl, Maxim becomes animated and mobilized out of his thoughts of Rebecca: the car journey they make together signifies this progressive characteristic. She, on the other hand, has been immediately raised into social recognition and commands deference as soon as she shares his table at the hotel. Once returned to Manderley, he is demobilized and becomes reactionary and regressive. His second wife participates in this, as is signified by the gaps in her days, her problem of filling out time. This relates, of course, to other factors such as society's determination that the upper-middle-class woman should do nothing useful; something else Rebecca violated by her extraordinary energy and powers of organization.

A considerable section of the narrative is devoted to this reactionary phase, marked by a series of references to charades, theatricals, disguises, masquerades, etc., all activities characterized by their being designed to simulate action and to produce the illusion of movement. This is why the costume ball is the culminating point of the narrative crisis. It serves several functions: first of all, it is reactionary in that it is an attempt to recover some of the traditional functions of the country house; it is also reactionary in so far as Mrs de Winter seeks to simulate the style and appearance of one of her husband's ancestors; and, finally, because in so doing she becomes at that moment a replica of Rebecca. Basically, the whole event is a Rebecca-like function. Dance is also, of course, a highly stylized form of movement, as it has no other purpose than as an activity in itself: it is simulated mobility. Significantly, Maxim does not wear fancy dress as this marks the moment when he is about to resume his 'real self'. This resumption cannot begin, however, until his second wife casts off her 'Rebecca costume' and stands by his side in her ordinary clothing. The action is simultaneously traumatic and progressive: the narrative can now be re-mobilized and reach a conclusion, a process arrived at by a highly complicated sequence of narrative plotting, in contrast with the relatively plotless (actionless) earlier sections.

The role of the second wife is to intervene in the Rebecca–Maxim catastrophe, and to produce a solution by arbitration (she is, in a sense, also the judge of his crime). Gramsci describes this as Caesarism: 'the particular solution in which a great personality is entrusted with the task of "arbitration" over a historico-political situation characterized by an equilibrium of forces heading towards catastrophe'.[11] The vital difference is that this particular situation is entrusted to a personality or personalities (remembering the mediation of Crawley, close to them at the ball) of low social status but of high moral and spiritual quality. In Gramsci's dialectic the problem is to see whether it is 'revolution' or 'restoration' which predominates. This dialectic of forces was potentially present in the crisis of transition in the period under discussion, as was the immobilization of the economy together with millions of the working class in the depression. The particular solution of the ruling class was not to restore the previous economic practices as some pressed for, nor, of course, was there revolution. No great personality emerged as the arbitrator of the conflict between labour and capital, but a third political solution was devised which involved the merging of certain of the forces in the potentially catastrophic conflict situation. As Gramsci points out, Caesarism is a polemical-ideological formula, and as a solution can exist without any great or heroic personality. The parliamentary system also provides a mechanism for a compromise solution. [. . .]

The Labour governments of Macdonald were seen by Gramsci as 'Caesarist' in character, and this fact was sharpened by what happened to the progressive forces (the labour movement in its parliamentary form) in the 1930s, particularly when Macdonald headed a government with a Conservative majority. The existence of the National Government in the 1930s was an intervention which, with compromises, limitations and modifications, helped in part to secure the reactionary forces of monopoly capitalism. Arguably, until 1957, it is this situation which marks the period as one of transition from contradictions, dissent and instability to an extended moment of consensus achieved through a mixed economy and state intervention. The process was evolutionary; the dominant social form had not exhausted its possibilities for development, but rather had exploited its marginal possibilities for further development and organizational improvement. The process was one of reciprocal fusion and assimilation which halted the organic struggle between the conflicting forces and transcended the catastrophic phase. [. . .] It may be that this equilibrium was/is of an intermediate and episodic character, but the historico-political period under consideration did produce some marked shifts in ossified and obsolete structures, and changes in the class composition of the ruling bloc, by introducing into national life and social activity a different and more numerous personnel. These personnel might be characterized by their being substituted as deputies or agents of the ruling bloc in the spheres of intellectual activity and bureaucratic organization. The fact that they are drawn from the working and lower middle class indicates the relative weakness of that class, and the ability of the dominant class to preserve and exploit that relative weakness through social mobility and an ideology of open access to the structures of power. [. . .]

It is this reciprocal fusion and assimilation which marks the resolution of the contradictions in the text of *Rebecca*. The actual country house may be burned, but this is a quantitative sacrifice – the necessary purging:

> 'It's funny,' I said. 'It looks almost as though the dawn was breaking over there, beyond those hills. It can't be though, it's too early.'
> 'It's the wrong direction,' he said, 'you're looking west.'[12]

So the fire heralds the breaking of a new 'day' in their relationship, in another direction from that which had previously seemed natural. Rebecca's death by 'drowning' might have been similarly accounted for – as baptismal – but it is a simulated drowning; the raising up of her body is but the prelude to another, final burial. Maxim is able to survive and adapt, to be reborn through a fusion with his second wife who represents the margins of possibility left to him as, in many ways, a peripheral social figure. The notion of relative weakness mentioned above is preserved by her being a woman – a 'real', that is spiritual, woman who, when the struggle is over, the catastrophe averted, is able to surrender to the arms of the dominant male, the *quality* of the patriarchal order guaranteed. Rebecca's conspicuous consumption, her life style, is an affront as it is a part of an immoral and doomed system, and is buried with her – a system emblematized by a pagan and non-moral (i.e. Christian) concept of gentility expressed in the figure of the Cupid, which Mrs de Winter breaks and guiltily hides, thus repressing and sublimating the erotic symbol of Rebecca. [. . .]

The relationship between Maxim and his second wife is lived out on *private means* (literally and metaphorically), it has to be experienced in personalized terms (what Althusser refers to as the 'interpellation of the subject' – hence the 'I' narrative) outside the space of the former conflict. This is the novel's 'conscience': the removal from public display of the signs of inequality and obvious wealth, to re-emerge in a narrative which itself is a testament of change and of a re-formation in the system of alliances which compose the hegemonic bloc. Above all, it is signified as a *qualitative* change: restorative but not reactionary.

Maxim loses his country house (a reference to a specific historical reality recognized by the text) and gives up many of the functions, political and social, consequent upon its ownership, for a personal life relatively confined and austere, and in some ways rootless. What he recovers and retains, through the fusion and assimilation of his 'lowly' second wife, is a transfusion of ideals and values, and a *style* with an important ideological function, that of the gentleman, signed by a morality of fair play, selflessness, courage, moderation and self-control, independence and responsibility. All of which can be summed up by the word *authority*, commanding deference. This authority is something which, incidentally, is bestowed upon the narrative by the nature of its being a personal testament (the ultimate reference in a liberal ideology): an 'I' for the truth, commanding acquiescence in its veracity. The text, therefore, has an authoritative structure as well as being about authority.

In the 1930s the total acreage of cultivated land continued to fall, but, at the same time, large farmers (subsidized by the government to a large extent) were more prosperous than at any other time in the century. Also, unearned income was still subject to relatively light taxation, which meant that the property-owning fraction retained a distinctiveness and was still very influential in social and political circles. The country house, with its pattern of social intercourse dependent on a supply of low-paid servants, was still significant and the depression had little effect on its patterns of consumption.[13] At the same time as this was true, though, the earlier failure in British agriculture had brought about a fundamental change in the landed society. The old landed aristocracy and gentry had abdicated. They sold their land to tenant-farmers, so much so that by 1927 36 per cent of the land of England was farmed by owner-occupiers: 'Precisely one quarter of England and Wales had therefore passed from being tenanted land into the possession of its farmers in the thirteen years after 1914.'[14] Such an enormous and rapid transfer of land and large-scale transformation of rural society contributed to the fact that the landed classes as such had ceased to be of national importance. This diminution and abdication marked the disappearance from sight and power of the landed gentry. Those who failed, or refused, to be assimilated into the realms of finance capital (via company directorships and shares) went 'underground' and became 'backwoodsmen', trying to live out anachronistic and displaced existences.

The hero of *Rogue Male* is one such figure: 'He disapproves of me on only two grounds: that I refuse to sit on the board of any blasted company, and that I insist upon my right to waste money in agriculture' (p. 47). In many ways the narrative explores the means whereby the displaced and unadaptable gentry figure seeks to find a place and a meaning in a society from which he is metaphorically exiled. The fact that both texts under consideration are 'written in exile' signals the recognition of the *displacement* of this particular class fraction from a real function in the dominant class. By the end of the 1930s the landed gentry could only have a cultural-fictional presence in the social formation.

> Now luck, movement, wisdom, and folly have all stopped. Even time has stopped, for I have no space. That, I think, is the reason why I have again taken refuge in this confession. I retain a sense of time, of the continuity of a stream of facts. I remind myself that I have extended and presumably will extend again in the time of the outer world. At present I exist only in my own time, as one does in a nightmare, forcing myself to a fanaticism of endurance. Without a God, without a love, without a hate – yet a fanatic! An embodiment of that myth of the foreigners, the English gentleman, the gentle Englishman. I will not kill; to hide I am ashamed. So I endure without object.
>
> (p. 122)

This seems to be a very precise articulation of the situation of the landed gentleman, defined through a series of absences and negatives, out of time and space. The narrative is an 'I' narrative, the testament of an unnamed (and, therefore, representative) figure attempting to register in a written record the conditions of his outlawry and the search for meaning and purpose. It is significant that it is only through the medium of writing, a cultural production, that the gentry figure can sign his existence, testify to his continuation. These fictions, through their structures of narrative coherence and continuity, act as a means of resolving the real historical contradictions rooted in the phenomena of rupture, discontinuity, and the incidence of interruptions. They *are* fictions of displacement and transformation, it is true, but their traditional, 'realist', structures seek to constitute a unity and to confer a validity on the subjects of their narrative. The presence of a traceable story and a discernible plot, the representations of a world that, despite modernist claims to the contrary, *is* capable of being re-presented, act as signs that life is meaningful and coherent, able to be 'put together again'. Every story, that is, tells a picture: the fictions are representational. The presences, the knowable characters, the resolvable conflicts, the well-charted time and space, the sheer weight of information mediated through the techniques of realism amount to a critique of the absences, fragmentations, contradictions and abstractions of avant-garde art and writing. [. . .]

So these texts not only seek to preserve and signify the continuing existence of absent and displaced figures in the social structure, but also through their very use of language, style and form seek to preserve and affirm a historical continuity in the context of real breaks, mutations and ruptures in the social formation. To paraphrase Foucault, what these texts undertake is to 'memorize' the monuments of the past, transform them into documents, and lend speech to those traces which, in themselves, are often not verbal, or which say in silence something other than what they actually say.[15] Primarily, they exist to indicate discontinuity as the stigma of temporal dislocation which it is the task of mass fictions to remove from visibility: though composed of discontinuities, contradictions and temporal dislocations, the text's ultimate reference is to *continuity*, to the fact that between all the events of a well-defined spatio-temporal area it is possible to establish a system of homogeneous relations. As Stedman Jones has pointed out: 'The differential temporality of linked historical structures has been obscured by the myth that all events are conjoined by the mere fact of continuous succession in time. Merely because parts of a social system are contemporaneous, they do not necessarily inhabit the same historical time.'[16] The function of these texts is to remove the differentials, to carve out a contemporary space for the displaced figure, and to enable the codes and styles of a past mode of behaviour to inhabit the same historical time as the radically transformed relations in society. In other words, the ideological thrust is to suggest that for all the appearance of difference, all events and classes symbolize one another and express one and the same central core. A more specific and concrete analysis of the class relations in both texts would, I think, reveal this ideology of a shared central core. In the face of dispersion in the real social relations, these, and comparable, texts seek to *totalize*, draw all phenomena around a single centre: the cultural analogy of the politico-ideological polemic of 'Caesarism'.

The significant fact that both texts use a first-person narra-

tive construction can also be related to other concepts developed by Foucault (in *The Archaeology of Knowledge*). This is
related to the role of cultural fiction as a locus of uninterrupted
continuities, for the forging of connections and syntheses that
can lead men towards a future. [. . .] This process provides a
shelter for the sovereignty of consciousness, as a continuous
cultural text is the indispensable correlative of the founding
function of the *subject*: the guarantee that everything that has
eluded him may be restored to him; the certainty that time will
disperse nothing without restoring it in a reconstituted unity;
the promise that one day the subject will once again be able to
appropriate all those things that are kept at a distance by
difference and change, and find in them what might be called his
abode. The 'I' of the narrative acts as such a guarantee, as does
the written testament, even if in the case of *Rogue Male* the hero's
destiny is certain death. The saving fact is that it is a death
which confirms his sovereignty against a series of crisis-ridden
experiences based on the *de-centrings* of the subject. It is the
resumption of the centrality of the subject that represents the
ultimate cultural meaning of both *Rebecca* and *Rogue Male*. Both
texts equally restore *rationality* as the *telos* of humanity. The
immobility of the formal structures, the closed systems of the
texts with their developmental narratives and their logical
endings, and the final synchrony of all the textual data (everything is explained) assert this rationality, the presence of the
unitary in discourse.

The narrator of *Rogue Male*, having escaped from an unspecified
European country after a failed attempt to assassinate the head
of state, records his search for a temporal and spatial *abode*. He is
the owner of a country estate in the West Country which has
been the property of his family for countless generations. Land-
ownership traditionally brought with it, and demanded, a series
of social rituals: landlord, sportsman and host; of these, he
retains only the role of sportsman. He is an explorer and
adventurer, and spends most of his time out of England. He
convinces himself that his attempt at assassination was itself a
response to a sportsman's hypothesis, a testing of the feasibility
of killing the biggest game of all. This marks his behaviour at the
outset as idiosyncratic and eccentric: his motivation was not

political, nor was he acting on behalf of any agency other than himself. So what is presented to us is the figure of the isolated and wandering hero, dislodged from his ancestral functions and seeking purpose through the hunt in foreign territory.

Having escaped, by means of the first of several ploys which necessitate his going 'underground', he arrives in England only to be pursued by agents of the enemy government. The main agent styles himself as Major Quive-Smith, and throughout the text this figure, in his upper-class guise, acts as the replica of the hero. At many points they overlap, and see each other not so much as enemies but as opponents, as figures, in other words, acting inside known and shared codes. Both are displaced aristocrats, the initial difference being that Quive-Smith has found a cause, a function within his own society. Forced to go on the run, the hero kills a man in an underground tunnel, which means that he is an outlaw in his own country (this is merely the literal placing of a larger metaphorical sense of exile and outlawry, which is the lot of the recalcitrant and unadaptive aristocrat). From that moment on he is forced to disappear underground, but not before he has equipped himself with a considerable sum of money and equipment appropriate to the exploring pioneer. An outlaw figure, he heads for a space which borders two farms in Dorset. He cannot return to his own estate, but he settles quite close to it and, effectively, rebuilds an estate of the self from the materials at his disposal in the natural environment. Without estate or family but *with* capital, he, with the resourcefulness of a Crusoe, re-constructs for himself a time, a space, and an identity in a rural milieu. His habitat is a burrow (a further reference to the fact of the gentry fraction being forced out of public sight) in which by an ingenious deployment of fieldcraft knowledge and the construction of an ancient form of weaponry, he plots the death of his opponent (the suggestions of the primitive are crucial in this text: man going back through historical time – to become a boy again in the womb of the natural – in order to re-constitute the sovereignty of the subject which has been dispersed, fragmented and divided in the modern world). The motivation for the killing, the impetus to emerge from his self-created tomb/womb, comes when he breaks from scepticism to commitment. This break comes under the interrogation of his *alter ego*, Quive-Smith. This is the latter's essential function: he offers *his* commitment to the hero, who in the act of rejection of it, because it lacks ethics, finds his own mission.

The work he is forced to undertake is a form of self-activity which has a recuperative effect, and is a necessary prelude to a mode of activity which goes beyond the self to a higher purpose. The hunter turned quarry has to re-define himself in the context of a changed situation. This re-definition, in the face of evacuation from actual political power, takes the form of a moral resurrection (the crucifixion, burial and resurrection motifs are interspersed throughout). The English gentleman resumes his position at the summit of society, but this is now in a spiritual/ moral incarnation. The role of disguise, simulation and substitution is significant in the text and refers to the way in which, in terms of cultural images, the ruling bloc is able to use the idea of a gentleman as a surrogate for itself in the ideological-cultural formation. His manners, his sense of fairness and his devotion to study and service together encode a socially legitimate character-type: a patriarchal definition of masculinity confirmed again and again in cultural masculine romances. It is worthy of note that in order to arrive at this renewal he is forced to impersonate a series of social types (elementary schoolmaster, company director, Professor of Christian Ethics, and author, all of which have recognizable functions in the contemporary social formation). His surfacings can only be in terms of socially valid currency, never as himself. The text itself explicitly recognizes that the landed gentry are no longer of the ruling class, but remain nevertheless inside what is termed as 'class X': characterized by the gentle voice. It is his voice which worries him as a barrier to the finding of new methods of effacing his identity. The narrative logic for this self-effacement is, of course, sustained consistently as is the physical disfigurement, but the larger cultural reference constitutes the *de facto* recognition of the effacement of the gentry in British society. The hero even draws up plans to distribute his land by the formation of a Tenants' Co-operative Society. This finally frees him from any dependants and completes his individual separation, the rogue male of the title.

The narrative structure enables the narrator to see himself at a distance, as a second self, through a mode of analysis located within the framework of *rationality* and coherence discussed earlier. In the course of analysis, it is revealed that the 'back-woodsman' has returned to the site formerly shared with his fiancée, a politically motivated woman from Spain killed by Quive-Smith's government. The going back gains in significance, as, unconsciously, his elaborate preparations and rehearsals in the hedgerows all serve later to propel him into a personal war of revenge for her death. The time spent in hibernation, full of uncertainty and misgivings, is significantly autumn. [. . .] The military/spiritual quality of his self-realization mimics the monastic stages of spiritual development, the emphasis on magic (craft) parallels the Catholic ritual, the love of the lady parallels the worship of Mary, and baptism (water is the hero's *querencia*) is secularized in the rebirth of the knight. This tradition of self-discovery reiterated here tries to affirm an uninterrupted development of history in the face of discontinuity, break and transformation.

The hero emerges from his historic test as 'captain of his soul', the supreme individualist with no need for any law but his own. The text then turns on a conflict between the *mass*, the State (bourgeois, fascist or socialist) and the individual. His final actions are those of the individual consecrated by his own anger to do justice 'where no other hand could reach'. He declares war as a spiritual offensive on behalf of the humanity which the woman has represented; finally, his whole existence has found purpose beyond that of landlord, sportsman and host (all discarded identities) by a process of personalization dignified by a spiritual crusade. He feels like a penitent after confession (as if what he has confessed has been the dereliction of the displaced and intransigent gentry). The narrative, at this point of resolution of crisis, is able to emerge from *its* metaphorical grave, hit the road and mobilize itself towards a conclusion: the object of *its* existence. [. . .] Unlike the bourgeoisie, he has no will to power, only a will to sovereignty of the subject, of consciousness not manipulated by a repressive totalizing apparatus, but a true totalizing harmony. This has been made possible by a search for and recovery of the origins of the historical subject, and the affirmation of the conservative function of a cultural totality which sees the recentred self as symbolic of all other selves by analogy. There is a kind of international synchrony in the resolution of the text (denoted by the journeys made) and the individualized ideology of war is rendered symbolic of a larger justification for war on behalf of 'freedom', unrelated to the territorial ambitions of competing forms of monopoly capitalism. 'I myself became a human being again' (*Rogue Male*, p. 169). A human being, one should add, marked by quality, breeding and membership of a chivalric élite committed to a mentality of war for the sake of his 'queen'. For all this, however, the hero leaves England in the guise of a bourgeois figure (a company director), so a level of embourgeoisment (linked with the ethic of individualism) has occurred: the gentry figure has to undergo certain transformations even if, at the level of the cultural fiction, he remains with his quintessential self. [. . .]

The hero goes into exile and death in order to assassinate the symbolic enemy of the personal, the individual. He becomes the 'great personality' of Gramsci's 'Caesarism' – the figure restored by a process of reciprocity and fusion. One final recognition and transformation must be noted. His original plan to kill the head of state was carried out in a rural terrain, where his own skill was acquired. The *education* the text testifies to is signified by the hero's decision to shift the quest from the country to the town (denoting the assimilation of the gentry into the urban space of the bourgeoisie) and to close the distance between self and target from 550 to 200 yards. This shift in terrain and scale marks the final effacement of the gentry fraction as a social reality, while at the same time the text constructs the memory of a scrupulously coded ideal: 'nobility as the symbol of mind' (Bagehot). The ruling class is still able to exercise its authority through a network of personalized agencies signed in some ways by the 'gentle voice' of class X, because we are still inclined to annex moral attributes to that voice and its style, which helps give society some of its ideologically cohesive power.

Notes

1   Daphne du Maurier, *Rebecca* (Gollancz, London 1938).
2   Geoffrey Household, *Rogue Male* (Chatto & Windus, London 1939).

3 Geoffrey Household, *Rogue Male* (Heinemann, London 1963), p. 159. All further references will be to this edition and will be included in the text.

4 Antonio Gramsci, *Selections from the Prison Notebooks*, trans. and ed. Q. Hoare and G. Nowell-Smith (Lawrence & Wishart, London 1971), p. 83.

5 Ernesto Laclau, *Politics and Ideology in Marxist Theory* (New Left Books, London 1977).

6 The phrase is Perry Anderson's.

7 Perry Anderson, 'Origins of the present crisis', *NLR*, 23, p. 36.

8 See the development of this argument by Richard Johnson in 'Barrington Moore, Perry Anderson and English Social Development', *Working Papers in Cultural Studies*, 9 (Centre for Contemporary Cultural Studies, Birmingham 1976).

9 This situation is well analysed by Eli Zaretsky in *Capitalism, Personal Relations and Family Life* (Pluto, London 1974).

10 Gramsci, *Selections*, pp. 219–23.

11 Ibid., p. 219.

12 Du Maurier, *Rebecca* (Pan edn, London 1975), p. 396.

13 For a full discussion of this situation see E.J. Hobsbawm, *Industry and Empire* (Weidenfeld & Nicolson, London 1968), and N. Branson and M. Heinemann, *Britain in the Nineteen Thirties* (Weidenfeld & Nicolson, London 1971).

14 Quoted in Hobsbawm, *Industry and Empire*.

15 Cf. Michel Foucault's introduction to *The Archaeology of Knowledge* (Tavistock, London 1972).

16 Gareth Stedman Jones 'The poverty of empiricism', in *Ideology in Social Science*, ed. R. Blackburn (Fontana, London 1972).

10

Agincourt 1944: readings in the Shakespeare myth
GRAHAM HOLDERNESS

We have for four years been fighting, alone or in partnership, the reptilian dragon-forces of unregenerate, and therefore unshaped and inhuman, instinct, energies breathing fire and slaughter across Europe, because such is our destiny, asserted by our own time-honoured national symbol, St George, the dragon-slayer, whose name our present sovereign bears.

G. Wilson Knight, 1944

The British nation and the British empire, finding themselves alone, stood undismayed against disaster. No one flinched or wavered; nay, some who formerly thought of peace, now think only of war. Our people are united and resolved, as they have never been before. Death and ruin have become small things compared with the shame of defeat or failure in duty. We cannot tell what lies ahead. It may be that even greater ordeals lie before us. We shall face whatever is coming to us.

Winston Churchill, 1940

We will go forward – heart, nerve and spirit steeled. We will attack; we will smite our foes; we will conquer; and in all our deeds, in this land and in other lands, from this hour on, our watchwords will be: urgency, speed, courage. Urgency in all our decisions; speed in the execution of all our plans; courage in the face of all our enemies; and may God bless our cause.

Laurence Olivier, 1943

> We few, we happy few, we band of brothers.
> For he today that sheds his blood with me
> Shall be my brother; be he ne'er so vile
> This day shall gentle his condition.

Henry V, 1415/1599/1944

Behind disorder is some sort of order or 'degree' on earth, and that
order has its counterpart in heaven.

E.M.W. Tillyard, 1944[1]

'Criticism' – signifying, in a limited but familiar definition, the
formally-written academic discourse of literary scholarship,
analysis and interpretation – is but one manifestation of the
general assemblage of social and ideological practices which
operate over the cultural ground we call 'literature'. But it
remains, however emphatically we deny its pre-eminence and
insist on its relativity, a privileged discourse claiming the status
of secondary function to the primary material of 'literature'
itself. Writing about literature cannot concern itself only with
texts, biographical factors, historical background: it must begin
by addressing that history which begins when a piece of writing
(or theatre) embarks on its career of consumption by readership
or audience: its long history of assimilation into the apparatus of
culture, its incorporation into received traditions of the 'canon'
of literature, in which context it can be immediately 'recognized'; its implementation into systems and structures of education. Any attempt to define what a literary work 'is' must be
preceded by an analysis of what it has become, what certain
cultural and educational processes have made of it, and of how
and why those operations took place. But can this history be
properly termed the history of 'criticism'? Can the science of it
be   properly   defined   by   Peter   Widdowson's   coinage
'critiography'?[2] Formal criticism is only a part of the totality of
cultural practices: does it remain the dominant, the determinant mode? If so, how and why does it secure and maintain
this dominant position? [. . .]

'Shakespeare' is a particularly rich field for this type of
investigation, since Shakespeare, conventionally the greatest of
English literary figures, has paradoxically been accorded the
most widespread and varied extra-literary existence. Readings
of Shakespeare which limit themselves to texts, criticism and
historical 'background' inevitably begin by implicitly claiming
that 'Shakespeare' is immediately accessible as an object of
investigation. Certain kinds of critical and pedagogic convention have convinced us that in the act of silent, individual

reading of a 'literary' text (the play as 'dramatic poem') we hear directly the voice of the bard, gain immediate access to the thoughts and feelings of his human heart, establish intimate connection with the past in which he wrote. But any attempt to discover the real Shakespeare – whether critical, historical or dramatic – involves peering through a vast and enormously complex system of refracting prisms: the whole multifarious body of ideas, attitudes, assumptions, images, which have accrued over centuries of cultural activity centred on the literary productions of this Elizabethan dramatist, and which constitute at any given historical moment the ideological problematic in which Shakespeare is 'recognized'. Every writer, every mode of writing, has this kind of history: in the case of Shakespeare it is not merely the visible history of a literary reputation, but the enormous residuum of centuries of constructing and reconstructing a symbol: a symbol, pre-eminently, of British national culture. 'Shakespeare' is everywhere: not only in criticism, scholarship and historiography, or in the apparatus of education, or in theatrical, television and film productions; but beyond these traditional media of national culture, the phenomenon appears in the fabric of everyday common life, a component of popular culture. It is probable that every English-speaking citizen of Britain has heard of Shakespeare: not necessarily from plays or books, but from tourist attractions, advertisements, television comedies, the names of pubs and beers. In this context 'Shakespeare' (a concept which, we can already see, is partly distinguishable from the writer of plays) appears as a universal symbol of high art, of 'culture', of education, of the English spirit. An agency offering elocution lessons advertises itself by a cartoon of a puzzled Shakespeare bewildered by the voice from a telephone receiver: to be understood by Shakespeare would be a guarantee of correct speaking. In the television series *Batman*, the entrance to the 'Batcave' is controlled by a switch concealed inside a bust of Shakespeare's head: the decorative property of a millionaire's house opens to activate an exotic world of drama and costume, of fantasy and adventure. Immediately we begin to look back at Shakespeare in a historical perspective, it becomes evident that what we see is not Shakespeare in history, but the history of 'Shakespeare'.

A theoretical question very much worth asking is: why is it that, despite the evident *universality* of the Shakespeare phenomenon, formal criticism can still claim to occupy the status of a privileged discourse; and is its power and influence as dominant as it so confidently assumes? If a literature like 'Shakespeare' exists self-evidently as a set of social practices, are some of those practices more determinant than others? School pupils all 'read' Shakespeare: they seldom read criticism, except in the form of Study Aids – Coles', Brodie's, and York Notes. Is their 'Shakespeare' a relatively criticism-free version? Is the Shakespeare who exists in theatrical productions (at all levels from RSC to school play) a more real and influential social fact than the Shakespeare of formal critical discourse? Is the Shakespeare of film and television broadcasts, which play to larger audiences than the plays have ever known, the truly constitutive activity of the present age? What is the relationship between criticism and other forms of cultural reproduction, and how constitutive in fact is it?[3]

The year 1944 represents an interesting focus of Shakespeare reproduction, and a decisive moment in the ideological reconstruction of the English history plays, especially *Henry V*. 1944 saw the appearance of three texts which represent three different ideological interventions into the culture of war-time Britain: all concerned generally with Shakespeare, particularly with the English history plays, and pre-eminently with *Henry V*. G. Wilson Knight published a patriotic essay *The Olive and the Sword*, which had been written in 1940, printed as a pamphlet in 1941, and performed as a play. Laurence Olivier's film of *Henry V*, in the making since 1943, was released. Finally there appeared the text which has proved by far the most influential, and which represents a much more conventional commitment to academic scholarship and formal criticism: E.M.W. Tillyard's *Shakespeare's History Plays*. I would like to explore this cultural moment through analysis of these texts, and suggest some reasons why 'criticism', however specialized and élitist an activity it may seem to be, remains the decisively constitutive discourse determining the nature of 'literature'. [. . .]

G. Wilson Knight's essay is as much a piece of war-time propaganda as an essay in literary criticism: if anything more propaganda than scholarship, since the starting-point of the argument is very explicitly not 'literature' but the contemporary situation. His language is not the mannered urbanity of scholarly discourse, but the fierce rhetoric proper to a national crisis: he begins with a direct appeal to the spirit of national unity ('our English heritage') which in his view was forged in 1940 by the imminent threat of invasion, and which he regards as the 'soul of the nation':

> Four years ago (1940) the sudden fusion of parties into a single united British Front gave confidence and purpose to a nation in peril. Only when all parties are felt as, in the depths, at one, can the soul of a nation be revealed; as in a human life, when different attributes, body, heart, and mind, pulse together, the soul is known . . . the soul of England has yet to find, or rather hear, its own voice.
>
> (p. 1)

In 1940 England found its soul of national unity. But the true *voice* of the authentic English soul is apparently to be heard in its literary tradition:

> We have for four years been fighting, alone or in partnership, the reptilian dragon-forces of unregenerate, and therefore unshaped and inhuman, instinct, energies breathing fire and slaughter across Europe, because such is our destiny, asserted by our time-honoured national symbol, St George, the dragon-slayer, whose name our present sovereign bears; and we shall first search out that destiny not in platitudes of half-belief nor any reasonings of our own fabrication, but where alone it rests authentic, in the great heritage we possess of English letters, the greatest accumulation of national prophecy; where the soul of England, which is her essential sovereignty, speaks clearly – in Shakespeare, Milton, Pope, Byron, Blake, Wordsworth, Tennyson, Hardy and many more.
>
> (p. 3)

Because Wilson Knight's ideological strategy here (setting aside his metaphysical language) is so explicit, there is little sense of mystification. Clearly 'English literature' is regarded as an object with its own independent mode of existence: it is the true voice of the nation. Yet the idea of the nation's soul 'finding' its voice implies something closer to a conscious and deliberate appropriation and reconstruction of a 'literature' for its usefulness in the contemporary crisis. Knight wishes to assert that literature has spoken of national unity all along – only its utterance has not been heeded. But the urgency of his concern with a pressing present reality suggests strongly that the voice is that of a ventriloquist, with Shakespeare his articulate dummy. The above passage negotiates an elusive slide from the political concept of national unity to the *metaphysical* idea of 'sovereignty'; metaphysical because Knight does not use it as a political term to define the heart of power in a state (in his Britain, constitutionally Parliament) but to allude rather to a spirit of national emotion which manifests itself in the sovereign (the king), but is possessed by the people as a whole. (It would be amusing to consider what some members of Knight's pantheon – Milton, Byron, Blake, Hardy – would have thought of his royalist 'sovereignty').

The greatest expression of this sovereignty, the most authentic expression of England's soul, is Shakespeare:

> If ever a new Messiah is to come, he will come, says the greatest of all American writers, Herman Melville, in the name of Shakespeare. We need expect no Messiah, but we might, at this hour, turn to Shakespeare, a national prophet if ever there was one, concerned deeply with the royal soul of England. That royalty has direct Christian and chivalric affinities. Shakespeare's life-work might be characterised as expanding, through a series of great plays, the one central legend of St George and the Dragon. Let us face and accept our destiny in the name both of Shakespeare and St George, the patron saint of our literature and nation.

(p. 3)

This rhetoric of metaphysical terminology seeks to identify a number of key terms – the nation, the nation's soul, and its voice (literature), the sovereign, Christ, Shakespeare and St George. The logical absurdity of this argument can easily be exposed: but such exposure does not exhaust its significance, which consists in the directness with which Knight defined the ideological function of literature as he conceived and practised it: 'I aim to show what reserves for the refuelling of national confidence exist in Shakespeare's poetry' (p. 4). Nothing could be clearer than that.

> Shakespeare wrote at a time when, after centuries of civil war, England first became nationally self-conscious . . . the voice of the new nation is Shakespeare.
>
> His historical plays are mainly studies of internal disorder during the centuries leading to the England of Elizabeth. Shakespeare's thinking functions continuously in terms of order. . . . The issues troubling Europe today are here in embryo; and the desire for world-order which fabricated the League of Nations is an expansion of a desire pulsing throughout Shakespeare.
>
> (p. 4)

Shakespeare's historical dramas were, for Wilson Knight, parables of 'order' and 'disorder': expressions of an unsentimental patriotism which faces up to the prevalence and the perils of 'disorder', and proudly affirms the potentiality and the imperative necessity of 'order'. Such political terms are used with an apparent innocence of political meaning: what social system constitutes this apparently unquestionable 'order'? In fact Knight's theory is metaphysical rather than political: social order is defined as the English nation united in the symbol of the Crown: 'The Crown symbolises the nation's soul-life, which is also the greater self of each subject' (p. 16).

This formulation recalls Matthew Arnold's theory of class: we all have a lesser self, which encourages us to consider our own personal interests or the interests of family, faction, social group or class; and a greater self, which urges us to identify with the corporate body of the nation. The form of that identification is the Crown: 'our sole final allegiance is to that whole of which all these are parts and whose symbol is the Crown' (p. 89). The category of 'order' is thus a substitute for the political definition of a social formation – in this case a bourgeois-democratic state governed by Parliament with an anachronistic figurehead in the form of a vestigial monarchy – and Shakespeare's plays are used to support and confirm an appeal to 'order' which signifies, in effect, a qualified adherence to the *status quo*. The appeal to order is exactly, in fact, that emotion of national unity which was fostered during the Second World War not just to defeat fascism but to secure the ideological unification of the bitterly-divided Britain of the 1930s. [. . .]

The relation of Laurence Olivier's film of *Henry V* to the contemporary war-time situation of its production (1943–4) is as explicit as that of Wilson Knight's jingoistic essay. The film bears an epigraph:

> To the Commandos and Airborne Troops of Great Britain, the spirit of whose ancestors it has been humbly attempted to recapture in some ensuing scenes, this film is dedicated.

Part of the film's intention was clearly identical with that of Wilson Knight's – 'to show what reserves for the refuelling of national confidence exist in Shakespeare's poetry'. Olivier, who was in Hollywood when the war began, learned to fly there in order to join the Fleet Air Arm. In uniform he played the role of patriotic orator to the Home Front: the quotation which precedes this essay is from a speech he gave in the Albert Hall in 1943. Too old for active service, Olivier obviously found opportunities for contributing to the war effort in the form of ideological and cultural service. According to Clayton C. Hutton he had to be persuaded by the Ministry of Information to abandon his duties in the Fleet Air Arm in order to make *Henry V*.[4] The film came out too late to coincide with D-Day (the date of which had of course been kept secret), but was still dedicated to the troops involved in the Normandy landings.

Those scenes of the film which seem to have made the maximum impact and to have lingered most strongly in the popular imagination (to judge by the number of ill-informed, unresearched published comments I have come across)[5] are those which belong to its patriotic application of the play to the current national crisis: Henry's Churchillian speeches before Harfleur and Agincourt; the dejection, courage and soul-searching of the long night before Agincourt (clearly recalling the mood of 1940); the inserted battle-scenes, filmed with all the resources of modern film technology – depicting what Shakespeare's Chorus despaired of depicting: the colourful panoply of chivalry, the glamour of historical pageant, the thrill of victory; the confident, militaristic emotions of 1944. Yet all these details belong to one part of the film: its dramatization of

Acts III and IV of Shakespeare's play; and by themselves do not by any means exhaust or even adequately describe the film's contribution to Shakespeare reproduction.

Shakespeare's Chorus speaks constantly of the difficulties involved in producing an 'epic' drama under Elizabethan stage conditions: the impossibility of presenting with any authenticity or realism the great national events and vivid historical spectacles which constitute the play's ostensible subject:

> But pardon, gentles all,
> The flat unraised spirits that hath dar'd
> On this unworthy scaffold to bring forth
> So great an object. Can this cockpit hold
> The vasty fields of France? Or may we cram
> Within this wooden O the very casques
> That did affright the air at Agincourt?
>   (*Henry V*, Chorus, Act I, 8–14)

Olivier came to the play equipped with all the formidable technology for portraying reality developed by the modern cinema: all the freedom of the camera to move from interior to exterior, studio to location; all the financial and material resources of setting and costume necessary to provide authentic historical colour; all the technology necessary to film something like the French cavalry charge at Agincourt. Why did Olivier not simply dispense with the Chorus – a testimony to aesthetic limitations long since transcended – and present the film 'realistically' within the conventions of historical reconstruction that Shakespeare's Chorus seems to yearn for? Why, with all these aesthetic resources at command, does the film begin with a reconstruction of an Elizabethan theatre – locking the play back into the constricting framework which its own poetry struggles so hard to escape?

The decision to incorporate into the film devices and aesthetic strategies derived from the dramatic technique of the Chorus provides the film with an ideological tendency which is quite different from – potentially contrary to – its ideology of patriotism, national unity and just war. The film's passage into a 'realistic' reconstruction of Agincourt is mediated by a series of devices which in their different ways distance the art of film from reality, displaying the artificiality of the medium in such a way as to qualify (though not, ultimately, to dispel) the passionate conviction of the patriotic emotion.

The most influential view of the Chorus in *Henry V* is that it is there to give the drama an *epic* character: to enlarge and elevate dramatic spectacle from the conflicts of persons to the conflict of nations, from the limited space of the stage to the territory of international war. The Chorus urges the audience to supply, by a sustained imaginative participation, the kind of scale and realistic narrative detail possible in epic poem and novel, but not in drama. Cued by the Chorus's poetry, the audience can fill in the sense of space and of enormous, farspread human activity (particularly of a military kind) proper to the epic; and thereby provide the necessary context of great achievement, heroic struggle, enormous human effort and significant space, in which the epic hero's destiny can be unfolded and admired. In addition the Chorus provides the play with a neo-classical unity of action; and the didactic purpose of holding up heroic action for admiration and imitation.[6]

But the Chorus has a double function. It is there to create an epic space for the drama in the imaginations of the audience. But it is there also to draw attention to the *theatrical* nature of this event; a performance, in which history is reshaped and transformed by actors, before an audience, on a stage. The Chorus is there to foreground the *artificiality* of the dramatic event, placing a barrier between action and audience. The audience's imaginations are invited inside that barrier to enjoy direct participation in the drama; at the same time, the play is limiting the freedom of reference from the events on the stage back to ordinary everyday reality.

> A kingdom for a stage, princes to act,
> And monarchs to behold the swelling scene.
> (Prologue, 3–4)

[. . .] The way to convince an audience of the truth of dramatic illusion is not, clearly, continually to insist on the illusory nature of the representation. By defining the nature of this dramatic 'mock'ry', the play diminishes rather than enlarges the audience's readiness to receive it as 'true'. The Chorus is concerned then not so much with bestowing epic qualities on the dramatic event, as with exposing the nature of theatrical illusion. The

Chorus has its own kind of heroic language; but it is up to the audience to create an epic experience:

> For 'tis your thoughts that now must deck our kings . . .

In a play, history is created by a peculiar conjuncture of the dramatist's words, the actor's speech and gesture, and the audience's response. If epic is produced, it is produced only in and by these specific theatrical conditions. There is no heroic view of life to be carried away from the theatre – one that would be confirmed and reflected back by the public morality of society, as for the audiences of Homer or of the *Beowulf*-poet. *Henry V* insists too strongly, through its Chorus, on the divergence between theatre and real events for any such simple relationship to hold.

Given these factors, it is no surprise to find that in *Henry V* epic qualities and heroic language are bestowed on unpromising material – on events and characters which cannot, in themselves, evoke anything like a wholehearted epic admiration. Patriotism, heroism, chivalry, the romance of war, can induce admiration and delight only when detached from their actual historical context and safely re-created in the security of the theatre purely as ideological entities. Once the real historical foundations of these ideologies are recognized, they lose their power to charm the imagination. The play is concerned both to isolate these ideologies and extract from them the maximum aesthetic and theatrical effect; while at the same time demonstrating the historical actualities from which they are in practice (though not in the theatre) inseparable. [. . .] What has been created here is the reverse of epic, where the epic hero enacts, for the admiration of the audience, some real problem of public morality; what has been created in this play is a self-mocking dramatic illusion, which inscribes a clear boundary between public morality and the ideological nature of its own 'celebration'.[7]

Various speculations have been attempted about Olivier's motives for locating the drama back into the historical context of the Elizabethan theatre. It has been suggested that the intention was primarily theatrical – to make a film of a stage production, rather than a screen adaptation of a play. Or perhaps the motive was more academic – the equivalent of a scholarly appendix on contemporary stage conditions. Or it was an exercise in cultural philanthropy – purveying the cream of high culture to a popular audience. It does not seem to have been realized that the film, in imitating Shakespeare's Chorus, also incorporates some of the aesthetic devices which work within Shakespeare's drama to undermine the play's traditionalist and official ideology.

The film begins with a shot of empty space – a scrap of paper is windblown through a vacant blue sky; whirled towards the camera, it resolves into a handbill advertising a performance of *Henry V* at the Globe Theatre. In so far as this device demands literal interpretation, it represents exactly that – a handbill tossed by the wind through the sky of Elizabethan London. But that blue sky is also empty space and time: the handbill, before it becomes the title-page of a play, is a scrap of paper arbitrarily carried forward from the past, indecipherable until it unfolds before the camera, meaningless until it is *read*. The film seems to begin by suggesting that the play floats in a turbulent vacuum of history until a process of visualization – of *reproduction* – transforms it into history of a new kind. The faintly disorientating character of this device contrasts sharply with the more familiar evocation of a firm, objectively existent historical tradition which is there to be read off from Shakespeare's text, or the legend of Henry V, or the soul of the English nation.

The camera then displays a reconstructed model (very obviously a model, patently artificial) of Elizabethan London, and a slow crane-shot comes to rest on the Globe Theatre. The camera then penetrates to the interior of the theatre, to show an audience collecting for a performance. A rich assemblage of visual detail seeks to portray a reconstruction of the theatre's atmosphere and tone in a very lively, noisy and sociable gathering, with much public self-display of the nobility, the sale of food and drink; all accompanied by William Walton's effective pseudo-Elizabethan music. The performance proper begins, not with a curtain raised to display a naturalistic *mise-en-scène*, but with a boy displaying a large printed card bearing the play's title – a convention of the Elizabethan theatre (and, incidentally, of Brecht's epic theatre) which disrupts any attempt at naturalistic illusion. There is no attempt at all to translate theatre into film: what is being filmed is a theatre in action.

Throughout Shakespeare's Act I the theatrical conditions are visible: sections of the audience, those seated on the stage and those on the floor or in the galleries; the Prompter, the tiring-room, and so on.

Critics committed to the independence of film as an art, and hostile to any dependence of film on the literary media, have shown impatience with what they see as the inappropriate survival here of theatrical form.[8] But it is much more important to describe the specific aesthetic and ideological effects of this foregrounding of productive devices. As long as the theatrical context remains visible (up to the end of Shakespeare's Act II) the audience can retain the possibility of seeing Henry primarily as an *actor* rather than as a historical character; and this is much more than the ostentatious virtuosity of a famous screen actor displaying itself before the cameras. With this suggestion supplied, the audience can easily make an imaginative jump from theatre to history: this is a king who seems to rule more by the accomplished deployment of theatrical techniques than by statesmanship or good government. The radical and subversive potentiality of Shakespeare's play consists mainly in this tendency of the drama to foregound the artificiality of its dramatic devices; and to create a perspective in which the king can display himself as an *actor* rather than a naturalistic character. Our first glimpse of Henry in the film is not on the stage as king, but in the tiring-room as a nervous actor, numb with stagefright, anxiously clearing his throat: prior to making his entrance to immediate and rapturous applause from a noisy and very visible audience. Henry presents himself to the audience as an actor: with scant respect for the conventions of naturalist drama.

The scene with the clergymen is played as farce, with continual and voluble interventions by the audience; and the high point of Henry's self-dramatization occurs in the film (as it does in the play) in his reaction to the Dauphin's insulting gift of tennis-balls. In this scene the camera employs a device developed by Olivier to overcome some of the difficulties involved in translating drama into film:

> The film climax is a close-up; the Shakespearean climax is a fine gesture and a loud voice. I remember going to George

Cukor's *Romeo and Juliet*. As a film director he did what seemed the right thing when he took the potion scene with Norma Shearer – he crept right up to a huge head, the ordinary film climax. But it was in fact a mistake. She, being a good technician in film-making, cut the power of her acting down as the camera approached her for the climax of that speech leading up to taking the potion – 'Romeo, I come! This do I drink to thee'.

At the moment of climax she was acting very smally, because the camera was near. That was not the way it should have been. So the very first test I made for *Henry V* I tried to see how it would work in reverse. It was in the scene with the French Ambassador, and as I raised my voice the camera went back.[9]

Olivier was speaking here primarily of the function of this technique as it concerned the actor; but the device also makes an important contribution to the 'epic' quality of the film, especially in the realistic, exterior location scenes used to represent Agincourt. The movement from close-up to long-shot doesn't just allow scope for the actor to intensify his performance; it also, more fundamentally, increases the size and multiplies the content of the frame: it supplies more abundance of visual detail thereby bringing more objects, images and characters into significant relationship. Henry's 'Crispin Crispian' speech (IV. iii) before Agincourt begins as a close shot from below depicting Henry himself (whose face, in close-up and soliloquy, has been dominating the screen in the previous sequence). As his speech rises to a climax the camera pulls back and up, to reveal the assembled masses of fighting men around him, all excited by his militaristic rhetoric and infected with his martial enthusiasm. The frame expands from a focus on the leader's personality to an image of the leader as centre of his loyal army: from the psychological to the epic; from the monarch to the nation.

The same technique, used to film the earlier scene with the French Ambassador, has an entirely different effect. A close-up shows Henry's controlled passion of indignation at the Dauphin's insult. As his speech of reply (I. ii. 259–97) rises to a climax, the camera pulls back to reveal – not a naturalistic social setting, but a stage, other costumed actors, an audience, a theatre. The effect is heightened by a deliberate emphasis on Henry as an actor playing to the audience: one shot taken from the back of the stage displays him *acting* before his enthusiastic spectators. His exit line at the end of the scene is delivered as a flourish directly to the audience.

As in Shakespeare's play, then, complete with its alienating device of the Chorus, the king can be characterized as an *actor* rather than a monarch: the drama displays his capacity to masquerade and perform, his ability to generate acclamation and excitement in the *theatrical* context. The *playing* is very obviously *play*. To see this, as many have done, as a naturalistic method of presenting theatre on the screen is seriously to underestimate the subtlety of the film's aesthetic devices; to see the film as concerned simply to offer a 'straight' patriotic version of *Henry V* is to interpret selected parts rather than the film's significant whole. [. . .]

Once the film settles into realistic locations for the battle of Agincourt (locations which occupy a small part of the film, yet which have, significantly, attracted a disproportionate amount of attention) the theatrical framework disappears completely, and with it the film's radical and subversive potentialities. The viewer is immersed in a *real* world which becomes increasingly analogous to the world of contemporary history. Scenes such as that between Henry and the soldiers (IV. i) with all the fear and anxiety of a night before battle – the naturalistically-presented military action showing the defensive preparation of the English and the showy chivalry of the French – were evidently too close to the contemporary experience of war for the film to free itself from, or even to offer qualification of, what becomes its dominant ideology. *Action* replaces *acting*; the serious business of fighting suppresses the freedom of theatrical play; the world of the film becomes more like the Britain of 1940. The critical exigencies of the contemporary situation pull the film back, away from its aesthetic experiments, into complicity with the ideologies of patriotism, war enthusiasm and national unity. This suspension of the viewer's complex awareness of the theatrical event, this immersion of the viewer into a carefully-constructed facsimile of a 'real' world, is so successful that it is with a shock that we see the theatre reappear at the end. The

illusions of naturalism and of conventional theatre have tem-
porarily succeeded in dominating the spectator's imagination:
and through the selectivity of collective memory have enabled
the film to be incorporated more readily into the prevailing
mythology of Britain at war.

Tillyard's study, despite sharing a common subject, common
preoccupations and – ultimately – a common ideology, differs
signally from the other two texts in displaying an apparent
innocence of contemporary engagement. The study is purely a
discourse of academic scholarship, giving the impression that a
characteristic and central activity of English culture has been
quietly proceeding, unravaged by the fierce reality of world
history. While Knight and Olivier were reconstructing
Shakespeare to point his relevance to the nation's crisis,
Tillyard, with a gesture of academic indifference to contemporary events, was patiently clearing the earth of history from the
roots of English culture, re-establishing a continuity with the
Elizabethan age unbroken by crisis, war, threatened invasion,
though this affirmation of continuity is nowhere explicitly
admitted.
    Tillyard's major argument – the legacy of which determined
almost all subsequent criticism of the history plays, and dominated school examining for decades – is that of *order*. The
ideological sources of Shakespeare's history plays lay in
dominant traditions of contemporary thought, expressed in
historiographical and philosophical writings of the Tudor and
Elizabethan period. These asserted that the existing political
state, the 'body politic', could not be considered merely as a
particular form of social organization, but was in reality a
function of a universal order, created and supervised by God,
ruled over, ultimately, by divine providence. A state or human
society occupied a median position in a cosmic hierarchy, with
God and the angels above, and the animal and plant kingdoms
below. The structure of a well-ordered state was itself a micro-
cosm of the hierarchical cosmos – containing within itself a
chain of being, from the monarch at the head, through various
gradations of social rank down to the lowest orders. The ruler of
a body politic possessed power which reflected, but was also
subject to, that of God: a king therefore ruled implicitly by

divine right. The natural condition of a state, therefore, like the natural condition of the cosmos, was order, defined primarily in terms of the maintenance of this rigid hierarchy. Any rupturing of this pattern would produce chaos – since the state was a component of a divine order, such alteration could not be mere social change, but a disruption of a divine and natural order, to the displeasure of God and the destruction of universal law. The extreme forms of such disruption, such as the deposition of a king and the usurpation of a throne, would constitute a gross violation of order, inevitably to be punished by the vengeance of God, operating through the workings of divine providence.[10]

According to Tillyard, this doctrine of order was a dominant Elizabethan ideology. Even the teaching of so influential a thinker as Machiavelli, with his view that 'disorder was the natural state of man', meant little to Shakespeare's contemporaries.

> Such a way of thinking was abhorrent to the Elizabethans (as indeed it always has been and is now to the majority), who preferred to think of order as the norm to which disorder, though lamentably common, was yet the exception.
>
> (Tillyard, p. 21)

This ideology (which, we notice, is *still*, in Tillyard's view, a 'majority' opinion) was Shakespeare's.

> In his most violent representations of chaos Shakespeare never tries to persuade that it is the norm: however long and violent is its sway, it is unnatural; and in the end order and the natural law will reassert themselves.
>
> (p. 23)

> It is not likely that anyone will question my conclusion that Shakespeare's Histories, with their constant pictures of disorder cannot be understood without assuming a larger principle of order in the background. . . . In the total sequence of his plays dealing with the subject-matter of Halle he expressed successfully a universally held and still comprehensible scheme of history: a scheme fundamentally religious, by which events evolve under a law of justice and under the ruling of God's providence, and of which Elizabethan England was the acknowledged outcome.
>
> (pp. 320–1)

Tillyard asserts what appear to be historical facts about a long-vanished age: there is little to suggest that his concern with 'order' – an unspecified and politically ambiguous vision of society – belongs as much to war-time Britain as to Elizabethan England. He never betrays any suggestion that his universal political moral might have relevance to his own time, though it clearly belongs with Wilson Knight's celebration of 'national unity'. The nearest Tillyard comes to an acknowledgement of the claims of contemporary history is this kind of ambiguous aside – discussing the tradition of sentimentalizing Falstaff, he attributes it to Victorian military optimism:

> The sense of security created in nineteenth-century England by the predominance of the British navy induced men to rate that very security too cheaply and to exalt the instinct of rebellion above its legitimate station. They forgot the threat of disorder which was ever present with the Elizabethans. Schooled by recent events, we should have no difficulty now in taking Falstaff as the Elizabethans took him.
>
> (p. 291)

The word 'schooled' matches the ambiguous portentousness of the academic mannerism: participation in history is a matter of education in moral and political wisdom. What Tillyard means by 'recent events' it is scarcely possible to know. 'Rebellion' could refer to the ascension and territorial expansion of fascism. Or it may more probably refer, as Wilson Knight refers, to the paramount necessity for maintaining order and national unity in face of the threat of foreign conquest. 'We' in 1944, in other words, have as much reason to value order, national unity, a strong but humane monarchy, as did the Elizabethans and Shakespeare.

Such an aside is however a flaw in the seamless unity of Tillyard's ideology, which masks its essential conservatism in an impenetrable disguise of academic scholarship. The object we are required to contemplate is not Tillyard thinking about *his* England (as Wilson Knight and Olivier openly declared their patriotic loyalties) but Shakespeare thinking about his:

> *Henry IV* shows a stable society and it is crowded, like no other play of Shakespeare, with pictures of life as it was lived in the

age of Elizabeth. . . . Those who, like myself, believe that Shakespeare had a massively reflective as well as a brilliantly opportunistic brain will expect these matters of Elizabethan life to serve more than one end and will not be surprised if through them he expresses his own feelings about his fatherland. It is also perfectly natural that Shakespeare should have chosen this particular point in the total stretch of history he covered, as suited to this expression. Henry V was traditionally not only the perfect king, but a king after the Englishmen's heart; one who added the quality of good mixer to the specifically regal virtues. The picture of England would be connected with the typical English monarch.

(p. 299)

The concept of Renaissance England as a well-ordered state is, however, infused with a sentimental attachment to the 'everyday' life of England dramatized in *Henry IV Part Two*: into Tillyard's discourse penetrates an emotional tone which declares, unmistakably, that Shakespeare's 'fatherland' is also his. This 'epic' drama offers a comprehensive cross-section of English life, linking the monarchy with the essential, unchanging rhythm of traditional rural society. The emphasis on the enduring quality of traditional social patterns is confirmed by Tillyard's quoting of Hardy's *In Time of the Breaking of Nations*:

'This will go onward the same
Though Dynasties pass.'
. . . From first to last Shakespeare was loyal to the country life. He took it for granted as the norm, as the background before which the more formal or spectacular events were transacted.

(p. 302)

Or, in the words of the popular song: 'There'll always be an England'. The argument and the quotation deliver us back into an organic, immutable 'English' society: a golden age which, though vanished, can yet linger and survive, unravaged by the fierce historical crisis of the present.

The remarkable logical slide from a description of Renaissance ideology to the celebration of an apparently immutable social and cultural entity called 'England' is Tillyard's most effective ideological strategy: it is, in fact, the quality which ensured that of all the cultural interventions of this period, Tillyard's piece of formal *criticism* would survive as the seminal, determinant text. Without making any explicit acknowledgement of the fact that the England of the Second World War is as much an object of address as that of the sixteenth century, Tillyard invokes and affirms values which were being assiduously – and much more openly – cultivated, especially by the works already discussed. [. . .]

Tillyard does not think highly of *Henry V*. He believes the character to be quite inconsistent with the Prince Hal of *Henry IV*, and the play itself to be forced and mechanical. A shying-away from the robust patriotism embraced by Wilson Knight and Olivier is characteristic of Tillyard: writing at a time when the epic heroism of the past could easily be affirmed as living in the present, the scholar relegates it to an inferior status: the play about the nature of 'England' is more important than the play about the military victories of a warrior-king. Tillyard's business was not with winning the war but with reconstituting the national culture in expectation of an Allied victory.

[. . .] A survey of the historical moment of Tillyard's production reveals that it stood in competition with other forms of cultural intervention in some ways more promising and powerful as strategies of ideological constitution. The timeless work of scholarship shares a common ideology with other works which confronted their society much more openly, addressed its problems much more directly, made no secret of the ideological foundation of their cultural productions. Wilson Knight made serious efforts to insert Shakespeare's prophetic vision directly into the texture of national life: he gave readings from Shakespeare with his own commentaries; and in July 1941, at the Westminster Theatre, he staged a bizarre production called *This Sceptred Isle*, which involved the actor Henry Ainley reading Knight's commentaries (from off-stage) and Knight himself acting various speeches from Shakespeare, under headings like 'St George for England', and 'The Royal Phoenix'. The programme announced the production as 'G. Wilson Knight's dramatisation of Shakespeare's Call to Great Britain in Time of War'. Olivier's role in *Henry V* was indistinguishable (apart from the uniform) from his real-life role as patriotic orator, a Churchillian inspiration to the Home Front. In each case there is a serious attempt to address the question of national unity directly, and to convey it through the more immediate, accessible and popular media of theatre, public reading and film.

Wilson Knight's grotesque patriotism and Olivier's martial rhetoric are now consigned to the margins of literary history: yet Tillyard's equally strange discovery of a governing philosophy of 'order' in Elizabethan society and in Shakespeare's plays lives on as a potent ideological force. Evidently the more *ideological* a work of criticism is (in the sense of its involving strong elements of concealment, deception and mystification) the more effective it will be in the long run as a constitutive element of cultural history. To declare a position too openly, as Wilson Knight did, is to render the work vulnerable as criticism: to talk of Shakespeare writing a 'call to arms' for Britain in 1944, or predicting the expansion of British power into world-order through ventures like the Falklands campaign, is to acknowledge far too openly that 'literature' is here being *invented* by the critic to serve a specific, contemporary, political purpose. The case of the Olivier film is different: though it also shows its hand by explicitly drawing analogies with the Second World War, it also contains elements which render it vulnerable in other ways. While its virile patriotism needs to be pushed into one margin of cultural history, it contains elements which demand marginalization in the opposite direction: its experimental foregrounding of aesthetic devices constitutes a subversive tendency which might well call into question the simplicity of its patriotic affirmations.

The distinctive quality of Tillyard's work is evidently its denial of contemporary history, its apparently timeless innocence of political orientation. Where Wilson Knight and Olivier declared, in their different ways, that Britain in her hour of need could turn to Shakespeare, Tillyard quietly affirmed that Shakespeare has always been, is, and always will be 'England'. The effectiveness of the enterprise can be measured by the fact that assent to that proposition can seem like recognition of the long familiar. Shakespeare has 'always' been the national poet, identifiable with the greatest of our cultural achievements, and with the greatest age of our history: what could seem more 'natural' than to invoke his presence in a time of national peril? Such familiarizing, with its absence of any explicit avowal of a determinant historical context, was peculiarly well-adapted to the task of establishing an image of 'Shakespeare's England' which would serve as an ideological power of social cohesion in Churchill's Britain. The scholarly imagination, revisiting a vanished past, severs the history it addresses from the exigencies of the present; and thus insidiously operates on the reader who, aware only of the attention he focuses on Shakespeare, is quite unaware of how an image of his own society is being implicitly celebrated and affirmed.

Many people felt during the Second World War that they were fighting for a new society of democracy, peace and justice: that the ordeal of the war could be made tolerable by assurance that the old society of poverty, inequality, unemployment, could never return. Tillyard offered his readers a different reason for fighting and enduring: to defend the society which existed once, still remains (implicitly) the 'natural' form of political order, and is visible in the works of Shakespeare. In the Labour victory of 1945, it seemed that the old world lay in ruins and was decisively rejected by the people. E.M.W. Tillyard's *Shakespeare's History Plays* was reprinted in 1948, 1951, 1956, 1959, 1961, 1964, 1969 and 1974.

Notes

All quotations from *Henry V* are taken from Gary Taylor (ed.), *The Oxford Shakespeare: Henry V* (Oxford University Press, Oxford 1984). I am indebted to Derek Longhurst's ' "Not for all time, but for an age": an approach to Shakespeare studies', in Peter Widdowson (ed.), *Re-reading English* (Methuen, London 1982). Terence Hawkes pursues a similar line of enquiry *vis-à-vis* J. Dover Wilson in 'Telmah' in *Shakespeare and the Question of Theory*, ed. Patricia Parker and Geoffrey Hartman (Methuen, London 1986).

1 G. Wilson Knight, *The Olive and the Sword* (Oxford University Press, Oxford 1944), p. 3; Randolph Churchill (ed.), *Into Battle: Speeches by Winston Churchill* (Cassell, London 1941), p. 256; Laurence Olivier, quoted from an interview, BBC, 17 October 1982; E.M.W. Tillyard, *Shakespeare's History Plays* (Chatto & Windus, London 1944), p. 8.

2 See Peter Widdowson, 'Hardy in history', *Literature and History*, 9: 1 (Spring 1983).

3 See Alan Sinfield, 'Shakespeare in education' and 'Royal Shakespeare', and Graham Holderness, 'Shakespeare in film and television', in *Political Shakespeare*, ed. Jonathan Dollimore and Alan Sinfield (Manchester University Press, Manchester 1985). See also Graham Holderness and Christopher McCullough, 'Boxing the Bard: the cultural politics of television Shakespeare', *Red Letters*, 18 (1985).

4 Clayton C. Hutton, *The Making of 'Henry V'* (Hutton, Englewood Cliffs 1944).

5 See e.g. Frederick Aicken, 'Shakespeare on the screen', *Screen Education*, (Sept.–Oct. 1963), p. 33; and J. Blumenthal, *'Macbeth into Throne of Blood'*, *Sight and Sound*, 34 (1965), p. 194.

6 See J. H. Walter (ed.), *King Henry V* (Methuen, London 1954), pp. xiv–xvii.

7 For further discussion of the Chorus see Graham Holderness, *Shakespeare's History* (Gill & Macmillan, Dublin 1985), pp. 136ff.

8 See Blumenthal, *'Macbeth'*, pp. 191–2 and 195n.; Aicken, 'Shakespeare', p. 34; and Michael Balcon *et al.*, *20 Years of British Film (1925–45)* (Falcon Press, London 1947).

9 Quoted in Roger Manvell, *Shakespeare and the Film* (Dent, London 1971), pp. 37–8.

10 For further discussion of Tillyard's influence see Alan Sinfield and Jonathan Dollimore, 'History and ideology', in *Alternative Shakespeares*, ed. John Drakakis (Methuen, London 1985).

Production and reproduction: the case of *Frankenstein*

PAUL O'FLINN

Mary Shelley's Gothic novel *Frankenstein* was published anonymously in 1818. In the same year, a couple of other novels – Peacock's *Nightmare Abbey* and Jane Austen's *Northanger Abbey* – also appeared and their derisive use of Gothic conventions suggested that the form, fashionable for fifty years, was sliding into decline and disrepute. There seemed good reason to suppose that *Frankenstein*, an adolescent's first effort at fiction, would fade from view before its print run was sold out.

Yet several generations later Mary Shelley's monster, having resisted his creator's attempts to eliminate him in the book, is able to reproduce himself with the variety and fertility that Frankenstein had feared. Apart from steady sales in Penguin, Everyman and OUP editions, there have been over a hundred film adaptations and there have been the Charles Addams cartoons in the *New Yorker*; Frankie Stein blunders about in the pages of *Whoopee* and *Monster Fun* comics, and approximate versions of the monster glare out from chewing gum wrappers and crisp bags. In the USA he forged a chain of restaurants; in South Africa in 1955 the work was banned as indecent and objectionable.[1]

None of these facts is new and some of them are obvious to anyone walking into a newsagent's with one eye open. They are worth setting out briefly here because *Frankenstein* seems to me to be a case where some recent debates in critical theory about cultural production and reproduction might usefully be centred, a work whose history can be used to test the claims that theory makes.[2] That history demonstrates clearly the futility of a search for the 'real', 'true' meaning of a work. There is no such thing as *Frankenstein*, there are only *Frankensteins*, as the text is ceaselessly rewritten, reproduced, refilmed and redesigned. The fact that many people call the monster Frankenstein and thus confuse the pair betrays the extent of that restructuring. What I would like to offer is neither a naive deconstructionist delight at the endless plurality of meanings the text has been able to afford nor a gesture of cultural despair at the failure of the philistines to read the original and get it right. Instead I'd like to argue that at its moment of production *Frankenstein*, in an oblique way, was in touch with central tensions and contradictions in industrial society and only by seeing it in those terms can the prodigious efforts made over the last century and a half to alter and realign the work and its meanings be understood – a work that lacked that touch and that address could safely be left, as Marx said in another context, to the gnawing criticism of the mice.

Frankenstein is a particularly good example of three of the major ways in which alteration and realignment of this sort happens: first, through the operations of criticism; second, as a function of the shift from one medium to another; and third, as a result of the unfolding of history itself. The operations of criticism on this text are at present more vigorous than usual. When I was a student twenty years ago I picked up the *Pelican Guide to English Literature* to find the novel more or less wiped out in a direly condescending half-sentence as 'one of those second-rate works, written under the influence of more distinguished minds, that sometimes display in conveniently simple form the preoccupations of a coterie'.[3] *Frankenstein* may have been on TV but it wasn't on the syllabus. A generation and a lot of feminist criticism later and Mary Shelley is no longer a kind of half-witted secretary to Byron and Shelley but a woman writer whose text articulates and has been convincingly shown to articulate elements of woman's experience of patriarchy, the family and the trauma of giving birth.[4]

The second instance – the way a text's meaning alters as it moves from one medium to another – is something I'd like to look at in more detail later in this essay by examining the two classic screen versions: Universal's movie directed in 1931 by James Whale and starring Boris Karloff, and Terence Fisher's picture for Hammer Films in 1957 with Peter Cushing. Literary criticism only metaphorically rewrites texts: the words on the page remain the same but the meanings they are encouraged to release differ. But a shift of medium means the literal rewriting of a text as novel becomes script becomes film. Scope for the ideological wrenching and reversing of a work and its way of seeing is here therefore even larger. [. . .] The third category is one I suggested earlier – namely the way in which the movement of history itself refocuses a text and reorders its elements. *Frankenstein*, I would like to argue, meant certain things in 1818, but meant and could be made to mean different things in 1931 and 1957, irrespective of authorial 'intention'. [. . .]

Mary Shelley's monster, in short, is ripped apart by one or more of at least three processes in each generation and then put together again as crudely as Victor Frankenstein constructed the original in his apartment. Faced with these processes, traditional literary criticism can either, with a familiar gesture, pretend not to notice and insist instead that *Frankenstein* 'spanned time' with 'timeless and universal themes' that 'live beyond literary fashion'.[5] Or it can pay attention to those changes but slip past the power and the politics that they imply, so that shifts in the work's presentation become a plain mirror of human evolution: 'the Monster . . . is no longer separate, he is quite simply ourselves';[6] 'it is a magnified image of ourselves.'[7] Capitalism creates and re-creates monsters; capitalist ideology then invites us to behold ourselves. I'd like to try to do something else.

First I would like to argue that much of the text's strength that continues to be released derives from certain issues in the decade of its composition, issues that the text addresses itself to in oblique, imaginative terms and that remain central and unresolved in industrial society. In that decade those issues erupted more turbulently than ever before: they were, briefly, the impact of technological developments on people's lives and the possibility of working-class revolution. Those issues fuel the

Luddite disturbances of 1811–17 and the Pentridge rising of 1817.

There had been instances of machine-breaking before in British history but never with the same frequency and intensity. The size of the army marshalled to squash the Luddites – six times as big as any used previously for internal conflicts in the estimate of one historian[8] – is a measure of the extent to which the new technologies, in the first generation of the industrial revolution, threatened traditional livelihoods and provoked violent resistance. There is the same sort of new and disruptive energy evident in the Pentridge rising of June 1817, when 300 men marched towards Nottingham on the expectation of similar marches, designed to overthrow the Government, occurring across the country. The group was soon rounded up by Hussars and three of its leaders executed in November. The revolt ended in shambles and failure but its significance for E.P. Thompson is epochal – it was 'one of the first attempts in history to mount a wholly proletarian insurrection, without any middle-class support'.[9]

The composition of *Frankenstein* needs to be seen in the context of these deep changes in the nature of British society. Mary began work on the novel in June 1816 at the Maison Chapuis, Montalègre, near Geneva, where she was living with Shelley. Byron lived nearby at the Villa Diodati and the book's impetus came from Byron's challenge – 'We will each write a ghost story' – during one of their regular evening visits. The point is that as Mary set about writing her first novel she was working alongside two men who had responded publicly and politically to the Luddite crisis. Byron's magnificent maiden speech in the House of Lords in February 1812 had attacked Tory proposals to extend the death penalty for machine-breaking, denouncing a process whereby men were 'sacrificed to improvements in mechanism'. And then in January 1813, when fourteen men were executed at York for Luddite activities, Harriet Shelley had written to the radical London bookseller Thomas Hookham on Shelley's behalf: 'I see by the Papers that those poor men who were executed at York have left a great many children. Do you think a subscription would be attended to for their relief? If you think it would, pray put down our names and advertise it in the Papers.'[10] Mary and Percy returned to

England from Geneva in September 1816 and Luddites were still being hanged in April 1817 as Mary made the last revisions to her manuscript. Before *Frankenstein*'s publication in March 1818, Shelley reacted to the execution of the leaders of the Pentridge rising with *An Address to the People on the Death of Princess Charlotte*, a forceful political pamphlet published in November 1817 and eagerly read by Mary, as she noted in her journal. The pamphlet lamented the 'national calamity' of a country torn between abortive revolt and despotic revenge – 'the alternatives of anarchy and oppression'.[11]

What was Mary Shelley's own response to these events and reactions? To try to pass *Frankenstein* off as a conservative riposte to the politics of Godwin and Shelley, as Muriel Spark has done,[12] is to ignore the book's brave dedication to the unpopular Godwin as well as Mary's own correct anticipation that a 'courtly bookseller' like John Murray would refuse to publish it when the manuscript was offered to him.[13] (It is also, as we shall see in a moment, to ignore most of the book's contents.) Similarly, to describe her politics at the time she wrote *Frankenstein* as 'innately conservative', as Jane Dunn does,[14] is to muddle her views in middle age with those she held at eighteen – often a mistake with Romantic writers and particularly so in Mary Shelley's case. Her letters around the time of *Frankenstein* reveal a woman who shared the radicalism of Byron and Shelley. The result was a politics shaped by a passión for reform, a powerful hatred of Tory despotism with its 'grinding & pounding & hanging and taxing' and a nervousness about the chance of the revolutionary violence such despotism might provoke. Thus, for example, she wrote to Shelley in September 1817 between the completion of *Frankenstein* in May and its publication the following March:

> Have you seen Cobbett's 23 No. to the Borough mongers – Why he appears to be making out a list for proscription – I actually shudder to read it – a revolution in this country would (not?) be *bloodless* if that man has any power in it. . . . He encourages in the multitude the worst possible human passion *revenge* or as he would probably give it that abominable *Christian* name retribution.[15]

Her politics here in short are those of a radical liberal agonizing in the face of the apparent alternatives of 'anarchy and oppression', to use the phrase which, as we have already seen, Shelley was to deploy six weeks later in his *Princess Charlotte* pamphlet. That politics also addressed itself to contemporary scientific and technological developments and their social implications. Discussion and speculation at the Villa Diodati ranged across galvanism and Darwin's experiments, as Mary carefully notes in her 1831 introduction to the novel. In the autumn of 1816, as she completed her manuscript, she read Davy's *Elements of Chemical Philosophy*.

It is out of these politics and this way of seeing that *Frankenstein* emerges. It is a multi-layered work; it includes odds and ends like her passing interest in recent British and Russian polar expeditions, and it is padded in parts with wads of her tourist's diary of a trip to Chamonix.[16] What I would like to show by turning to the text itself in the next two sections is that one of these layers, a layer that accounts for a lot of the story's vigorous, protean life, is an imaginative rendering of the two issues – scientific-technological developments and working-class revolt – which, as we have seen, asserted themselves violently in the half-dozen years preceding the text's production. It is a layer whose boundaries are drawn by the author's politics.

Mary Shelley's interest in scientific questions has been well documented[17] and this interest is built into the very narrative structure of her novel. Frankenstein's story is itself framed by the story of Walton, the polar explorer whom Frankenstein meets and to whom he tells his tale. Through the twin narratives of Walton and Frankenstein Mary Shelley presents two models of scientific progress. Both men are obsessed by the urge to discover and both pursue that obsession, enticed by the possibility of 'immortality and power' that success would bring. In the end the pursuit kills Frankenstein whereas Walton survives. What is the difference?

The difference is the sailors on Walton's expedition ship. Frankenstein works alone but Walton works with a crew and it is the crew who force Walton to turn back when they realize that the reckless drive through the polar ice will cost everyone's lives. Several things are worth noting at this point. First, Frankenstein makes a forceful speech aimed at changing the sailors' minds by reminding them of the honour that even failure will bring and still holding out the dream of heroic success. Second, Walton turns back not, as has been argued, for altruistic reasons or for the sake of his sister,[18] but simply because he is forced to by the threat of mutiny, to his own fury and frustration:

> The die is cast; I have consented to return, if we are not destroyed. Thus are my hopes blasted by cowardice and indecision; I come back ignorant and disappointed. It requires more philosophy than I possess, to bear this injustice with patience.

> (p. 215)

And third, Mary Shelley takes care to distance her readers' sympathies from both Frankenstein's pleas and Walton's anger by pushing those sympathies towards the sailors. [. . .] What the text then appears to offer is a straightforward contrast. Scientific development subject to some form of strong democratic control – even in the violent form of mutiny – can avert the dangers its researchers encounter and save human beings from the possibly fatal consequences of those researches. That is Walton's story. But scientific advance pursued for private motives and with no reining and directing social control or sense of social responsibility leads directly to catastrophe. That is Frankenstein's story. The text does not, contrary to Christopher Small's claim, offer us hand-wringing about some abstracted and reified 'irresponsibility of science'.[19] Rather it sees scientific development as neutral, its results tolerable or disastrous entirely depending on the circumstances in which they are produced.

Seen from this angle, the function of certain elements in the text becomes clearer – in particular those elements which emphasize the dangers of acting alone and illustrate the help that can be provided by other people. Walton's project is especially perilous because it 'hurries me out of the common pathways of men, even to the wild sea and unvisited regions I am about to explore' (p. 22) but he has to go with a crew and they save him, as we have seen. From the start he is aware of the need of a colleague 'to approve or amend my plans' (p. 19) and hence his delight on meeting Frankenstein. The latter, by contrast, works deliberately alone. His move to Ingolstadt where he begins his research cuts him off from Geneva where he had 'ever been surrounded by amiable companions' (p. 45) and he stays away from them for two years. He constructs the monster 'in a solitary chamber, or rather cell, at the top of the house . . . separated from all the other apartments' (p. 55), just as later he goes to 'the remotest of the Orkneys' (p. 163) to begin building the monster's mate.

Studded through the text as miniatures of its central message are moments when disaster, threatening a lone individual, is avoided by the interventions of others. The ship's master provides the solution to the tangled affairs of the young Russian Lady; Frankenstein's father rescues Caroline Beaufort from a life of beggary and she in turn pulls Elizabeth Lavenza and Justine Moritz out of similar misery. Frankenstein's life is saved when he appears to be mortally ill by the ministrations of his friend Clerval, and then there is the complex story, told by the monster, of Felix who liberates the Turk facing execution. The text's thrust on a series of levels is naively clear: for people together, problems can be solved; for the man alone, they can overwhelm.

The monster describes a crucial part of his education as follows:

> Every conversation of the cottagers now opened new wonders to me. When I listened to the instructions which Felix bestowed upon the Arabian, the strange system of human society was explained to me. I heard of the division of property, of immense wealth and squalid poverty; of rank, descent, and noble blood.
>
> The words induced me to turn towards myself. I learned that the possessions most esteemed by your fellow-creatures were high and unsullied descent united with riches. A man might be respected with only one of these advantages; but, without either, he was considered, except in very rare instances, as a vagabond and a slave, doomed to waste his powers for the profits of the chosen few! And what was I? Of my creation and creator I was absolutely ignorant; but I

knew that I possessed no money, no friends, no kind of property.

(pp. 119–20)

Looking at that passage, it is perhaps worth remembering that the first person to offer the text as a straightforward allegory of the class struggle is not some vulgar Marxist in the twentieth century but one of the book's protagonists. Read as the monster suggests, the novel argues that, just as Frankenstein's creation drives him through exhausting and unstinting conflicts to his death, so too a class called into being by the bourgeoisie and yet rejected and frustrated by it will in the end turn on that class in fury and vengeance and destroy it.

This way of seeing the work, as well as being overtly stated by the work itself, is rendered more likely if we look again for a moment at the text's context. Lee Sterrenburg has documented the extent to which the populace as a monster, bent on the destruction of the ruling class and its property, figures as a standard trope in conservative journalism in the generation after the French Revolution.[20] During the Luddite years, the monster appeared to some to be on the loose. Factories in Yorkshire were fired in January and April 1812 and in March and April in Lancashire; there were murders, attempted assassinations and executions again and again between 1812 and 1817. During the most famous attack, on Rawfolds mill in the Spen Valley in April 1812, two of the Luddites were killed and 'Vengeance for the Blood of the Innocent' appeared chalked on walls and doors in Halifax after one of the funerals.

In the midst of this crisis, Mary Shelley picks up a way of seeing – the populace as a destructive monster – provided by Tory journalism and tries to re-think it in her own radical-liberal terms. And so in the novel the monster remains a monster – alien, frightening, violent – but is drenched with middle-class sympathy and given central space in the text to exercise the primary liberal right of free speech which he uses to appeal for the reader's pity and understanding. The caricatured people-monster that haunts the dominant ideology is re-produced through Mary Shelley's politics and becomes a contradictory figure, still ugly, vengeful and terrifying but now also human and intelligent and abused.

In addition, incidents in the class struggles of the 1810s are projected into the text. The monster too turns on the De Lacey family he has worked for and, in chapter 16, burns their property to the ground. That pattern of murders and reprisals that characterizes the history of the decade also constitutes much of the plot of the novel. The demand for vengeance flared on the walls of Halifax in 1812 and again and again the terms 'vengeance' and 'revenge' erupt in the text to describe the relations of Frankenstein and monster–on, for example, pages 92, 136, 138, 142, 145, 168, 202 and 220. It is of course precisely a violent class politics fuelled principally by 'the worst possible human passion *revenge*' that Mary wrote in fear of to Shelley, as we saw earlier, shortly before the publication of *Frankenstein*.

To see the text in these terms is not, as I have argued already, a daft left-wing distortion but a reading suggested by the text itself and one that is also apparent if we turn to the way the text was taken up in the nineteenth century. In 1848, for example, the year of revolutions and of the *Communist Manifesto*, Elizabeth Gaskell published *Mary Barton*, the first English novel with a Communist as its protagonist. Describing John Barton she writes at one point:

> And so on into the problems and mysteries of life, until, bewildered and lost, unhappy and suffering, the only feeling that remained clear and undisturbed in the tumult of his heart, was hatred to the one class, and keen sympathy with the other.
>
> But what availed his sympathy. No education had given him wisdom; and without wisdom, even love, with all its effects, too often works but harm. He acted to the best of his judgment, but it was a widely-erring judgment.
>
> The actions of the uneducated seem to me typified in those of Frankenstein, that monster of many human qualities, ungifted with a soul, a knowledge of the difference between good and evil.
>
> The people rise up to life; they irritate us, they terrify us, and we become their enemies. Then, in the sorrowful moment of our triumphant power, their eyes gaze on us with mute reproach. Why have we made them what they are; a powerful

monster, yet without the inner means for peace and happiness?[21]

What is intriguing about this reference is that Elizabeth Gaskell obviously hasn't read the book – she confuses Frankenstein with the monster and she doesn't know that the monster has a very clear knowledge of the difference between good and evil. What she has absorbed instead and passes on is the dominant political reading of the text, the sense that the middle classes are threatened by a monster of their own making. That monster, as we have seen, was manufactured out of the violence and anxieties of the Luddite decade; a generation later, at the peak of the Chartist decade, Elizabeth Gaskell reaches into cultural mythology to find the imaginative terms for her own predicament and that of her class.

It is significant that this political reproduction of the text persists and tends to surface at times of sharpening conflict. The 1961 Supplement to the *Oxford English Dictionary* notes Sidney Webb's use in *Fabian Essays*, published in 1889 at the height of the socialist revival: 'The landlord and the capitalist are both finding that the steam engine is a Frankenstein which they had better not have raised.' And the 1972 Supplement quotes the *Daily Telegraph*, 3 May 1971: 'There are now growing indications that the Nationalists in South Africa have created a political Frankenstein which is pointing the way to a non-white political revival.' Again, in both cases, monster and Frankenstein are muddled, indicating a level in ideology at which the text itself has ceased to exist but a myth and a metaphor torn and twisted from it is being strenuously put to work.

This separating of myth and metaphor from text and constructing something entirely new in ideology begins very early. In September 1823, Mary Shelley wrote to Leigh Hunt that she found herself famous – not for her novel but for a stage adaptation of it called *Presumption, or the Fate of Frankenstein* by Richard Brinsley Peake that was having a successful run in London. The title betrays the way the work is already being realigned as one idea in the complex structure is pulled out and foregrounded, and this foregrounding is underscored by a statement on the playbills for the opening performance on 28 July at the English Opera House: 'The striking moral exhibited in this story is the

fatal consequence of that presumption which attempts to penetrate, beyond prescribed depths, into the mysteries of
nature.'[22] Frankenstein certainly concludes from his own experience that the pursuit of knowledge ought to be prohibited,
but the text does not endorse that kind of obscurantist morality,
particularly by its placing of the contrasting Walton story. But
the later, more conservative and religious Mary Shelley slides
towards this position, so that we find her insisting in the 1831
introduction: 'supremely frightful would be the effect of any
human endeavour to mock the stupendous mechanism of
the Creator of the world'. She herself, in fact, is among the
first to nudge the text into the space occupied by the dominant
ideology, and we can also see that nudging going on in some
of the revisions she makes for this third 1831 edition; for example,
Elizabeth Lavenza is no longer Frankenstein's cousin, so that the
potentially offensive hint of incest is deleted, while the orthodox
notion of the family as moral and emotional sanctuary is
boosted by the addition of several passages in the early chapters
idealizing the domestic harmony of Frankenstein's childhood.[23]
If ideology has taken hold of *Frankenstein* and remade it for its
own purposes, Mary Shelley led with her own suggestions about
how it might be done.

What I would like to do in the rest of this essay is to look at the
two most famous reproductions of *Frankenstein* in the twentieth
century, namely Universal's *Frankenstein* directed in 1931 by
James Whale and starring Boris Karloff as the monster, and
Hammer Films' *The Curse of Frankenstein* directed by Terence
Fisher with Peter Cushing as Baron Frankenstein. The constructions and the operations of ideology are complex, and
within the scope of an essay I cannot hope to do more than
gesture at what seem to me to be the implications of the content
of those two versions; wider questions about, for example, the
precise relationship within the movie industry between honest
popular entertainment, calculated profit-seeking, capitalist
propaganda and painstaking aesthetic practice must inevitably
be left to one side. [. . .]

That said, there seem to me to be at least three different types
of shift that need to be borne in mind when looking at the gap
between Mary Shelley's book and twentieth-century films;

those shifts concern medium, audience and content. In the case of *Frankenstein*, the shift of medium is particularly important because it must inevitably obliterate and replace what is central to the novel's meaning and structure – namely the patterned movement through three narrators as the reader is taken by way of Walton's letters into Frankenstein's tale and on to the monster's autobiography before backing out through Franken-stein's conclusions to be left with Walton's last notes. That process cannot be filmed and so the very medium demands changes even before politics and ideology come into play.

The turning of novel into film also involves a change in the nature of the work's audience. David Punter has convincingly argued that the Gothic novel is pre-eminently a middle-class form in terms of authors and values as well as readership.[24] The films in question are middle-class in none of these senses, produced as they are by large businesses in search of mass audiences. That different site of production and area of distri-bution will again bear down on the work, pulling, stretching and clipping it to fit new needs and priorities.

Where this pulling, stretching and clipping appears most obviously is in the alterations in the third category mentioned earlier, namely the work's content, and I would like to detail some of those in a moment. What needs emphasizing here is that the radical change in the class nature of producer and audience hacks away at the content of the original, so that the book is reduced to no more than an approximate skeleton, fleshed out in entirely and deliberately new ways. This makes it quite different from, for example, a BBC serial of a Jane Austen novel, where some attempt is made at a reasonably faithful reproduction of the text. It is therefore a traditional critical strategy in reviewing such serials to ask questions about how 'true' to the text, how 'accurate', is the portrayal of, say, Fitzwilliam Darcy or Emma Woodhouse. It is the failure to see this difference that makes one reviewer's querulous response to the 1931 film quite laughably beside the point:

> Mary Shelley's story has artistic interest as an essay in German horrific romanticism and I think that if *Frankenstein* had been produced by a historically-minded German the result would have been much more interesting. . . . What is

the object of taking Mary Shelley's story and then removing the whole point of it before starting to make the picture?[25]

The object, of course, is precisely to remove the whole point of it – and substitute other ones. Other ones are necessary for several reasons – not least because there are no immutable fears in human nature to which horror stories always speak in the same terms. There is not, for all David Punter's strenuous arguing, 'some inner social and cultural dynamic which makes it necessary for those images to be kept alive' (p. 424); rather, those images need to be repeatedly broken up and reconstituted if they are to continue to touch people, which is one of the reasons why horror films that are 30 or 40 years old can often seem simply boring or preposterous to a later audience.

The Universal movie was calculated quite precisely to touch the audiences of 1931. At that time Universal was not one of the front-rank Hollywood studios; its rather cautious and unimaginative policies had left it some distance adrift of the giants of the industry at the end of the 1920s, namely Famous Players, Loews and First National.[26] But a way out of the second rank seemed to offer itself with the huge box office success of Universal's *Dracula*, starring Bela Lugosi, which opened in February 1931 and soon grossed half a million dollars. In April Universal bought the rights of Peggy Webling's *Frankenstein: An Adventure in the Macabre*. The play had run in London in 1930 and its title already suggests a tilting of the work away from Mary Shelley's complex scientific and political statement towards those conventional terror terms for which *Dracula* had indicated a market. *Frankenstein*, filmed in August and September 1931, was an even bigger profit-maker than *Dracula*. Costing a quarter of a million dollars to make, it eventually earned Universal 12 million dollars, was voted one of the films of 1931 by the *New York Times* and confirmed a fashion for horror movies that was soon to include Paramount's *Dr Jekyll and Mr Hyde* and Universal's *The Murders in the Rue Morgue*. In looking at the content of this movie I'd like to confine my comments to those three areas where the shifts from the novel seem to me most important in terms of the ideological and political re-jigging that they betray; those areas are the Walton story, the nature of the monster and the ending.

The point about the Walton story is a simple one: it has gone.

It is not there in the immediate source of the movie, namely Peggy Webling's play, where its disappearance is partly prompted by the need to cram a novel into the average duration of a play. But the fact is that to take away half of Mary Shelley's statement is to change it. It was argued earlier that the function of the Walton story within the text's meaning is to offer a different model of scientific and technological progress, one in which human survival is ensured as long as that progress is under firm and effective popular control. Remove that narrative and the work collapses into Frankenstein's experience alone which can then be presented as a universal model, replete with the sort of reactionary moralizing about the dangers of meddling with the unknown and the delights of tranquillity which are implicit in that tale and made explicit at more than one point. The film can then more easily slide towards a wider statement about the perils of any kind of progress and change, feeding fears of the unknown that change brings and reinforcing those conservative values that stand in its way.

On the question of the nature of the monster, the most important revision here concerns the creature's brain. The film adds a new episode in which an extra character called Fritz, Frankenstein's assistant, is sent to a laboratory to steal a brain for the monster. In that laboratory are two such pickled organs, in large jars boldly labelled NORMAL BRAIN and ABNORMAL BRAIN. Before the theft, the audience hears an anatomy lecture from Professor Waldman in which he draws attention to various features of the normal brain, 'the most perfect specimen', and contrasts them with the abnormal brain whose defects drive its owner to a life of 'brutality, of violence and murder' because of 'degenerate characteristics'. Its original owner was, in fact, 'a criminal'. The lecture over, Fritz creeps in, grabs the normal brain and then lets it slip so that jar and contents are smashed on the floor. He is forced to take the abnormal brain instead.

The implications for the monster and his story are immense. A central part of Mary Shelley's thesis is to insist that the monster's eventual life of violence and revenge is the direct product of his social circumstances. The monster summarizes his own life in terms that the text endorses: 'Every where I see bliss, from which I alone am irrevocably excluded. I was benevolent and good; misery made me a fiend. Make me happy, and I shall again be virtuous' (p. 100). The film deletes this reading of the story through its insistence that the monster's behaviour is not a reaction to its experience but biologically determined, a result of nature, not nurture.

Most commentators on the film are bewildered by this change, one not found in Peggy Webling's play. It has been variously dismissed as an 'absurd and unnecessary sequence . . . a cumbersome attempt at establishing motivation', 'ridiculous' and 'the main weakness.'[27] If seen from Mary Shelley's stance, these comments are true; seen in terms of the film's ideological project, they miss the point. At one level in the text, Mary Shelley was concerned to suggest, in the imaginative terms of fiction, that Luddite violence was not the result of some brute characteristics of the nascent English working class but an understandable response to intolerable treatment. The Universal film, consciously or unconsciously, destroys the grounds for such a way of seeing with its radical political implications and instead sees violence as rooted in personal deficiencies, to be viewed with horror and to be labelled, literally, ABNORMAL and so sub-human. Bashing the monster ceases to be the problem but becomes instead the only way that the problem can be met and solved. So it is that Mary Shelley is stood on her head and *Frankenstein* is forced to produce new meanings for 1931.

This upending of Mary Shelley's book and its meaning explains two other profound changes in the monster's presentation that the film introduces. In the text, the monster spends chapters 11 to 16 describing his life – a huge speech that is placed right in the centre of the novel and fills over 20 per cent of its pages. In the film the monster can't speak. Again, in the novel, the monster saves a child from drowning in chapter 16; in the film, the monster drowns a child. Both reversals are of a piece with the Abnormal Brain scene and flow from it in that both deliberately seek to suppress audience sympathy for the monster. (Hence, when in the 1935 sequel *Bride of Frankenstein* the monster did speak, Boris Karloff protested that it made him seem 'more human', so that in the second sequel, *Son of Frankenstein* in 1939, he is again wordless.) The changes sharpen a re-focusing which is itself part of the shift from novel to film: reading the book, we hear the monster at eloquent length but we don't see him except vaguely, in imagination, and so reader sympathy is easily evoked; watching the film, we hear nothing from him but instead we see a shambling goon with a forehead like a brick wall and a bolt through his neck, and so audience revulsion is promptly generated. Thus the novel makes him human while the film makes him sub-human, so that in the novel his saving of the drowning child is predictable while equally predictable is his drowning of the child in the film.

The way the film ends flows directly from the drowning of the child and so brings me to the third and last piece of ideological restructuring in the Universal movie that I'd like to look at. In the novel, Frankenstein dies in his pursuit of the monster across the icy Arctic while the latter, in the final sentence, is 'borne away by the waves, and lost in darkness and distance'. In the film, the drowning of the child provokes the villagers to pursue the brute and trap it in an old windmill which is then burnt down; a brief, single-shot coda shows a recovered Frankenstein happily reunited with his fiancée Elizabeth. The politics of the mill-burning scene are overt: as the blaze engulfs the blades they form a gigantic fiery cross that deliberately suggests the Ku Klux Klan, virulently active at the time, and so, as Tropp crudely puts it, 'points up the mob violence that does the monster in' (p. 97). Similarly, another observer sees the film ending 'with what Whale called "the pagan sport of a mountain man-hunt"; at the finale, the film's sympathies are with the monster rather than with the lynch mob'.[28]

These may have been Whale's intentions but there is a wide gap between director's aims and the movie as distributed. In Whale's original version, in the drowning scene, the girl dies because the monster innocently tries to make her float on the water like the flowers they are playing with and then searches frantically for her when she sinks. But these moments were chopped from the print of the film put out for general release: there we simply see the monster reaching out towards the girl and then cut to a grief-stricken father carrying her corpse. Child rape and murder are the obvious assumptions, so that the immediate response of the community in organizing itself to eliminate the savage culprit comes across as a kind of ritual cleansing of that community, the prompt removal of an inhuman threat to civilized life which is comfortably justifiable within routine populist politics and at the same time provides the firm basis for and so receives its sanction from the conventionally romantic final scene of hero and heroine at last happy and free from danger. If Mary Shelley's monster alludes indirectly to working-class insurrection, one answer to that canvassed in the 1930s was counter-revolutionary mob violence.

Political readings of the film tend to see it either in simple reflectionist terms (Tropp, for example, regards the monster as 'a creature of the '30s shaped by shadowy forces beyond its control, wandering the countryside like some disfigured veteran or hideous tramp' (p. 93), while another finds 'a world in which manipulations of the stock-market had recoiled on the manipulators; in which human creatures seemed to be abandoned by those who had called them in being and those who might have been thought responsible for their welfare'[29]) or as escapist – 'Large sections of the public, having difficulty in dealing with the Depression, were glad to spend some time in the company of a monster that could more easily be defeated.'[30] Readings of that sort can only be more or a lot less inspired speculation. I'd prefer to look within the film and see it as a *practice*, as an intervention in its world rather than just a picture of it or a retreat from it, a practice whose extent is marked out by the reconstruction of the text that I have indicated. Certainly it was released in the depths of the Depression, depths which can shock even when seen from Thatcherite Britain. The value of manufactured goods and services produced in the USA in 1929 had stood at 81 billion dollars and output at 119 (1923 = 100); as the film criss-crossed the nation in 1932, the value of goods and services had more than halved to 40 billion dollars and output was down to 64. There were 14 million unemployed. How the film reflects that catastrophe or seeks to escape from it is less important than what it says to it. As we saw earlier, it is historically at precisely such moments of crisis that Frankenstein's monster tends to be summoned by ideology and have its arm brutally twisted till it blurts out the statements that ideology demands. What Universal's *Frankenstein* seeks to say specifically to the mass audience at whom it is aimed concerns above all mass activity in times of crisis: where that activity might be assertive and democratic and beneficial (the Walton story), it is removed and concealed; where it is violent and

insurrectionary (the monster's story), it is systematically deni-
grated; and where it is traditional and reactionary (the mill-
burning), it is ambiguously endorsed. The extent to which the
film powerfully articulates those familiar stances of the dominant ideology in the 1930s is measured by its box-office success.

The fact that Frankenstein's monster is most urgently hailed at
times of crisis perhaps accounts for the fact that, with the jokey
exception of Universal's *Abbott and Costello Meet Frankenstein* in
1948, the English-speaking movie industry left the brute alone
between 1945 (Universal's *House of Dracula*) and 1957 (Hammer's *The Curse of Frankenstein*) as the long post-war boom slowly
built up. The Hammer film marked the end of the lengthiest
break in Frankenstein pictures in the past fifty years and was the
first attempt by a British studio to reproduce the story.

The relationships between, say, *Roderick Random* and early
capitalism are complex and highly mediated. The links between
Hammer Films and late capitalism are less obscure; the execu-
tive producer of *The Curse of Frankenstein*, Michael Carreras,
whose family founded Hammer Film Productions in 1947 and
have run it for three generations, has put it simply enough: 'The
best film is the one that makes money. Our job is to entertain
and promote something that is really exploitable. Exploitation
is the thing.'[31] Hammer's policy proceeded directly from this
philosophy and has been well analysed by David Pirie.[32] It
specialized in stories that were already 'pre-sold' to the public
by tradition or by radio or television so that public recognition
of the product was not a problem – hence early films like *PC 49,
The Man in Black, Robin Hood* and so on. At the same time, it
sought for itself an area of the market left untouched by the
dimpled complacencies of Rank and Ealing Studios. These two
strands of policy combined to push it towards horror films, first
with *The Quatermass Experiment* in 1955, a spin-off from the 1953
BBC serial *Quatermass*. The success of both serial and film
prompted Hammer to explore the genre further, and the filming
of *The Curse of Frankenstein* began in November 1956.

The result was a cultural phenomenon whose scale and
importance has certainly been noted but whose significance has
not really been investigated. *The Curse of Frankenstein* is, it has
been claimed, 'the biggest grossing film in the history of the

British cinema in relation to cost.'[33] When it opened in the West End in May 1957 it at once started breaking box-office records and it did the same across the USA that summer. One consequence was that the connections that Hammer had with the American market were rapidly reinforced: in September, for example, Columbia Pictures put Hammer under contract to make three films a year and by 1968 Hammer found itself a recipient of the Queen's Award to Industry after three years in which they had brought a total of £4.5 million in dollars into Britain – this at a time, of course, when most of the rest of the British film industry was in a state of vigorous collapse. In the decade and a half after the success of *The Curse of Frankenstein* Hammer made six sequels, all starring Peter Cushing as the eponymous hero.

In looking at the first of this series, it's Cushing and the part he plays that I would like to focus on, because it is there that the efforts of ideology in putting the myth to work for fresh purposes are most strenuous. At other points – the dropping of the Walton framework, for example – the film simply follows previous practices whose implications have been argued already. It is in the reconstruction of the protagonist that the Hammer film is distinctive, and here the director Terence Fisher was not encumbered by any sense of the original which indeed he had not read. Thus, although Fisher's script (by Jimmy Sangster) was based on the novel, the way was clear for an alignment of the material that was not inhibited by considerations of accuracy, of being 'faithful to the text', but which was free to rework the elements towards those broad Hammer policies of exploitation and money-making.

The singularity of Cushing's role has been spotted by several observers without much attempt being made to see why this should be so.[34] The fact that the film is centred on creator rather than monster in this version is signposted by the way that Boris Karloff, the monster in the Universal movie, at once became a star while Colin Clive, who was Frankenstein, remained obscure; conversely, in the Hammer picture, it was Peter Cushing who featured in the sequels, whereas Christopher Lee never took the part of the monster again.

Central to the specificity of Cushing's part is the way he makes Frankenstein unambiguously the villain of the story and this shift is produced by at least three major changes in his presentation. First and most obviously there are the crimes he commits which have no basis in the text or in previous film versions: to get a brain for his creature he murders a colleague, Professor Bernstein, and later on he sets up the killing of his servant Justine to conceal from his fiancée Elizabeth the fact that he has got her pregnant. Second, there is a marked class mutation that takes a tendency that is apparent in earlier versions several stages further. Mary Shelley's hero is a student, the son of a magistrate; in the Universal movie he becomes the son of a baron; in the Hammer film for the first time he himself is styled Baron Frankenstein and is given decadent aristocratic trappings to go with his title – he becomes, in Pirie's eyes, 'a dandy'. And then thirdly there is the change in age: Mary Shelley's youthful student is turned into Peter Cushing's middle-aged professor. The relevance of that emerges if we remember that 70 per cent of the audience for horror movies in the 1950s were aged twelve to twenty-five, a fact of which the commercially alert Hammer were well aware. A film pitched largely at adolescents could evoke hostility towards the protagonist more easily by transforming him from one of their own kind into a standard adult authority figure.

In short, the ambiguity of earlier readings of the story is removed by these revisions and we are given a Frankenstein to hate – a Frankenstein who, as Martin Tropp points out, is the real monster, a villain who ends the film facing the guillotine and straightforwardly enacting Terence Fisher's own way of seeing: 'If my films reflect my own personal view of the world . . . it is in their showing of the ultimate victory of good over evil, in which I do believe.'[35] Peter Cushing's Baron Frankenstein is a lethal nutter, an archetypal mad scientist.

It is here that the break with the Universal version is sharpest. James Whale had worked specifically to avoid a mad scientist reading of the story and had written to actor Colin Clive insisting that Frankenstein is 'an intensely sane person . . . a sane and lovable person'.[36] And the one moment in Whale's film when this analysis wavers – namely Frankenstein's megalomaniac cry of 'Now I know what it feels like to be God' as his creature moves for the first time – was chopped by pious censors before anybody else got to see it.

What I'd like to argue is that close to the root of this transformation in the reading and reproduction of *Frankenstein* is a shift in the structure of fears within the dominant ideology. The possibility of working-class insurrection that had concerned Mary Shelley and terrified Universal was no longer a prime source of anxiety in 1956. To take one crude statistical indicator of working-class discontent: the number of working days lost, or rather won, in strikes in Britain in the 1940s and 1950s was the lowest in the twentieth century. But on the other hand the development of atomic and hydrogen bombs created a new and dire nightmare of the risk of world destruction flowing from a single, deranged individual – a cultural neurosis that the James Bond novels and films, for instance, were to run and run again through the 1960s and beyond. To imagine a universal catastrophe initiated by one mad scientist was a fear that was simply unavailable to Mary Shelley granted the level of scientific capacities in 1818; indeed, the very word 'scientist' was not coined until 1834. *The Curse of Frankenstein*, by contrast, was made at a time when the processes of science seemed to threaten human survival. As David Pirie points out, six months before filming began, a headline in *The Times* on 21 May 1956 had read: 'Giant H-Bomb Dropped, Luminosity More Than 500 Suns.' Equally importantly, we need to remember events in the very week that filming began. The cameras turned for the first time on 19 November; two days earlier, the first Hungarian refugees had arrived in Britain driven out by the Russian tanks that smashed their revolution; a fortnight earlier, on 5 November, Anglo-French airborne troops had landed at Port Said at the depths of the fiasco of the Suez invasion.

The Curse of Frankenstein was therefore made at a unique and overdetermined conjuncture in world history when, for the first time, both the technology and the crises existed to threaten the very survival of the planet. Once again Mary Shelley's novel was pulled off the shelf and ransacked for the terms to articulate cultural hysteria. In one sense, of course, the movie represents a flight from the politics of Eden and the Kremlin into a spot of escapist Gothic knockabout; but to see it and then dismiss it as no more is to wipe out a series of factors including Fisher's ideology, Hammer's business sense, American investment and contemporary critical responses,[37] all of which mark out the seriousness of the project at one level. To put it baldly, at a time of genuine and multi-layered public fears, *The Curse of Franken-stein* addresses itself to a predominantly young audience and locates the source of anxiety in a deranged individual, focuses it down to the point where its basis is seen as one man's psychological problem. Wider systematic and social readings and other possibilities (the Walton story for one) are repressed, as a structure whose values go unquestioned is presented as threatened by a loony rather than as being itself at the root of instability. Responsibility for imminent catastrophe is limited to a single intellectual standing outside both ordinary lives and the political establishment, so that the film can flow from and then feed back into a populist politics and a scrubby anti-intellectualism frustrated by its own impotence. *The Curse of Frankenstein* is the curse of blocked democracy looking for a scapegoat and being sidetracked from an analysis.

What I have tried to show is that there is no eternal facet of our psyche that horror stories address themselves to. The reworkings of Frankenstein's story in the last century and a half prove that if there are, in Mary Shelley's phrase in the 1831 introduction, 'mysterious fears of our nature' to which her tale seeks to speak, those fears, like our nature itself, are produced and reproduced by the processes of history itself. Elsewhere in the same introduction Mary Shelley insists that 'invention, it must be humbly admitted, does not consist in creating out of void, but out of chaos; the materials must, in the first place, be afforded; it can give form to dark, shapeless substances but cannot bring into being the substance itself'. To look for those materials, that chaos, that substance, elsewhere in literature alone and so to read *Frankenstein* simply as shuffling round the themes and structures of earlier Romantic and Gothic texts is to fail to account for the way the novel, ceaselessly reconstituted, vigorously survives while those other fictions are long forgotten – forgotten, indeed, even by Mary Shelley herself by 1831.[38] I suggest that the chaos and the materials were there in the struggles of the Luddite decade, just as other materials and other kinds of chaos were there first in the 1930s and then in the 1950s to produce new meanings in a process that continues. (In 1973, for example, Brian Aldiss took Mary Shelley's book apart and reconstructed it in his novel *Frankenstein Unbound* around the notion that 'man has power to invent, but not to control'.[39] This is an idea which, luckily for Walton, would have sounded daft to his crew.)

What conclusions can we draw from all this? First, surely, we need to see that here as in any text there is no 'real', 'true' reading waiting for a sharp academic to nail it down for ever in the pages of a monograph; even for its own ostensible creator, *Frankenstein* meant certain things in 1818 and began to mean other things by 1831. A historically informed criticism needs to see those meanings, not abolish them. And then what, in the face of those meanings? S.S. Prawer concludes his study of horror movies by calling for 'standards' that will enable us to distinguish the work of the likes of James Whale from those mindlessly misusing the conventions of horror 'for the sake of profit' (p. 279). Such a search is likely to prove futile, especially if it begins with the odd assumption that somehow Universal weren't trying to make a lot of money. The standards that will distinguish between meanings – that will struggle for some and that will detect but resist others – are politically informed ones; standards that are based on a politics that knows where meanings come from and where they lead and is not afraid to fight on the grounds of that knowledge.

Notes

1 Details from W.H. Lyles, *Mary Shelley: An Annotated Bibliography* (Garland, New York 1975), and Peter Haining (ed.), *The Frankenstein File* (New English Library, London 1977).
2 See in particular Tony Bennett, *Formalism and Marxism* (Methuen, London 1979), chs 7, 8 and 9; Catherine Belsey, *Critical Practice* (Methuen, London 1980), chs 2 and 6; and Terry Eagleton, *Walter Benjamin: Or Towards a Revolutionary Criticism* (Verso, London 1981), part II, ch. 3.
3 D.W. Harding, 'The character of literature from Blake to Byron', in Boris Ford (ed.), *The Pelican Guide to English Literature. Vol. 5: From Blake to Byron* (Penguin, Harmondsworth 1957), p. 45.
4 See, for example, Ellen Moers, *Literary Women* (The Women's Press, London 1977); Kate Ellis, 'Monsters in the garden; Mary Shelley and the bourgeois family', in George Levine and U.C. Knoepfl-

macher (eds), *The Endurance of Frankenstein: Essays on Mary Shelley's Novel* (University of California Press, Berkeley 1979); and Sandra M. Gilbert and Susan Gubar, *The Madwoman in the Attic: The Woman Writer and the Nineteenth-Century Literary Imagination* (Yale University Press, New Haven 1979).

5 Jane Dunn, *Moon in Eclipse: A Life of Mary Shelley* (St Martin's Press, New York 1978), pp. 131, 134.

6 Christopher Small, *Ariel Like a Harpy: Shelley, Mary and Frankenstein* (Gollancz, London 1972), p. 331.

7 Martin Tropp, *Mary Shelley's Monster* (Houghton Mifflin, Boston 1976), p. 156.

8 Malcolm I. Thomis, *The Luddites: Machine-Breaking in Regency England* (David & Charles, Newton Abbot 1970), p. 144.

9 *The Making of the English Working Class* (Penguin, Harmondsworth 1968), p. 733.

10 Frederick L. Jones (ed.), *The Letters of Percy Bysshe Shelley. Vol. I: Shelley in England* (Oxford University Press, Oxford 1964), p. 351.

11 Roger Ingpen and Walter E. Peck (eds), *The Complete Works of Percy Bysshe Shelley. Vol. VI* (Benn, London 1965), p. 81.

12 See *Child of Light: A Reassessment of Mary Wollstonecraft Shelley* (1951), ch. 11.

13 Betty T. Bennett (ed.), *The Letters of Mary Wollstonecraft Shelley. Vol. I: A Part of the Elect* (Johns Hopkins University Press, Baltimore 1980), p. 36.

14 *Moon in Eclipse*, p. 134.

15 *The Letters of Mary Wollstonecraft Shelley. Vol. I*, pp. 138, 49.

16 For details, see Appendix C of Mary Wollstonecraft Shelley, *Frankenstein or The Modern Prometheus*, ed. M.K. Joseph (Oxford University Press, London 1969). All subsequent references to the text are to this edition.

17 See Elizabeth Nitchie, *Mary Shelley, Author of Frankenstein* (Greenwood, Connecticut 1953), pp. 26–33.

18 See, for example, Tropp, *Mary Shelley's Monster*, p. 82, and Mary Poovey, 'My hideous progeny: Mary Shelley and the feminization of romanticism', *Proceedings of the Modern Languages Association*, 95 (May 1980).

19 Small, *Ariel Like a Harpy*, p. 328.

20 See 'Mary Shelley's Monster: politics and psyche in *Frankenstein*', in Levine and Knoepflmacher, *Endurance of Frankenstein*.

21 *Mary Barton* (Penguin edn, Harmondsworth 1970), pp. 219–20.

22 Quoted in App. IV, 'The stage history of *Frankenstein*', Nitchie, *Mary Shelley*, p. 221.

23 For details, see Poovey, 'My hideous progeny'.

24 See the concluding chapter, 'Towards a theory of the Gothic', in

David Punter, *The Literature of Terror, A History of Gothic Fictions from 1765 to the Present Day* (Longman, Harlow 1980).

25 *New Statesman* (30 January 1932), p. 120.

26 Information from J. Douglas Gomery, 'Writing the history of the American film industry: Warner Brothers and sound', *Screen*, 17, 1 (Spring 1976). Facts about the making of the Universal *Frankenstein* in this section are derived from P. Haining, *Frankenstein File* (New English Library, London 1977); Levine and Knoepflmacher, *Endurance of Frankenstein*; Paul M. Jensen, *Boris Karloff and His Films* (Barnes, San Diego 1974); and Donald F. Glut, *Classic Movie Monsters* (Scarecrow, Metuchen 1978).

27 See, respectively, Tropp, *Mary Shelley's Monster*, pp. 87, 90; David Pirie, *A Heritage of Horror: The English Gothic Cinema 1946–1972* (1973) p. 69; and Jensen, *Boris Karloff*, p. 30.

28 Jensen, *Boris Karloff*, p. 41.

29 S.S. Prawer, *Caligari's Children: The Film as Tale of Terror* (Oxford University Press, Oxford 1980), p. 22.

30 Jensen, *Boris Karloff*, p. 44.

31 Quoted in Prawer, *Caligari's Children*, p. 241.

32 See Pirie, *Heritage of Horror*, p. 26.

33 Allan Eyles, Robert Adkinson and Nicholas Fry (eds), *The House of Horror: The Story of Hammer Films* (Barnes, San Diego 1973), p. 16.

34 See, for example, Pirie, *Heritage of Horror*, pp. 69 ff.; Tropp, *Mary Shelley's Monster*, pp. 125 ff.; Donald Glut, 'Peter Cushing: Doctor Frankenstein I presume', in Haining, *Frankenstein File*; and Albert J. LaValley, 'The stage and film children of *Frankenstein*: a survey', in Levine and Knoepflmacher, *Endurance of Frankenstein*.

35 Quoted in Eyles *et al.*, *House of Horror*, p. 15.

36 Quoted in Jensen, *Boris Karloff*, p. 35.

37 *Tribune*, for example, found the movie 'depressing' and 'degrading', and for C.A. Lejeune in *The Observer* it was 'among the half-dozen most repulsive films I have encountered'. The inadequacy of a dismissal of horror stories as merely escapist has recently been powerfully argued by Rosemary Jackson, *Fantasy: The Literature of Subversion* (Methuen, London 1981).

38 For evidence of Mary Shelley's forgetfulness of her literary sources, see James Rieger, 'Dr Polidori and the genesis of *Frankenstein*', *Studies in English Literature*, 3 (Autumn 1963), pp. 461–72.

39 Brian Aldiss, *Frankenstein Unbound* (Granada, London 1982), p. 77.

12

Re-imagining the fairy tales:
Angela Carter's bloody chambers
PATRICIA DUNCKER

I started to write short pieces when I was living in a room too small to
write a novel in. So the size of my room modified what I did inside it
and it was the same with the pieces themselves. The limited trajectory
of the short narrative concentrates its meaning. Sign and sense can fuse
to an extent impossible to achieve among the multiplying ambiguities
of an extended narrative.

Angela Carter, Afterword to *Fireworks: Nine Profane Pieces* (1974)

The Afterword to *Fireworks* (1974) and the Polemical Preface to
The Sadeian Woman (1979) are both literary manifestos, maps for
the territory and enterprise of Angela Carter's fiction. In her
most recent work two strands sever and combine; first, her
translations of the fairy tales of Charles Perrault (1977), ancient
wisdom reborn as didactic little pieces of enlightened self-
interest, the short tale in which sign and sense become utterly
fused, with the moral, often a contradictory one, chugging along
behind like the guard's van; and second, her critique of the
mythology of sexuality in her novel, *The Passion of New Eve*
(1977), a fantastic Gothic quest across an America riven by
approaching apocalypse, an invading voyage into the forbidden
places of sexual taboo. The psychology of pornography and the
Gothic, submerged in the sexual translations of Eve, are sub-
jected to speculative, non-fictional treatment in *The Sadeian*

Woman; out of the last metamorphosis come the fairy tales of Charles Perrault, rewritten by the woman disguised, self-styled as the moral pornographer, the tales in *The Bloody Chamber*.

We must stand back to applaud her ambition, for the success of her enterprise, re-shaping and re-imagining the archetypes of imagination, re-casting the bricks of our inner worlds, would require extraordinary resourcefulness. The lure of her chosen form, tales rather than short stories, is easily explicable. For Carter the strength of the tale lies in the fact that it does not sink into the slough of dailiness, rather it unfetters the imagination. For the tale interprets rather than presents everyday experience, through 'a system of imagery derived from subterranean areas behind everyday experience, and therefore the tale cannot betray its readers into a false knowledge' (Afterword to *Fireworks*). But here, I believe, she is wrong. The unconscious is not a treasure vault containing visionary revelations about ourselves. It is rather the cesspool of our fears and desires, filled with the common patterns that are also projections of the ways in which we have been taught to perceive the world. And the deep structure of those patterns will reflect the political, social and psychological realities within which we exist as best we can. The unconscious mirrors these changing realities. Nothing else. And the fairy tales, the received collective wisdom of the past, which, as Carter rightly perceives, reflect the myths of sexuality under patriarchy, have been and still are used as the text books through which those lessons are learned. Thus the tale, especially the fairy tale, is the vessel of false knowledge or, more bluntly, interested propaganda. Andrea Dworkin, in *Woman Hating* (1974), discusses the process by which women are taught fear, through the fairy tales, as a function of their femininity.

> The lessons are simple, and we learn them well.
> Men and women are different, absolute opposites.
> The heroic prince can never be confused with Cinderella, or Snow-white, or Sleeping Beauty. She could never do what he does at all, let alone better . . .
> Where he is erect, she is supine. Where he is awake, she is asleep.
> Where he is active, she is passive. Where she is erect, or awake, or active, she is evil and must be destroyed.[1]

The fairy tales, with all the unfettered cruelty that is permissible in fantasy, spell out the punishment for rebellion or dissent. Dworkin again:

> There are two definitions of woman. There is the good woman.
> She is a victim. There is the bad woman. She must be destroyed.
> The good woman must be possessed. The bad woman must be killed, or punished. Both must be nullified.
>
> (ibid.)

Her analysis is perfectly correct. So far as she goes. She sees the fairy tales as parables handed out to children as working tools, ways of dealing with the world, the way to knuckle down into uncongenial shapes, rather than as weapons of understanding and change. The fairy tales are, in fact, about power, and about the struggle for possession, by fair or magical means, of kingdoms, goods, children, money, land, and – naturally, specifically – the possession of women. And even the fairy (more properly folk) tale itself, as the narrative art of the people, communally owned, has been appropriated by the ruling class at a specific point in history, transformed, rewritten, possessed. For the fairy tales became children's literature at a particular moment in the history of their transmission. Originally, they were nothing of the kind.[2]

The German term *Märchen* – fairy tale – comes from the Old High German word, *mâri*, or Gothic *mêrs*, Middle High German *Märe* – which means news or gossip. The term *Volksmärchen*, or folk tale, acknowledges the people – *das Volk* – as its rightful owners. The term fairy tale comes from the French *conte de fées*, most probably derived from the Countess d'Aulnoy's collection *Contes de Fées* (1698), translated into English in the following year as *Tales of the Fairys*. The term fairy tale is now used to describe both the orally transmitted folk tales and the literary productions of bourgeois and aristocratic writers in the late seventeenth and eighteenth centuries. This important distinction lies smothered under the blanket term fairy tale; it is a split which occurred gradually in Europe, coinciding with the invention of childhood and the rise of the bourgeoisie. The classical notion of *paideia*, education, and of childhood as a time of

preparation and initiation into the adult world was not generally held during the Middle Ages. [. . .] But during the Renaissance there was a new emphasis on education for the middle and
upper classes. The reinforcement of patriarchy under Prot-
estantism endorsed a more rigid hierarchy within the family
and the state – eventually the fairy tales became part of that
order and were absorbed into the structure of educational
propaganda for children. Thus, a radical current in popular
culture was appropriated and contained. But it is of course
extremely difficult to gauge the intention behind these aristocratic borrowings from popular culture. [. . .]

In Germany there is a significant distinction between the
Volksmärchen, the traditional tales of the people, and the *Kunst-
märchen*, a specifically literary form which was of crucial importance to the German Romantic movement.[3] The Romantiker
grasped the revolutionary potential of the folk tale; they wrote
their own. Particularly in the work of Novalis, Brentano,
Eichendorff, Chamisso and Hoffmann the *Märchen* becomes a
critique of bourgeois society and the vehicle for philosophical
and aesthetic theories.[4] But alongside this radical reclaiming of
a current in German literature went the larger process through
which the tales, trapped in the anthologies by literary archaeol-
ogists like the Brothers Grimm, were captured for consumption
by an educated audience and finally relegated to the nursery.[5]
The original folk tales were a collective enterprise, produced by
both audience and narrator, which articulated the aspirations
of the people and their fight against social injustice. The world of
these tales reflects the solid walls of feudalism; it is ruled by kings
and queens, bound by fixed class hierarchies, filled with peasants,
soldiers, dragons and magic. It is a predominantly rural order;
there are no signs of industrialization. The trades are traditional, weavers, spinners, millers, merchants. And the tales stress
inequalities in superlative terms;[6] the kings are always the
wealthiest and most powerful in the world, the poor shepherds
and peasants the most helpless, destitute and underprivileged
mass nature ever suffered to survive upon the earth. And yet
fairyland is also an unstable world in which appearance crum-
bles before magic; Cinderella becomes a princess, the miller's
youngest son becomes the Marquis of Carabas, the frog becomes
a prince. Fairy tales deal in transformations which subvert

the apparently unalterable social realities; magic translates, fragments, inverts; the lower classes are upwardly mobile; official morality is calmly set aside, cunning or deception pays off, as it does for Puss-in-Boots, his master, and for the common soldier who deceives the twelve dancing princesses.

But although the fairy tales show a fantastic inverted world where every pretty chamber maid can aspire to be queen, the hierarchies themselves remain resolutely intact. The King (the Father) will always rule over absolute subjects. Translation is always a process of forgetting. The wicked may be deposed, but the memory of the peasant/swineherd/shepherd's previous existence cannot influence the rule of the New Prince; except that he will govern wisely and well, in order to forestall another fairy tale revolution.

Charles Perrault and the Countess d'Aulnoy, both writing in the last years of the seventeenth century, transcribed the tales from a living oral tradition, as did the Brothers Grimm, who rewrote and reshaped the Rhineland tales in their collection for a supposedly more sophisticated audience. But the tales, coming out of history, continue to mirror the times which produced them. There was nothing particularly remarkable about stepmothers in a period when lives were short, childbirth often fatal and a surviving husband would probably marry again; nor, in a medieval community, is there anything extraordinary about wells as the centre of village life or marriage at puberty. But, inexorably, the fairy tales became the property of childhood. And now, whether they are read or told, they have become narratives passed on from adults to children. The teller traditionally bears the face of age. They are the parables of wisdom and experience addressed to the apprehension of innocence, in which the pleasure of fiction is carefully fenced off and contained within the ritual parentheses, 'Once upon a time . . .', 'They lived happily ever after. . . '. These are the limits of fantasy, and the fairy tale is necessarily fantastic, a world of extremes, excess, an inversion of dailiness. But the tales continue to expose the raw nerves of real conflicts between classes, families, men and women, mothers and daughters, fathers and sons. The transition from adolescence through puberty to adulthood is brutally taught through the tales in which inequalities are painted unambiguously in the characters of excess. The sexual symbolism of the fairy tales may now appear to us to be ludicrous, transparent, but to the child their meanings remain mysterious. Carter's rewriting of the tales is an exercise in making the mystery sexually explicit.

Apart from 'The Erl-King', which she presumably adapts from Goethe's ballad, Carter chooses a sequence of classic tales most of which are to be found in Perrault; the story of Bluebeard and his wives in 'The Bloody Chamber', two versions of 'Beauty and the Beast' in 'The Courtship of Mr Lyon' and 'The Tiger's Bride', an operatic Puss-in-Boots which deliberately suggests the Baroque ornamentation of Rossini's music, Snow-White in 'The Snow Child', Sleeping Beauty as a Gothic vampire in 'The Lady of the House of Love', two versions of Red Riding Hood and a tale that combines motifs from several of these, 'Wolf-Alice'. The animal aspects of human sexuality are her particular concern; thus the wolf and the lion roam through the tales seeking whom they may erotically devour. Carter's style is genuinely original; perhaps this is the most startling departure from the simplicity of form and directness characteristic of Perrault's narratives, as stark and uncompromising as ballads. Perrault's morals may be knowingly smug: his narratives are not. Carter's method is quite deliberate; the tales are rewritten as elaborate pieces of pure Gothic, in the manner of Poe. 'Character and events are exaggerated beyond reality, to become symbols, ideas, passions. Its [the Gothic tradition of Poe] style will tend to be ornate, unnatural. . . . Its only humour is black humour' (Afterword to *Fireworks*). But the infernal trap inherent in the fairy tale, which fits the form to its purpose, to be the carrier of ideology, proves too complex and pervasive to avoid. Carter is rewriting the tales within the strait-jacket of their original structures. The characters she re-creates must to some extent continue to exist as abstractions. Identity continues to be defined by role, so that shifting the perspective from the impersonal voice to the inner confessional narrative, as she does in several of the tales, merely explains, amplifies and reproduces rather than alters the original, deeply, rigidly sexist psychology of the erotic. The disarming of aggressive male sexuality by the virtuous bride is at the root of The Frog Prince and Beauty and the Beast. Carter transposes this moral into the narrative 'The Company of Wolves', so that the erotic confrontation and reversal at the end becomes a meeting of sexual aggression and the cliché of female erotic ingenuity. Red Riding Hood sees that rape is inevitable – 'The Wolf is carnivore incarnate'[7] – and decides to strip off, lie back and enjoy it. She wants it really. They all do. The message spelt out in 'The Tiger's Bride' argues a variation on the original bargain; the heroine is sold to the highest bidder in the marriage pact, but she too strips off all artifice, the lies inherent in borrowed garments, and reveals herself as she is, the mirror image of his feline predatory sexuality. Authorial comment surrounding this encounter is contradictory; on the one hand Beauty's body is 'the cold white meat of contract' (p. 66) but on the other, 'I, white, shaking, raw, approaching him as if offering, in myself, the key to a peaceable kingdom in which his appetite need not be my extinction' (p. 67). I would suggest that all we are watching, beautifully packaged and unveiled, is the ritual disrobing of the willing victim of pornography.

Carter's tales are, supposedly, celebrations of erotic desire. But male sexuality has too long, too tenaciously been linked with power and possession, the capture, breaking and ownership of women. The explicitly erotic currents in her tales mirror these realities. Pornography, that is, the representation of overtly sexual material with the intention to arouse prurient, vicarious desire, uses the language of male sexuality. Even the women's equivalent of soft porn, romance novels and 'bodice-rippers', all conform to recognizably male fantasies of domination, submission and possession. Heterosexual feminists have not yet invented an alternative, anti-sexist language of the erotic. Carter envisages women's sensuality simply as a response to male arousal. She has no conception of women's sexuality as autonomous desire.

One of the deftest, most disturbing pieces in the book is her version of Snow-White, 'The Snow Child'. Here Carter exposes the Oedipal conflict between Mother and Daughter: the snow maiden is the father's child, 'the child of his desire' (p. 92) who threatens to usurp the Mother's place. With one small touch Carter reveals the Mother as a sister to Sade's Juliette, the sexual terrorist, with a motif taken from the literature of pornography, 'she wore high, black shining boots with scarlet heels and spurs' (p. 91). If the Mother ever fails the child in the fairy tales that child's life is always in jeopardy. In Carter's version the Mother offers up the child, as her sexuality blossoms in the rose, to the Father's lust, which destroys her. Carter removes the supposedly comforting denouement to the tale in which the Mother is destroyed and the child successfully navigates the dangerous transition into sexual maturity. But she doesn't question the ideology implicit in the story, that the Mother and Daughter will – necessarily – become rivals for the Father's love and be prepared to countenance one another's destruction. The division between Mother and Daughter, and between Sisters, is one of the cornerstones of patriarchy. The fact that so many of the tales suggest and endorse those old enmities is both sinister and predictable. Cinderella, Snow-White, Beauty and the Beast all argue the case for 'women, beware women'. The logic of the fairy tales travels on into the structures of orthodox literature; *King Lear* is cast in the fairy-tale mould of the old father dividing his kingdom between the three daughters. Two are destructive and predatory, and only the youngest daughter, carefully constructed out of masculine desire as the Snow Child had been, remains loyal to the father. Carter rings the sexual changes cheerfully enough. Red Riding Hood sleeps between the paws of the Wolf, the Grandmother actually *is* the Wolf, Beauty becomes the Beast; but she still leaves the central taboos unspoken. Some things are unthinkable. She could never imagine Cinderella in bed with the Fairy Godmother.

Carter's extraordinary fascination with de Sade simmers at the root of what is both disturbingly reactionary and sadly unoriginal in her work. She knows that 'the tale has relations with the subliterary forms of pornography, ballad and dream'.[8] In *The Sadeian Woman* she suggests that the Devil is best slain with his own weapons and argues the case for the moral pornographer, who is, curiously, envisaged as male.

The moral pornographer would be an artist who uses pornographic material as part of the acceptance of the logic of a world of absolute sexual licence for all the genders, and projects a model of the way such a world might work. A moral pornographer might use pornography as a critique of current relations between the sexes. His business would be the total demystification of the flesh and the subsequent revelation, through the infinite modulations of the sexual act, of the real relations between man and his kind. Such a pornographer would not be the enemy of women, perhaps because he might begin to penetrate to the heart of the contempt for women that distorts our culture even as he entered the realms of true obscenity as he describes it.[9]

This is, I would suggest, utter nonsense. Pornography, indeed the representation of all sexual relations between men and women, will necessarily 'render explicit the nature of social relations in the society in which they take place'.[10] That is why most bourgeois fiction concentrates upon the choices surrounding courtship and marriage, for it is there that the values and realities upon which a society is based will be most sharply revealed. The realities of power perhaps, but not the imagined experience of desire. Pornography, heightened, stylized, remote, mirrors precisely these socially-constructed realities. The realities of male desire, aggression, force; the reality of women, compliant and submissive. Where then shall imagined desire, the expression of feminist eroticism, be found, apprehended, expressed? Andrea Dworkin argues that this can only emerge when the division of sexual polarity is destroyed, when male and female sexual identities are reborn.

we will have to abandon phallic worth and female masochism altogether as normative, sanctioned identities, as modes of erotic behaviour, as basic indicators of 'male' and 'female'.

As we are destroying the structure of culture, we will have to build a new culture – nonhierarchical, nonsexist, non-coercive, nonexploitative – in other words, a culture which is not based on dominance and submission in any way.

And as we are destroying the phallic identities of men and the masochistic identities of women, we will have to create, out of our own ashes, new erotic identities.[11]

This passage, taken from her essay 'The politics of fear and courage', is very much to the point in that the fairy tales are used to teach precisely these things; phallic worth, female masochism, fear and courage. The fairy tales are bridges across the straits of adolescence. The child becomes a man or a woman; the rite of passage is marriage and sexual maturity, but within the architecture of the fairy tale this will have a different meaning for a boy and a girl. Tom Thumb, Puss-in-Boots carry the classical Oedipal message of puberty; the Father, the ogre, must be slain by the adolescent who then possesses his inheritance, the ogre's castle, the princess. The Father is never killed by name in the fairy tales, but his threatening, confining destructiveness is emphasized. He is masked by superlatives, but with courage, ingenuity and strength he may be overcome. So the tales send the boys out into the world to seek their fortunes, create their wealth, possess their women. The boys must be taught courage. The girls must be taught fear. For girls the critical metamorphosis is sexual: menstruation, puberty, marriage. For Sleeping Beauty the symbolic curse that comes upon her is puberty, the first shedding of blood, the curse that can only be redeemed by marriage, her rightful place. This is the first of the tales in Perrault's collection *Histoires ou contes du temps passé* (1697). Perrault tells the tale up to the 'happy ending' of the Prince's kiss which redeems the time and awakens the Princess from her long stupor of adolescence. All the woman has to do is wait. She must not initiate sexual activity, a potential she now possesses that is fraught with danger. She must wait and sleep out the years until she is possessed. Perrault, with all the unctuousness of a civil servant, adds the moral. 'The Tale of Sleeping Beauty shows how long engagements make for happy marriages, but young girls these days want so much to be married I do not have the heart to press the moral.'[12]

But Perrault only tells us a version of an older Neapolitan story to be found in Basile's *Pentamerone* (1636). In that version a king is out hunting, he passes the locked and deserted castle, his falcon flies in through the open window, he follows the bird and comes upon the sleeping princess, he is unable to rouse her or to control himself, rapes her, leaves and forgets her. The result of this little exploit is twins, Sun and Moon, who awaken their mother. The king eventually returns, but he is, unfortunately, already married to an ogress, a sister of Medea who tries to organize a meal in which his two children are served up in a pie and the Sleeping Beauty is to be burnt. The link here between Sleeping Beauty and Snow-White is clear; in both cases she is the Oedipal child who arouses the desire of the Father and the hatred of the Mother. Perrault's desire to curtail the narrative before it became too unpleasant need not be attributed to prudery; his stories were addressed to the Court where it was scarcely tactful to speak of cannibal queens and raping kings.

Carter's Gothic version of the tale is a peculiar nemesis for radical feminism. The lady of the House of Love is both the Sleeping Beauty and the Vampire Queen, the voracious witch of Hansel and Gretel. [. . .] In fact what the Countess longs for is the grand finale of all 'snuff' movies in which the woman is sexually used and ritually killed, the oldest cliché of them all, sex and death. She can abandon her predatory sexuality, the unnatural force, as her own blood flows, the symbolic breaking of the virgin hymen, the initiation into sexual maturity and then into death. [. . .] Only in death does she pass into womanhood, and the handsome British cyclist passes out of the innocent security of fairy tale into the terror of history and the trenches of the First World War.

The most successful narrative in Carter's collection is the most elaborate and expansive, the modern Bluebeard, 'The Bloody Chamber'. This is a tour de force. The confessional voice of the tale is that of experience, the girl recalling her initiation into the adult world. Carter's story – and indeed all the earlier versions – is about women's masochistic complicity in male sexual aggression; and about husbands. Perrault was in no doubt about this either. He draws the moral from the story; an admonition to nosy women who seek to know the truth about the men they marry. 'Curiosity is the most fleeting of pleasures; the moment it is satisfied, it ceases to exist and it always proves, very, very expensive. It is easy to see that the events described in this story took place many years ago'.[13] He then adds, embarrassed, 'no modern husband would dare to be half so terrible'.[14] Carter's Bluebeard is simply a husband; he is given no other name.

There may well have been a historical Bluebeard. One possibility is Gilles de Rais (1404–40), a Breton aristocrat who fought alongside Joan of Arc at Orleans. But this seems un- likely, for although he was hanged in 1440 for multiple murder – his victims were numbered at 140 – he only had one wife and she survived him. Apparently his beard was red and not blue and his victims were usually little boys, whom he liked to fondle as they died. The other candidate for the role of Bluebeard is Comorre the Cursed, another native of Brittany who lived in AD 500. He was given to murdering his wives as soon as they were pregnant, and supposedly decapitated the last one, Tryphine. She was restored to life by St Gildas, a local abbot, eventually founded a convent, and was, in the fullness of time, canonized by the Church.[15]

Carter's 'Bloody Chamber' uses all the iconography of the Gothic; the remote castle, the virgin at the mercy of the tormented hero-villain, the enclosed spaces, hidden atrocities, women voraciously, masochistically eager for the corruption of sexuality. All the pervading themes of pornography are there too; domination, control, humiliation, mutilation, possession through murder. All perpetrated on willing, eager victims. The marriage bargain becomes explicit, the bride as the bought woman, acting out the 'ritual from the brothel' (p. 15). Carter's tale carefully creates the classical pornographic model of sexuality, which has a definite meaning and endorses a particular kind of fantasy, that of male sexual tyranny within a marriage that is grossly unequal; the child bride responsive to her husband's desire, ready to be 'impaled' among the lilies of death, the face with its 'promise of debauchery', a rare talent for corruption. Here is the sexual model which endorses the 'normal and natural sadism of the male, happily complemented by the normal and natural masochism of the female.'[16] The husband of 'The Bloody Chamber' is a connoisseur, a collector of pornography. When the child bride peers at the titles in his bookcase she finds the texts for the knowledge she reads in blood, a guide to her fate, *The Initiation*, *The Key to Mysteries*, *The Secret of Pandora's Box*, imaged in the Sultan's murdered wives.

But there are two other figures that Carter has created in her rewriting of the tale whose actions and presence alter the terms of the unequal conflict between husband and wife. In Perrault's original version the bride's sister Anne, about whom we are told nothing but her name, looks out from the tower as Bluebeard sharpens his cutlass in the courtyard, to proclaim the galloping arrival of the bride's two brothers. In Carter's version this figure becomes the blinded piano tuner, Jean-Yves, who loves the child bride not for her ambiguous beauty, the veil across corruption, but for her single gift of music. Only with the

blinded boy who humbly serves her music can Carter envisage a
marriage of equality for Bluebeard's bride. Men as invalids are
constant figures in women's fiction,[17] most remarkably in the
writing of Charlotte Brontë: her heroes suffer on the point of her
pen, she blinds them, maims them, drowns them. This is easy to
understand: if a man is damaged and hurt a woman is released
from the habitual sexual constraint forced upon her, she can
take action, initiate contact, speak out, and the power imbalance inherent in all heterosexual relationships is levelled off.

This attempt to break down the traditional erotic identities is
also implied by the pervasive transvestitism in Brontë's
novels:[18] Rochester dressed as a gypsy woman, De Hamal as a
nun, Shirley, behind the ambiguous sexuality of her name,
talks, acts, commands, swaggers like a man, Ginevra Fanshawe
is wooed by Lucy Snowe, taking the part of a man in the school
play. The man whose eyes are extinguished can no longer
evaluate, dominate, control. He is reduced to dependence. Only
when Rochester is blinded can Jane Eyre return. Blindness is
the curse of Oedipus, a symbolic reckoning. But the blinded
man has further significance. This figure suggests that although
men observe women constantly they do not see us; they do not
perceive who we really are, we remain invisible. But while
blindness, as symbolic castration, may signal the end of male
sexual aggression, it is also mutilation. As such it cannot be
offered as the answer, the new male erotic identity. In the case of
Bluebeard's bride it is as well that her lover cannot see her, for
she carries the mark of her complicity and corruption forever,
the complicity of women who have been made in man's image,
who have desired to be possessed, who walk after the diva of
Isolde, the model of Montmartre, the Romanian Countess, who
meet the reward of that complicity in the bloody chamber.

It is not the brothers who arrive armed with muskets and
rapiers to save Bluebeard's bride, but a figure who never
appears in the fairy tales, the mother as travelling heroine. [. . .]
This is the mother who invests in her daughter's career rather
than her price on the marriage market; and it is the mother's
spirit, the courage incidentally of the Gothic heroines who pass
unraped, unharmed down into the dungeons of the castle,
which accompanies her daughter to learn the truth of the bloody
chamber. [. . .] And the hand of vengeance against Bluebeard is

the woman's hand, the mother's hand bearing the father's weapon. Only the women have suffered, only the women can be avenged. [. . .] Here Carter is transforming the sexual politics of the fairy tales in significant ways. The mother of Bluebeard's bride never deserts her child. She has the wisdom to give her child the freedom demanded by sexual maturity, the freedom denied to Sleeping Beauty by her royal parents when they seek to protect her from the fairy's curse, that her hand shall be pierced by a spindle. But the mother arrives with melodramatic timeliness, giving the lie to Papa Freud's Oedipal realities. 'I felt a pang of loss as if, when he put the gold band on my finger, I had, in some way, ceased to be her child in becoming his wife' (p. 7). In fact, the bond between Mother and Daughter is never broken. Carter's tale, perhaps unwittingly, carries an uncompromisingly feminist message; for the women's revolution would seal up the door of the bloody chamber forever.

All Carter's books are either short novels or tales, fantastic narratives. *The Sadeian Woman* and her collected essays, *Nothing Sacred* (Virago 1982), are her only non-fictional work to date. Her style is as lavish and ornate as the detail on the architecture Puss-in-Boots finds easy to climb – 'Nothing to it once you know how, rococo's no problem' (p. 69). This is her great strength. Her rewriting, re-imagining of the fairy tales could have been more intriguing than it is, had she studied the ambivalent sexual language that is there in the original tales. Perrault's Red Riding Hood is – in French – designated by a masculine name, Le Petit Chaperon Rouge. At the moment when the ritual words are uttered – 'draw the bolt and the latch will open' – she is the one who enters; the wolf wears the grandmother's clothes. In later versions the woodcutters find both Red Riding Hood and the grandmother safe in the womb of the wolf. These ambiguities are partially acknowledged in 'The Company of Wolves', but follow the sexual symbolism of Cinderella thrusting her foot into the envoy's slipper, of Bluebeard's wife penetrating the secret space of the bloody chamber. These currents are there too in Carter's tales. She cannot avoid them. And she could go much further than she does.

Carter chooses to inhabit a tiny room of her own in the house of fiction. For women, that space has always been paralysingly, cripplingly small; I think we need the 'multiplying ambiguities of an extended narrative' to imagine ourselves whole. We cannot fit neatly into patterns or models as Cinderellas, ugly sisters, wicked stepmothers, fairy godmothers, and still acknowledge our several existences, experienced or imagined. We need the space to carve out our own erotic identities, as free women. And then to rewrite the fairy tales – with a bolder hand.

Notes

1 Cited in Andrea Dworkin, *Our Blood: Prophecies and Discourses on Sexual Politics* (The Women's Press, London 1982), p. 55.

2 See Roger Sale, *Fairy Tales and After* (Harvard University Press, Cambridge, Mass. 1978), p. 26.

3 Jack Zipes, *Breaking the Magic Spell: Radical Theories of Folk and Fairy Tales* (Heinemann, London 1979), p. 23 ff.

4 See Zipes, *Breaking the Magic Spell*, especially ch. 3.

5 *Kinder und Hausmärchen* (1812–14).

6 I am indebted here to an essay by Michel Butor, 'On fairy tales', in *European Literary Theory and Practice: From Existential Phenomenology to Structuralism*, ed. Vernon W. Gras (Dell, New York 1973).

7 Angela Carter, *The Bloody Chamber and Other Stories* (1979, but all references are to the Penguin edition, Harmondsworth 1981).

8 Angela Carter, Afterword to *Fireworks: Nine Profane Pieces* (Quartet, London 1974), p. 122.

9 Angela Carter, *The Sadeian Woman* (Virago, London 1979), pp. 19–20.

10 Carter, *Sadeian Woman*, p. 20.

11 Dworkin, 'The politics of fear and courage', in *Our Blood*, p. 62.

12 *The Fairy Tales of Charles Perrault*, trans. Angela Carter (Gollancz, London 1977), p. 71.

13 *Fairy Tales of Charles Perrault*, p. 41.

14 *Fairy Tales of Charles Perrault*, p. 41.

15 Iona and Peter Opie, *The Classic Fairy Tales* (Oxford University Press, Oxford 1974).

16 Andrea Dworkin, *Pornography: Men Possessing Women* (1981; The Women's Press, London 1982), p. 109.

17 See Rosika Parker, 'Images of men', *Spare Rib*, 99 (November 1980), pp. 5–8.

18 Patricia Beer's lecture to The Brontë Society at Haworth, June 1981, dealt with precisely this topic, about which she has also written a poem. See her collection *The Lie of the Land* (Hutchinson, London 1983).

13

Marxism and popular fiction
TONY BENNETT

Literature, popular fiction and the bourgeois literary formation

It is usual to assume, when confronted by the formula 'Marxism and . . .', that a relationship is to be argued for in which Marxism will figure as the analytical donor and the other bit, the bit which comes after the 'and', as the beneficiary. In this case, it suggests that what might be on offer is a Marxist theory of popular fiction. I should stress, therefore, that this is not the approach adopted here. Indeed, rather than proposing a Marxist theory of popular fiction, I want to argue against the need for such a theory or for a theory formulated in those terms.

To be more specific, my overriding purpose – although I shall come to this only toward the end of this essay – is to outline the part that the study of popular fiction (so-called) might play within a critical strategy aimed at deconstructing the category of Literature and at dismantling those critical procedures which currently produce for literary texts their political and ideological effects. By 'Literature' here, I have in mind not the literary as, in Tony Davies's words, 'a neutral totality of imaginative or fictional writing', but Literature as 'an ideologically constructed canon or corpus of texts operating in specific and determinate ways in and around the apparatus of education';[1]

in short, the canonized tradition. And I would regard such a
project as a Marxist one; indeed, it is perhaps the most important task currently facing Marxist criticism. As Stuart Hall has
argued, the conventional ordering of the system of intertextual
relationships implied by the concept of Literature needs to be
made 'the first object of interrogation' within any radical
critical practice:

> Why is it that the text, the many texts, the many signifying
> practices which are present in any social formation have
> yielded, as the administered curriculum of literary studies,
> these ten books up to the top; then these twenty books with a
> question mark above them; then those fifty books which we
> know about but which we only need to read very quickly; and
> then those hundreds and thousands of texts nobody ever
> reads? That hierarchy itself, which constitutes the selective
> tradition in literary studies, becomes the first object to be
> interrogated.[2]

While there are signs that such a critical project is well underway, it should be stressed that it is the full range of that
hierarchy and not just the top of it – not just 'Literature' – that
needs to be problematized. Indeed, this is unavoidable: to take
on the concept of Literature by way of analysing its critical
effects *necessarily* involves a critical reconsideration of those
other categories – such as 'popular fiction' – which have conventionally been ranged alongside or opposed to it. For 'Literature'
does not merely denote a particular body of texts. It is, rather,
the central, co-ordinating concept of the discourse of literary
criticism, supplying the point of reference in relation to which
relationships of difference and similarity within the field of
writing are articulated. So much so that most other forms of
writing have been defined negatively: only in the respects in
which they differ from Literature. Thus the concept of popular
fiction conveys – beyond the notion of numerical appeal –
nothing so much as that it is *not* Literature. It is, in fact, a
residual concept – the residue which remains once the sphere of
Literature has been described and accounted for: in most
instances, attempts to articulate the specific qualities of popular
fiction consist of a listing of those attributes (such as lack
of character or standardization of plot) which supposedly dis-

tinguish it from the already established characteristics of Literature.

It follows that any attempt to unsettle the concept of Literature necessarily and simultaneously involves unsettling the concept of popular fiction in that it calls into question the ways in which relationships of difference and similarity within the field of writing have conventionally been constructed. What is at issue, then, is not just a dismantling of the category of Literature, or the ways in which the texts thus labelled have usually been studied, but a study and critique of the bourgeois literary formation – of the ways in which the relations of intertextuality have been constructed within that formation; of the ways in which different practices of writing have been caught, held and defined in relation to one another; and of the ways in which critical and institutional practices have borne upon the reproduction of those differences. It also involves an attempt to think outside that formation, to construe the internal economy of the field of writing in terms which by-pass the distinctions posited by the concept of Literature.

My purpose, then, is not to develop a Marxist theory of 'popular fiction', but to suggest some ways in which what is commonly referred to as popular fiction may be analytically occupied by Marxists in order to call into question the system of critical concepts of which popular fiction itself forms a part. As a prelude to doing so, however, it will be necessary to indicate that Marxist criticism has, for the greater part of its history, been an essentially bourgeois enterprise at the level of its founding theoretical assumptions, if the kind of critical strategy suggested above is to be developed and inserted within Marxism as part of a substantially reformulated critical problematic. It will also be necessary to consider the relationship between Marxism and popular fiction from another angle: historical and critical rather than strategic. My contention, here, will be that the neglect of popular fiction within Marxist criticism (or, where it has been dealt with, the terms in which it has been addressed) is regrettable not merely in itself and not merely for political reasons, but because it is symptomatic of a faulty conception of the Marxist critical project, which has proved debilitating even for the way the study of canonized texts (ever the Marxist critic's preferred stalking ground) has been conceived and executed.

Against Literature

I have stated that popular fiction has been a neglected area of study within Marxist criticism; that the bulk of Marxist critical attention has focused on the canonized tradition is incontestable. However, and especially of late, there *are* Marxists who have concerned themselves with the study of popular texts – Eco and Barthes, for example. Even so, it is noticeable that popular texts have figured more prominently within the project of developing a general semiology than within the distinctively literary-critical region of Marxist theory. So far as the *historical formation* of Marxist criticism is concerned, however, the degree of critical attention devoted to the study of recognizably popular forms within those major schools of Marxist criticism which – at least until recently – have defined the central terms of reference of Marxist critical debate has been, to say the least, cursory.

Take Lukács. He has nothing at all to say on the subject, not a word. His critical attention moves unremittingly within the confines of 'world historical literature', pausing only momentarily to take the odd, largely uninformed, swipe at the degenerate 'mass culture' of the West; or, in the gestures of a familiar organicism, to invoke 'the people' – creative, it would seem, not in their own right but only by proxy – as a necessary support for all truly great world literature. Goldmann makes one or two oblique references to popular fiction in attempting to explain why the methods of world-view analysis should be 'valid only for the great works of the past'.[3] But in resolving this problem definitionally – Goldmann squares his circle with remarkable candour: world-view analysis can only be used in relation to great works because, so it happily turns out, only great works contain or express world-views – he puts popular fiction safely back in the box labelled 'ideology' from whence he took it. And Althusser, having posited an unargued-for distinction between 'authentic art' and 'works of an average or mediocre level', ignores the latter entirely.[4]

The only major school of Marxist criticism that can claim to have seriously and sustainedly studied the domain of non-canonized texts – although more in the field of music than of fiction – is the Frankfurt School. However, the Hegelianized version of the mass-culture critique which informed the Frankfurt theorists' approach to popular texts resulted chiefly in a leftward-inflected version of the terms in which such texts had already been condemned. All the elements which inform the mass-culture critique – the lack of a controlling centre of culture, aesthetic barbarism, and so on – are present in the Frankfurt critique, but shuffled to the left in being recast within the Frankfurt perspective of containment. [. . .]

There are other exceptions: Gramsci and, perhaps most notably, Raymond Williams, who, at a theoretical level if not at the level of his 'practical criticism', has done more than any other single figure to contest the concept of Literature by tracing the stages and processes of its historical formation. None the less, the point that Marxist critics have, for the greater part, merely mirrored bourgeois criticism, accepting its valuations and duplicating its exclusions, remains valid. If the gravitational pull of the concept of Literature has proved well-nigh irresistible with regard to the way the 'canon' has been approached and conceptualized, the pull of the mass-culture critique has proved equally strong in relation to the way Marxists have studied popular forms. The result has been, for a science which claims to be revolutionary, a highly paradoxical history in which Marxist criticism has functioned largely corroboratively in relation to the distinctions forged by bourgeois criticism: approving of the same body of canonized works but for different reasons, and disapproving of the rest – lumped together as a residue – but, again, for different reasons. Bourgeois criticism has thus been simultaneously patted on the back for having recognized which works are truly great and taken to task for having misrecognized the reasons for their greatness. The *real* reason for Tolstoy's greatness, it turns out, has nothing to do with the eternal verities of the human condition, but to his having given coherent expression to the world-view of the peasantry (Lukács) or to his supplying us with a vision of the contradictions inscribed in the ideology to which his works allude (Macherey). Mulhern has warned that 'it would be astonishing if the judgements of Marxist criticism turned out to be so many materialist *doppelgänger* of those made current by the foregoing idealist tradition'.[5] Yes, astonishing indeed; none the less, so far as the question of literary evaluation is concerned, that has been the main heritage of the tradition so far.

This mimicry of the evaluations of bourgeois criticism is symptomatic of the complicity with the defining assumptions of bourgeois criticism which marked the foundation of Marxist criticism. For a variety of reasons, Marxist criticism's basic orientation in relation to bourgeois criticism has been to compete with it on its own ground rather than to dispute or displace that terrain.[6] At the level of ideological polemic, the main claim of Marxist criticism has been that the central problem of bourgeois criticism – the specificity of Literature – can be satisfactorily accounted for only by the application of Marxist (that is, historical and materialist) principles of analysis. It would be mistaken to argue that this strategy (as distinct from a theoretical position) has been wholly in error or wholly negligible in its consequences. If bourgeois criticism is currently in crisis (and I do say 'if'), this is due in no small part to the fact that it has been forced, by the challenge of Marxism, to evacuate, or at least to share, the critical terrain over which it once reigned supreme. Yet the price paid for this has been that Marxist criticism has distinguished itself from bourgeois criticism solely at the level of method, addressing the same set of problems by means of different analytical principles, and not at all at the crucial level of the theoretical constitution of its object. [. . .]

Quite apart from being a mistaken problem in itself, this concern with 'Literature' has seriously distorted the ways in which other areas of critical interest have been conceived and addressed within Marxism.[7] It has resulted, first, in an obsessive degree of concern with the problem of value. This, at least in the way it has usually been formulated, is, I shall contend, not a proper problem for Marxism and, more important, has impeded the development of what should occupy its place – the analysis of the *social contestation of value* as a means of making *strategically calculated* interventions within that process of contestation. Equally debilitating, the degree of centrality accorded the problem of value has 'overdetermined' – and with harmful consequences – the way in which three related areas of Marxist critical concern have been conceptualized: the analysis of the historical determination of literary forms; the calculation of the political and ideological effects that might be attributed to different practices of writing; and the problem of the relative autonomy of literature (as a general category) and of the diverse relations which exist between the literary and the ideological.

Marxist criticism: a deformed materialism

The problem of value

The statement that Marxists have been obsessively concerned with the problem of value is, of course, contestable. Terry Eagleton, for one, has argued that Marxism 'has maintained a certain silence about aesthetic value'.[8] While it is true that attempts to pose the problem of value at an explicitly theoretical level have been few and far between, the problem of value has none the less saturated Marxist critical practice in the sense that it has been routinely there, present in the background, even when other problems have been addressed. It has been massively present in the way the problem of reductionism has been posed within Marxist criticism. For this has been conceived as a problem only in relation to valued texts; outside this restricted sphere of writing, reductionist formulations have been actively embraced. Reductionism, that is to say, has been shunned less for theoretical reasons than for tactical ones, particularly – in the context of an ideological contest with bourgeois criticism – the need to ward off the ever-ready equation between material-ism and philistinism.

I will return to this point later. Meanwhile, it should be noted that to maintain that the problem of value is an improper one for Marxism is not thereby to assert the equivalence or parity of all forms of writing – a self-evident absurdity. Statements to the effect that Joyce opened up the possibilities of language in a way that Conan Doyle, say, did not seem to me to be quite unprob-lematic. However, such purely technical assessments of the formal effects of different practices of writing do not, of them-selves, offer grounds for valuing the one above the other. That is a further step which requires the intervention of a discourse of value which argues reasons for preferring forms of writing which stretch the possibilities of language over those which do not (for not all discourses of value have produced such criteria for valuation). Still less is it to advocate a neo-Kantian stance which abdicates the realm of value in the name of a pseudo-neutrality. This is not merely a question of arguing that judgements of value can and should be made; it is more one of recognizing that they inevitably *will* be made and that Marxists cannot afford to stand aloof from the ever ongoing process of the social valorization – and counter-valorization – of texts.

Rather, my chief objection is to the form which the debate about value has predominantly taken within Marxist criticism where it has been conceived as *identical with* and *addressed through* the problem of Literature. This has resulted in the conflation of a whole series of analytically separate problems: the problem of explaining the source of a work's value has been run in with that of explaining its 'literariness' – those formal characteristics which uniquely distinguish it from other forms of fiction – and, worse, problems of aesthetic evaluation and political calculation have been implicitly merged, as in Lukács's attempt to construct a realist aesthetic that would recruit all great realists to the banner of progressivism in art. Most disquieting of all, however, has been the tendency – consistent with an acceptance of the valuations of bourgeois criticism – to view value as essentially *static*, at least over large periods of time; to regard it as a property that is inherently inscribed within conventionally revered texts; and, as a part of an ideological polemic with bourgeois criticism, to contend that such properties can only be explicated by returning the text, analytically, to the conditions of its production.

This way of posing the problem is mistaken for a number of reasons, all of which cluster around the fact that value is not – nor, logically, can it be – a property of the text *alone*. One cannot pose the question of value without introducing into the analysis the problem of the valuing subject. Texts do not *have* value; they can only *be valued* by valuing subjects of particular types and for particular reasons, and these are entirely the product of critical discourses of valuation, varying from criticism to criticism. What has been offered within Marxist criticism, under the guise of *theories of value*, are in fact merely *specific reasons for valuing*, specific discourses of value begetting valuing subjects of particular types, which cannot logically (although they may, of course, politically) be preferred above those produced by competing critical discourses of valuation.

In the case of Lukácsian aesthetics, for example, texts are valued – that is, they are alleged to contain a value which Marxist critical judgement merely accurately reflects – in proportion to the degree to which they approximate the norm of historical self-knowledge which constitutes the Lukácsian model of literariness. In the case of the Althusserians, value is explained in terms of the extent to which texts distance or rupture the ideological discourses to which they allude; if they do this significantly, they're 'in', they count as Literature and are valued; if they do not, they are consigned elsewhere. As specific political reasons for valuing, such arguments are unexceptionable; they can be debated politically at the level of a strategic calculation of their effects – of the practices of writing they support, of the types of valuing subject they produce, of the categories of readers they imply and so on. However, in so far as they are presented as theories of value (and they *are* so presented) they are singularly impertinent. For such are not at all the grounds upon which the revered texts of the great tradition have, predominantly, been valorized. It is only possible to present such *reasons for valuing* as *theories of value* by simply discounting the positions of valuing subjects produced by and within competing critical discourses. We can see here the way in which the logic of false-consciousness has exerted its presence in Marxist aesthetic debate. For attempts to construct a theory of value have necessitated that the valuing subjects produced by the discourses of bourgeois criticism should be dismissed as illusory subjects, mistaken in their reasons for valuing.

A theory of value (as opposed to an analysis of the social and ideological processes of valorization) is only possible on condition that one escapes from the plurality of different reasons for valuing, the plurality of discourses producing different valuing subjects, by means of the discursive construction of the category of a universal valuing subject. This, of course, has been the central tactic of bourgeois criticism: value resides in the relationship between the universal values embodied in great works and the universal subject buried deep within us all. The more usual tactic within Marxism has been that of historicism as manifested in the formation of teleological theories of value pivoted on the construction of a universal valuing subject which, situated at the end of history, beyond the conflict which currently separates us as valuing subjects (and, of course, as much more than that), will, come the day, vindicate the provisional judgements currently made on its behalf. This is very clearly the case with Lukács, whose entire critical practice – where texts are conceived as being historically related to one another as the baton of aesthetic totalization is passed on from class to class – required, for its very constitution, the concept of the proletariat as the identical subject-object of history waiting with its judgements in hand – but always just around the next historical corner. [. . .]

In his review of *History and Class Consciousness*, Josef Révai argued that the conception of the proletariat as the identical subject-object of the historical process meant, in regard to the totality of past history, 'an unsupersedable transcendence of its historicity with respect to its being for itself',[9] as the real history that has taken place is overridden by and referred to the history that is yet to be. In the same way, the categories required to sustain a Marxist theory of value – chiefly, the category of a universal valuing subject in its historicist variant – necessarily undercut any materialist *credo*. The real history of valuation – of competing and contesting evaluations – is retrospectively nullified by the impending integrative judgements of a posthistorical valuing subject. Clearly, the effect of any such theory is to exorcize conflict from the sphere of the aesthetic – even if only in the form of a visionary goal looming at the end of history.

In place of a theory of value, then, Marxism's concern should be with the analysis of 'the ideological conditions of the social *contestation* of value'. So far as the *making* of evaluations is concerned, this is a matter for strategic calculation – a question of politics and not of aesthetics.

The literary and the ideological

I would not pretend to have disposed of the problem of value in the above remarks; rather, I have aimed merely to open up a debate which seems long overdue. To avoid misunderstanding, I should therefore stress, once again, that to take issue with the problem of value does not entail arguing that the sphere of writing is lacking in internal differentiation. Faced with this problem by his *New Left Review* inquisitors, Raymond Williams replied:

> The mistaken assumptions which lie hidden in the old concepts have to be cleared away for us to be able to begin searching again for a more tenable set of emphases within the range of writing practices – I agree that you could not go on with an undifferentiated range. On the other hand it seems to me that from now on we have to accept it as a true range, without any categorial division between what is done on one side of a line and what is done on the other.[10]

Clearly, then, relationships of similarity and difference within the sphere of writing need to be established. The crucial questions concern the criteria which should govern the construction of such relationships. In subscribing to the problem of value, as mediated through the category of Literature, Marxist criticism has taken on board an already established principle for their construction. And it is one which sits ill at ease with – and has, indeed, seriously distorted or obfuscated – the contending principles, dictated by Marxism's own theoretical and political requirements, which ought to govern the way in which these relationships are articulated. The price that the centrality accorded the problem of value has exacted can be seen in relation to the way adjacent areas of Marxist critical concern have been conceived and addressed.

I have already alluded to its influence on the way in which problems of determination have been posed. Its most discernible effect is that Marxists have been less concerned with explaining specific works (those of, say, Tolstoy or Racine in the case of Lukács and Goldmann respectively) as the product of specifically constrained signifying practices, than with the problem of explicating their 'greatness'; or, more accurately, the foregrounding of the latter concern has 'overdetermined' the way in which the former has been posed. The result has been a highly paradoxical enterprise in which the role allotted to the conditions of textual production has been to explain why and how some conditions of production enable the texts produced within them to break free from their restraining hold in order to achieve a universal appeal. Either that, or, as with Plekhanov, the towel is thrown in from the outset: materialist principles of analysis can take one only so far – up to the text but not into it or into the source of the aesthetic pleasure it affords.

It is easy to see how, in both options, the problem of value has distorted the way in which the issue of relative autonomy has been posed in the literary-critical region of Marxist theory. For it has resulted in this issue being regarded not as one pertaining to the *specificity of the determinations bearing on literary practice* but, rather, as one concerning the *limitations of any account which focuses on the analysis of determinations per se*. It has been viewed not as a problem of how to articulate the relationships between those determinations specific to literature and the more general economic, political and ideological determinations which Marxism sees as relevant to the analysis of any practice, but of how to resolve the tension between any determinist account which focuses on the analysis of conditions of production and the apparently contradictory evidence afforded by those texts which continue to register their effects when the originating conditions of their production have passed away.

In sum, it has been posed less as a problem *within* Marxism than as one *between* Marxism and bourgeois criticism; less as a problem concerning the articulation of different levels of determination within a social formation, than as one of reconciling Marxism's materialism with the idealist theories of value propounded within pre-Marxist criticisms. The result has been that the role allotted to conditions of textual production has been shamefacedly curtailed, as it has been acknowledged that texts do break free from the conditions of their production in registering continuous and long-term effects within a culture, while, at the same time, it has been ludicrously extended as it has been argued that whether or not texts do thus break free from their conditions of production is 'finally' determined by those conditions of production themselves. Such a materialism is a materialism purchased at a price: first, because it results in a one-sided historical approach to the study of literary texts, as if the history that flowed into the text through the conditions of its production were the only one that counted, overriding or cancelling out in advance the history which might bear on it through the history of its consumption; second, because the reductionism that is avoided in one area of fiction is actively endorsed in relation to others since, by the *very force of the argument*, non-canonized texts are *necessarily* collapsed back into the conditions of production from which they derive. Here, it would seem, culture works by reflex – not so much because detailed textual study has supported this conclusion but because it is *necessitated* by the attempt to render a materialist account of the specificity of Literature in terms of the uniqueness of its relations to the conditions of its production.

This 'necessitarianism' is most clearly seen in the way Marxist critics have addressed the problem of the relative autonomy of 'the literary' and the diverse modes of its relations to the ideological. No matter which school of criticism – Lukácsian, Frankfurt, Althusserian – the position advanced is substantially the same: Literature is not ideology and is relatively autonomous in relation to it, whereas popular fiction is ideology and is reduced to it. Literature, it is usually argued, either rises above ideology because of its social typicality or the depth of its historical penetration (Lukács), or consists of a specific set of formal operations upon it (Althusser); but 'popular' or 'mass' fiction is viewed as simply a reflection or formulaic reproduction of the ideology on which it is dependent and which it simply passes on. 'Popular literature', as Roger Bromley has put it, ' is one among many of the material forms which ideology takes (or through which it is mediated) under capitalism, and is an instance of its social production through the medium of writing.'[11]

The difficulties with such formulations are numerous. It is just not possible to contend, to take Althusser's proposition, that it is only in the case of 'truly authentic' art, and not at all in the case of 'average or mediocre' works, that a distance is opened up between the 'literary' and the 'ideological'. For instance, quite an elaborate play with the dominant forms of narrative ideology is to be found in the detective novel,[12] whereas the detective film, as Stephen Neale has put it, 'dramatizes the signification process itself as its fundamental problem'.[13] More generally, the entire field of popular fiction – especially film and television – is replete with parodic forms in which considerable 'distancing', 'alluding', 'foregrounding' and so on takes place. Whilst an exact categorization of pro-grammes such as *Monty Python's Flying Circus*, *Not the 9 o'clock News* and *Ripping Yarns* may be difficult, it is clear, first, that they are *popular* and they are *fiction*; and, second, that they are not *just* ideology: they disrupt not merely conventional narrative forms but are often profoundly, if anarchically, subversive of the dominant ideological discourses of class, nation, sexism and so on.

Such empirical difficulties apart, the very attempt to found a distinction between Literature and popular fiction – so that one is differentiated from, and the other flattened against, ideology – results in a crucial theoretical inconsistency according to which the effectivity that is granted to formal and aesthetic strategies in relation to ideological categories in one area of fiction is withheld from often not dissimilar strategies in other areas of fiction. Such a formulation is, at best, illogical: any area of writing in which fictional devices and strategies are in evidence must, in some way or other, effect a specific *production* of the ideological discourses contained within it. It cannot, if the concept of 'fiction' is to retain any usefulness as a differentiating term, simply be equated with such ideological discourses. Nor, if the logic of reflection theory is faulty elsewhere, can it be construed as a mere reflection or formulaic reproduction of them. At worst, however, it is self-fulfilling, the product of a rift within the critical strategy of Marxism which guarantees that popular texts be viewed reductively. If 'literary' texts have been distinguished from ideology whereas popular texts have been collapsed back into it, this is partly attributable to the fact that these different regions of textual production have received different types of critical attention which serve to buttress the supposition that the distinctions between them are, indeed, organized and explicable in these terms. In their treatment of canonized texts, Marxists have focused on the specifically for-mal means and mechanisms by which such texts either distance themselves from, or lift themselves above, the merely ideologi-cal. When dealing with popular texts, however, they have tended to read through such specifically formal operations, to plunder the texts for the evidence of the 'falsifications' of reality which they contain, and, in doing so, have joined hands with bourgeois criticism in reproducing, in the very form of their critical practice itself, the Literature/popular fiction distinction in its ideological form.

Such contradictions are attributable, ultimately, to the pressure which 'Literature' has exerted on the way the problem of relative autonomy has been conceived and addressed. Rather than being posed as a problem concerning the complex and diverse articulation of two different regions of the ideological, the literary (or fictional) and the discursive, it has been construed as a problem concerning the relationship between Literature (as a specific and privileged area of fictional practice) and Ideology viewed, variously, as the domain of false-consciousness, as the opposite of Marxism, or as a specific practice producing specific 'imaginary' subject positions which give rise to the effect of 'misrecognition'. Such a project is misconceived because the categories with which it deals – Literature and Ideology – are, in as much as they have their provenance in different bodies of theory (bourgeois criticism and Marxism respectively), mismatched from the outset. Put simply, there is no *necessary* reason why a space should exist within Marxist theory for the concept of Literature, and the attempt to clear such a space has resulted in the problem of the relationship between the literary or the fictional (in their diverse modes) and the ideological being resolved by definitional *fiat*. Ultimately, the proffered equation of popular fiction with ideology within Marxism is a tautology, a *necessary* definition entailed by the way in which the relations between Literature, Science (Marxism) and Ideology have already been constituted. Once Literature has been distinguished from Ideology and from Science (Marxism) in the formulations of classical Marxism's favoured 'holy trinity of the superstructure', then there is, quite simply, *nowhere that popular fiction can be placed*, other than within the ideological, which does not call into question the category of Literature and the terms in which its specificity has been theoretically constructed. The effect of the category of Literature has been to so constrain Marxists theoretically that they have had *no option* but to argue, time and again, that since popular fiction is not Marxism (it does not contain any analysis of social relationships), and since it is not Literature either (it does not have the critical 'edge' of Literature), then it *must* be ideology. [. . .]

But it is, of course, politically that the effects of this approach are most damaging. For its *en bloc* categorization of popular fiction as a sphere of writing which contributes to the reproduction of dominant ideological formations entails that it be abandoned as a field of struggle. The only relation of political calculation it permits is that of struggling *against* popular fiction (by unmasking it, by opposing to it the knowledge of Marxism or the critical insights of Literature), rather than *within* it. It is necessary to insist, in the face of the essentialism that has blighted much Marxist discussion of the internal economy of the superstructure, that conflict and struggle take place *within* and not just *between* the different regions and spheres of the superstructure. Beating popular fiction over the head with the three volumes of *Capital* is, politically, beside the point; what is needed are terms of theorization which will enable writers and critics to intervene, in a strategically calculated way, *within* the processes of popular reading and writing. Hegemony is to be won, not by sailing against the prevailing wind but by plotting a course across it.

Questions of political calculation

This brings me, by way of concluding this part of my argument, to the influence that the problem of value (and, through that, the category of Literature) has had on the way in which questions of political calculation have been posed within Marxist criticism. If the problem of value has been implicitly equated with, and addressed through, the problem of the specificity of Literature, questions of political calculation have been merged with both in the assumption that the determination of an aesthetic carries with it the determination of a politics. This has yielded a series of competing equations (different in substance but similar in kind) proffered by contending theoretical tendencies; equations of the type 'politically progressive texts' = 'valued texts' = 'those texts which most closely approximate to the model of literariness' (as posited by the critical tendency concerned). Political debates have thus been inextricably bound up with debates as to what, precisely, constitute the distinguishing characteristics of the aesthetic, with the result that political calculations have been advanced from within, and as emanations of, opposing theories of the specificity of the aesthetic. In fact, in Marxist criticism it is with aesthetic issues that the real base-lines of disagreement have been drawn, political disputes often being epiphenomenal in relation to these.

The assumption of a correlation between the determination of an aesthetic and of a politics has supported the view that a text's political effects can be read-off from, or calculated solely on the basis of, an analysis of its formal properties. This assumption lies behind those debates whereby one is expected to decide, in an abstract way, either for or against realism or modernism, for or against texts of *plaisir* or texts of *jouissance*, or to weigh in the balance the effects of the semiotic chora; in short, behind that entire tradition in which essentialism vies with essentialism. It is easy, as Terry Eagleton has admonished, to struggle free of such essentialism only to fall foul of 'an "extreme conjuncturalism" which merely collapses the work into its various moments of reception'.[14] None the less, the decisive objection to such purely formal approaches to literary politics is that the conjuncture constitutes *the only possible political 'place'* into which a text can play and register its effects. Still, Eagleton is right to warn against an unpardonable reduction of the conditions of reception to the political circumstances of the conjuncture. The way in which the text is inserted and has effects in relation to any given conjuncture needs to be viewed as being mediated through the systems of intertextuality – the changing articulations of text–ideology relations – which bear upon the moment of reception. It is as it is accessible through these that the text enters back into history – is historically 'redetermined' – during the process of its reception, figuring not as the *source* of *an* effect, but as the *site* on which *plural and even contradictory* effects may be produced during the course of its history as a received text.

The calculation of political effects, however, requires not only that the conjuncture or the prevailing system of intertextual relations be taken into account; there is also the question of the reader – of his/her position in the conjuncture, and of how s/he is placed in relation to the systems of intertextuality which regulate the act of reading. While the 'effects' tradition within media sociology is seldom laudable, it has given serious consideration to questions of the audience; and in recent years, the input of semiological perspectives to the process of 'decoding' has yielded a climate of opinion in film and television studies which is more cautious than that discernible in literary-critical circles concerning the extent to which effects can be inferred from form. Put simply, there are, as yet, no serious readership studies, a project which the literary left has culpably neglected.

This is not to suggest that readership studies should replace textual analysis; the text clearly constrains the possible ways in which it may be read, albeit these limits can never be specified in advance. Nor is it to suggest that existing models of audience research should simply be borrowed; these clearly place too much reliance on simple-minded questionnaire techniques. It is rather to recognize that the ground on which the text produces its effects consists not of naked subjectivities but of individuals interpellated into particular subject positions within a variety of different – and sometimes contradictory – ideological formations. This further entails recognizing that such positions vary in accordance with considerations of race, class and gender and, concerning their insertion within the system of intertextual relations, on the degree to which, within the educational apparatus, the institution of Literature has borne upon their ideological formation, upon their positioning as readers. [. . .]

If such considerations are not allowed a determining role in relation to the process of reading, the result is liable to be an approach to the calculation of the text's effects which, implicitly, is orientated to an assumed reader: white, male and bourgeois. Indeed, only too often (think of Adorno) the implied reader has been none other than the critic himself. More than a theoretical point is at issue here; consideration of the reader also requires that the very practice of Marxist criticism itself be re-thought. If texts do not have effects but serve as the site on which effects may be produced, then the question of effects is pre-eminently a practical problem; the problem of how best to intervene within the social process of the production of textual effects. 'In analysing literature', Colin MacCabe has argued, 'one is engaged in a battle of readings, not chosen voluntaristically but determined institutionally. The validity of interpretation is determined in the present in the political struggle over literature.'[15] The object of Marxist criticism is not that of producing an aesthetic, of revealing the truth about an already pre-constituted Literature, but that of intervening within the social process of reading and writing. It is no longer enough, if ever it was, to stand in front of the text and deliver it of its truth. Marxist critics must begin to think strategically about which forms of critical practice can best politicize the process of reading. This may mean different forms of criticism, and different forms of writing, for different groups of readers. As Brecht said: 'You cannot just "write the truth"; you have to write it *for*, and *to* somebody, somebody who can do something with it.'[16] Not a sufficient antidote, perhaps, to a theoreticism which has made, in Willemen's words, 'discursive activities immune from the necessity of planning and strategy in favour of a radical a-historicist opportunism that abdicated, in theory, any responsibility for the effects discursive practices may have'[17] – but a start.

Popular fiction/Literature: by-passing the categories

My main purpose so far has been to suggest that the concept of Literature has intruded an inescapably idealist dimension into the structure of Marxist critical debate, frustrating its historical and materialist ambitions at every turn. Such ambitions can be realized, I want now to argue, only if questions concerning the determination and effects of literary forms, and the articulation of the relations between them, are put in a way that sidesteps the conventional ordering of the relations between texts which 'Literature' implies. In doing so, I shall attempt to outline the part that the study of popular fiction might play within the development of a critical strategy which aims at 'by-passing the categories'.

First, however, I must comment on the spirit in which such an enterprise should be conducted, for there is a sense in which simply to speak of 'popular fiction' is to sell the pass from the outset. No matter how much one might wish to contest the assumption that the internal economy of the sphere of writing is organized in relation to the concept of Literature, the mere use of a term derived from the inherited vocabulary of criticism keeps that assumption alive by and through the very process of contesting it. It is to commit oneself in advance to a position within the system of concepts that should itself be the object of problematization. The problem I face here is one which Derrida has made familiar; it is that of 'the status of a discourse which borrows from a heritage the resources necessary for the deconstruction of that heritage itself'.[18] And that problem, as Derrida goes on to note, is one of *economy* and *strategy*. In the absence of a better alternative, then, I use the term 'popular fiction' for reason of economy, and mean by it that massive, exceedingly heterogeneous, body of texts which is conventionally defined as a residue in relation to 'Literature proper' and which is not normally encompassed within the purview of criticism. Strategically, however, the response that the marginalization of this area of texts requires is not simply one of developing it as an area of study, if it then continues to be regarded as a separate (and marginal) enclave of fiction whose determining characteristics are still defined negatively in relation to the focal point of reference supplied by the concept of Literature. Nor is the development of a fully-fledged theory of popular fiction an appropriate response, for this axiomatically concedes the theoretical and political pertinence of conventional constructions of relations of difference and similarity in the sphere of writing. Instead, it is necessary to dispute the cartography of the field, to question where the centre is and what the margins are. This means treating 'popular fiction' as merely a convenient stop-gap concept that can fulfil an economical (if misleading) denotative function until more adequate terms are to hand.

It is possible to distinguish two levels of study at which such strategies might be realized. First, the critical and institutional procedures bearing on the production and reproduction of the Literature/popular fiction distinction need to be interrogated. Work in this area is, of course, already well underway, particularly as regards the connections between the problematic of Literature and the development of universal schooling and literacy.[19] Similarly, our understanding of the way in which, within the practice of criticism, the Literature/popular fiction distinction is routinely reproduced by the contrasting ways in which 'literary' and 'popular' texts are analytically focused is rapidly increasing. Stephen Neale, for example, has convincingly argued that within film theory the concept of genre has functioned contradictorily so that, although apparently opposed to the ideology of high art, it has, in practice, underwritten its effects. Viewed, in *auteur* theory, as a mere external constraint which the director subjects to his or her creative will, imbuing it with a personal vision and thereby extending its expressive possibilities, the same genre conventions have, in the field of commercial cinema, been regarded as self-reproducing formulae, totally regulating the practice of the director by virtue of the industrially based requirement to 'maximise the profitability of capital assets and to repeat the formulae marking previous financial successes'.[20] In the case of 'film as commerce', that is to say, the concept has been used consistently as a part of extremely reductionist formulations, whereas in the case of 'film as art' it has remained complicit with the ideology of high art in its conceptualization of the artistic subject.

This schismatic use of the concept of genre is merely a specific example of the role played by the differential functioning of the category of the 'author' within the discourse of criticism. As Foucault has argued, the concept of the 'author' functions, discursively, as a means of valorizing texts:

> Discourse that possesses an author's name is not to be immediately consumed and forgotten; neither is it accorded the momentary attention given to ordinary, fleeting words. Rather, its status and its manner of reception are regulated by the culture in which it circulates.

But the 'author-function' is neither universal nor constant:

> Even within our civilization, the same types of texts have not always required authors; there was a time when those texts which we now call 'literary' (stories, folk tales, epics, tragedies) were accepted, circulated and valorized without any question about the identity of their author.[21]

It is clear – witness the stage of *auteur* theory within film criticism – that the process of canonization is, in essence, the process by which a group of texts, hitherto unauthored, comes to be regarded as authored. This is not merely to say that a name is assigned to the text (most texts, at least within capitalist society, have a name affixed to them); it is more a question as to how this sign of the writer's identity functions in relation to the texts which bear it as a signature. For the constitution of a text as an authored text is essential to the ideology of criticism, to that hermeneutic project of reading through the workings of the text to uncover the meaning that is secreted within it which still characterizes the socially dominant forms of criticism. The critic, as the interpreter of meaning, requires the author as a necessary fiction; necessary because, in order that meanings might be taken out from the text, there needs to be constituted a place – the author as the site of diverse influences – through which meanings pass into the text, and because the completion of the hermeneutic exchange between past and present, between life and life, requires that a text that is valuable for life should be seen as the product of a valuable life.

The concept of the 'author', however, does not merely distinguish valuable from non-valuable text; in so doing, it also effects a differential distribution of critical procedures. Although serving a need, the category of the 'author' also exacts a price: the demand for unity of meaning. [. . .] It is thus no accident that such hermeneutic procedures have scarcely ever been deployed in relation to forms of fiction where the name of the writer does not function under the sign of the 'author'; such texts have been regarded as, by definition, without 'real meaning'. Nor is it any accident that the primary hermeneutic demand for unity or consistency of meaning, which has borne so heavily on the study of canonized texts, has scarcely impinged on the study of non-canonized forms. Nor, finally, that biographical criticism has articulated the relations between life and work differently as between the two categories: tying life, work and meaning into an indissoluble unity in the case of one, connecting the life to the work only at the level of miscellaneous anecdote in the case of the other (contrast Meyer on Ibsen with Pearson on Fleming, for instance).[22]

Only by considering, in detail, the way different regions of texts have been differentially constituted by the procedures of criticism is it possible both to reveal and to contest its ideological effects. If much of this seems familiar ground, the point I particularly want to stress is the insufficiency of work which concentrates solely on those major critical traditions which have been most influential in relation to the canonized tradition. Admittedly, there is a shortage of works even in this area: Francis Mulhern's *The Moment of 'Scrutiny'* and John Fekete's *The Critical Twilight* are the only recent studies that spring readily to mind.[23] However, an exclusive focus on the upper echelons of criticism is misleading in that their effects can only be determined if they are placed within a knowledge of the full internal economy of the sphere of criticism, one which includes a knowledge of the way non-canonized texts have been routinely criticized in weekly reviews, the daily press, etc. Nor is this required solely for theoretical reasons. The political value of any critical practice depends on the way it intrudes upon and modifies the relationship between text and reader. It is necessary, therefore, to consider how that relationship is already constituted: how, in supervising the relations between text and reader, the socially dominant forms of criticism help to structure the ideological field into which the text plays and in which its – always variable – effects are registered. In doing so, it should be appreciated that there are other readers than university literature students, and that a knowledge of the critical mediations which intervene between such readers and the texts they read would be a by no means politically negligible contribution to critical theory.

There is also a need for specific strategies of textual analysis to be developed and deployed alongside the investigations outlined above. Most obviously, the assumptions embedded within the dominant critical practices are ones that need to be consciously opposed in the way popular texts are addressed. What, therefore, are the features which have most clearly distinguished the study of 'popular' from 'literary' texts? Apart from the strongly reductionist tendencies exhibited within Marxist criticism, five major lines of approach to the study of popular fiction can be distinguished:

1. In his *Thrillers*, Jerry Palmer argues that 'one of the main functions of literary criticism, at least in its academic version, has been to separate the wheat (deserving of extended analysis), from the chaff (the subject of generalization)'.[24] Without doubt, the most important single distinguishing feature of popular fiction criticism is the absolute preponderance of generic over textual analysis, of generalized surveys of the history of a genre over detailed studies of specific and historically circumscribed bodies of work.

2. Sociology, held in tight check with the great tradition, has

been given free reign in the study of popular fiction – but, as Terry Eagleton has noted, only in a form which deals with the 'outworks' of the text and fails to relate these to the inner processes of the text's workings.[25] Histories of the reading public and of the book trade are common enough, but few make any serious attempt to relate such histories to formal developments within the sphere of popular writing. True, Q.D. Leavis's *Fiction and the Reading Public* is an exception in so far as it allows the sociological outworks of literary practice a bearing on form by way of explicating the deterioration of standards. But the evidence for this deterioration depends on critical procedures which, when applied to the 'lower depths', can, at best, be described as casual.

3.   The claim – always held off in the case of Literature – that works of fiction might provide, in a more or less direct way, evidence of the customs, mores, manners, etc. of the period in which they were originally produced has been strongly present in the study of popular fiction since the days of Mme de Staël and Hippolyte Taine.

4.   The question of 'effects' (on attitudes and behaviour) has been especially prevalent and noteworthy in the study of popular fiction (it has rarely been put, except in Marxist circles, in relation to Literature). But the debate about effects has consistently manifested a tendency to treat popular works as if their effects could be read-off from their manifest content. The bleak history of content analysis, from its beginnings in American media sociology to the current cavortings of the National Viewers and Listeners Association, displays in a clear, albeit exaggerated, way the prevalent assumption that informs 'effects' research: namely, that popular writing *has no form*.

5.   Structuralism acquired much of its early influence in critical circles in Britain via its application to popular texts. Although welcome in that it has increased our knowledge of the formal complexity of popular texts, structuralism has tended to deprive them of their specificity (formal and historical) by regarding them as merely the manifestations of structures (the structures of language or myth) which have their central determinations and provenance elsewhere.

These are, admittedly, quite crude generalizations. None the less, they sustain the central point I want to derive from them: that virtually all approaches to the study of popular fiction have shared the common absence of any serious consideration of the *specific forms of writing* associated with popular texts. These are pushed to one side as mere surface impedimenta which get in the way of the critic's quest for historical or sociological evidence, mythic or linguistic structures, universal patterns of narrative, inferior or harmful values, or whatever. Richard Hoggart perfectly exemplifies the critical temper I have in mind when, in *The Uses of Literacy*, he condemns virtually the entire sweep of contemporary popular fiction on the basis of his own, wholly contrived, specimens of the thriller and romance forms. That Hoggart was obliged to resort to this expediency by the copyright difficulties he incurred in connection with the popular texts he had originally intended to discuss does not exonerate him. For it is inconceivable that he, or anyone else, would, even under such circumstances, have been willing to discuss Lawrence or Shakespeare on the basis of contrived textual excerpts.

Practically speaking, the implication of these considerations is that the conventional priorities need to be concretely challenged via the production of a criticism which focuses on the specifically formal properties of different types of popular fiction, and which does so at the level of specific texts rather than at the level of genre or period studies. Yet there is a danger here: that of merely aestheticizing a selection of popular texts, of producing a 'little tradition' beneath the 'great tradition'. In conditions of near-universal literacy, Eagleton has argued: 'Literature presents itself as a threat, mystery, challenge and insult to those who, able to read, can nonetheless not "read". To be able to decipher the signs and yet remain ignorant: it is in this contradiction that the tyranny of Literature is revealed.'[26] Any strategy which compounded that tyranny by producing, so to speak, a new category of cultural illiterates would clearly be anything but progressive; it would merely be to do criticism's dirty work for it, in extending the range of its repressive effects. There is also the further danger that such a strategy might result in a theory of popular fiction *ranged alongside* a theory of Literature. Against this, it is necessary to insist that any strategies of textual analysis should aim to 'occupy' the domain of popular fiction merely provisionally; to treat it as a strategic site upon which to deconstruct the entire system of concepts of which popular fiction is at once a part and the excluded term; and thereby to propose new terms for the theorization of the internal economy of the sphere of fiction as a whole.

The resolution of both difficulties requires that the issue of relative autonomy be radically re-thought; indeed, the very form of the problem needs to be altered. The phrase 'relative autonomy' always presupposes an answer to the question: 'relatively autonomous in relation to what?' Usually, it has been conceived as a matter of levels: of the relative autonomy of literature in relation to ideology, and of both in relation to the economy or politics. And, classically, the problem of levels has been retrieved as one of categories: of the relative autonomy of the category Literature in relation to the category Ideology. The inconsistencies resulting from this – especially as regards the way popular fiction has been viewed – have already been discussed. More fundamentally, however, it is the very attempt to conceive the internal economy of the superstructure as a set of relations between abstract and static categories that needs to be questioned. For, politically speaking, it is not the analytic separation but the diverse and historically specific modes of articulation of the various elements of the superstructure that should be brought in focus.

The problem of relative autonomy, then, should not be viewed as one that concerns the relations between two 'abstract' categories, Literature and Ideology, but as one concerning the diverse and specific forms of the play and interaction between two spheres of the ideological: the *discursive* (those discourses which produce imaginary orderings of the relations of men and women to one another, to the conditions of their social existence, and to their history), and the *fictional* or *literary* (those discourses which allude to the *discursive* and recombine its elements by means of specific formal devices). To construct a rigid categorial distinction between these two spheres of the ideological is misleading (for the precise mode of their articulation varies historically) and is politically beside the point: the effects of literature are located not in its separateness from the discursive region of ideology but in the way literary practices connect with that region.

A mere formalism on these questions, however, is not enough. It is not enough to show, within the text, how practices of writing can be distinguished from one another in terms of the differing and specific ways in which they re-combine elements of the ideological by means of the formal strategies peculiar to them. True, to construct relations of similarity and difference in accordance with principles and procedures of this kind would be a considerable advance on the simple Literature/middle-brow/popular division which constitutes the only available alternative. But it would still stop short before the point at which analysis can engage, concretely, with the political: the point of the connection between the articulation of the ideological elements contained in the text and those obtaining within the social formation at large. It is here, in the interface between the formation of subjects within the text and the (diverse and plural) formation of subjects outside the text, that the (diverse and plural) effects of literary texts are located. In order to engage with such issues the very notion of textual analysis needs to be jettisoned in favour of an approach which will *reinscribe* the text within, and theorize its action in relation to, the modes of articulation which comprise specific and determinate moments or types of hegemony. Posed in this way, the question of relative autonomy no longer concerns the specificity of determinations or the specificity of effects; nor is it a question of defining one category in relation to another. It is rather a question of articulation: it concerns the diverse ways in which different practices of writing are *bound into* the struggle for hegemony; their *imbrication with* and not *separation from* other regions of ideological struggle.

In a recent presentation of Gramsci's writings on literature, Colin Mercer has argued that these constitute 'a semiotic reading of texts' and 'of the ways in which hegemony, far from being reflected in these texts, is actually, although unevenly, distributed and *inscribed* within them'; a method concerned not 'with the text as product or as object but as a *process* . . . [as] articulated elements of hegemony' rather than as evidence of it.[27] It is always tempting these days – and especially at the end of long essays – to wheel on Gramsci as a 'hey-presto' man, as the theorist who holds the key to all our current theoretical difficulties. Whether or not Gramsci's writings will bear the burden Mercer places on them remains to be seen (they are as yet untranslated). None the less, the concept of hegemony (as it has been reworked and handed down to us since Gramsci) affords a means of rethinking the concerns of Marxist criticism so as to yield, not a theory of Literature, but a 'political economy' of writing – and one which will open up the sphere of popular reading to a politics which goes beyond merely opposing it in the name of either Literature or Science.

Notes

1 T. Davies, 'Education, ideology and literature', *Red Letters*, No. 7 (1978), p. 13.

2 S. Hall, 'Some paradigms in Cultural Studies', *Annali Anglistica*, (Naples 1978), vol. XXI, no. 3, p. 26.

3 L. Goldmann, *The Hidden God: A Study of Tragic Vision in the Pensées of Pascal and the Tragedies of Racine* (Routledge & Kegan Paul, London 1964), p. 314.

4 L. Althusser, 'A letter on art', in *Lenin and Philosophy, and Other Essays* (New Left Books, London 1971), p. 204.

5 F. Mulhern, 'Marxism in literary criticism', *New Left Review*, no. 108 (1978), p. 86.

6 This emerges very clearly from Anderson's synoptic sketch of the history of Marxism. See P. Anderson, *Considerations on Western Marxism* (New Left Books, London 1976).

7 My reasons for holding the question of Literature's specificity to be incompatible with the concerns of Marxism are outlined in T. Bennett, *Formalism and Marxism* (Methuen, London 1979).

8 T. Eagleton *Criticism and Ideology* (New Left Books, London 1976), p. 187.

9 J. Révai, 'A review of Georg Lukács' "History and Class Consciousness"', *Theoretical Practice*, vol. 1 (1971), p. 28.

10 R. Williams, *Politics and Letters* (New Left Books, London 1979), p. 326.

11 R. Bromley 'Natural boundaries: the social function of popular fiction', *Red Letters*, no. 7 (1978), p. 40.

12 See the discussion of the Sherlock Holmes stories in C. Belsey, *Critical Practice* (Methuen, London 1980).

13 S. Neale, *Genre* (British Film Institute, London 1980), p. 26.

14 T. Eagleton, 'What is literature?', *New Statesman*, 6 July 1979, p. 20.

15 C. MacCabe, *James Joyce and the Revolution of the Word* (Macmillan, London 1978), p. 26.
16 Cited in P. Slater, *Origins and Significance of the Frankfurt School: A Marxist Perspective* (Routledge & Kegan Paul, London 1977), p. 141.
17 See Willemen's introduction to Neale, *Genre*, p. 4.
18 J. Derrida, *Writing and Difference* (Routledge & Kegan Paul, London 1978), p. 282.
19 See, for example, R. Balibar, *Les Français fictifs: le rapport des styles littéraires au français national* (Librairie Hachette, Paris 1974), and R. Balibar and D. Laporte, *Le Français national: politique et pratique de la langue nationale sur la Révolution* (Librairie Hachette, Paris 1974).
20 Neale, *Genre*, p. 10.
21 M. Foucault, 'What is an author?', *Screen*, vol. XX, no. 1 (1979), pp. 19–20.
22 See M. Meyer, *Ibsen* (Penguin, Harmondsworth 1974), and J. Pearson, *The Life of Ian Fleming* (Jonathan Cape, London 1966).
23 See F. Mulhern, *The Moment of 'Scrutiny'* (New Left Books, London 1979), and J. Fekete, *The Critical Twilight: Explorations in the Ideology of Anglo-American Literary Theory from Eliot to McLuhan* (Routledge & Kegan Paul, London 1977).
24 J. Palmer, *Thrillers: Genesis and Structure of a Popular Genre* (Edward Arnold, London 1978), p. 2.
25 See Eagleton, *Criticism and Ideology*, p. 48.
26 Ibid., p. 165.
27 C. Mercer, 'After Gramsci', *Screen Education*, no. 36 (1980), pp. 11–12.